# CORSICA

**ROUGH GUIDES**

Written and researched by
**Zoë Smith**

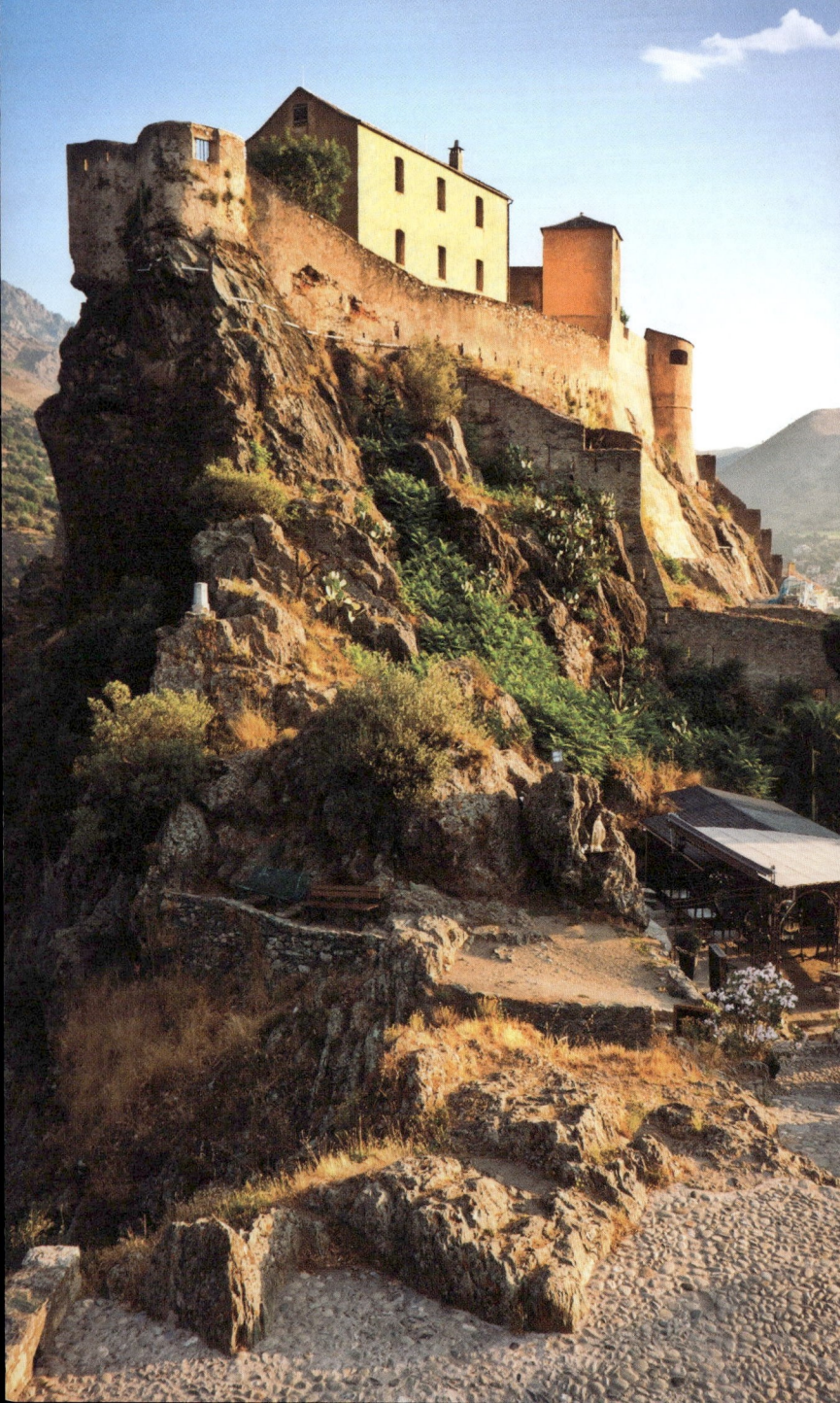

# Contents

THE CITADEL OF CORTE

# Introduction to
# **Corsica**

Known to the French as the "*Île de Beauté*" (Island of Beauty), Corsica doesn't disappoint. Burly rock-hewn canyons and forest-clad valleys dominate the mountainous interior, while marbled turquoise seascapes unfold along the coast, buttressed by swaggering cliffs and calanques that tumble down to half-moon bays of white sand. Nowhere in the Mediterranean promises such diverse topography, and the tourism boom hasn't tempered its wild side. Outdoor adventures remain the main allure for the 3.5 million travellers that visit France's southernmost region each year, and many of the island's beauty spots can still only be reached on foot or by boat.

Marooned between the French and Italian mainland, within spitting distance of Sardinia, Corsica's strategic setting has shaped its tumultuous history. Greeks, Romans, and Byzantines all staked their claims to the island before the Genoese arrived in the thirteenth century. Almost 500 years of often-contested Genoese rule followed, during which the island's coastal **defence towers** (now the focal point of numerous coastal hikes) were built, mostly in the sixteenth century to ward off barbary pirates.

The island didn't become French until 1769, just in time for the birth of Corsica's most notorious son, **Napoleon Bonaparte**. For locals, however, it's homegrown hero **Pascale Paoli**, leader of the short-lived but much-reminisced Corsican Republic of 1755, who is most revered. Paoli, allied with the British monarchy, was also responsible for the briefly established Anglo-Corsican Kingdom of 1794, although the French quickly stamped out the possibility of a British takeover.

Centuries of changing hands have left the island with an assortment of historical sites and architectural styles, from Genoese citadels and Pisan-style churches to French bourgeois buildings. Culturally, it's just as much a mixed bag. French might be the official language, but the island's Catholic brotherhoods, native language and beloved **cuisine** have more in common with Italy than *le continent* (mainland France). More

# CORSICA

LIGURIAN SEA

N

Rogliano
Centuri
Macinaggio

CAP CORSE

Nonza

Bastia

Désert des Agriates
St-Florent

NEBBIO

L'Île-Rousse

Murato

Calvi

BALAGNE

Calenzana

Ponte-Leccia

CASTAGNICCIA

Piedicroce

Moriani-Plage

Galéria

Haut'Asco

Monte Cinto
(2706 m)

HAUTE

CORSE

Cervione

Paglia
Orba
(2525 m)

NIOLO VALLEY

Porto

Évisa

Corte

Monte
Rotondo
(2622 m)

BOZIO

Piana

Cargèse

Sagone

Monte
d'Oro
(2389 m)

Vizzavona

Ghisoni

Aléria

Tavignano

Fium'Orbo

Ghisonaccia

Monte
Renoso
(2352 m)

Gravona

TYRRHENIAN SEA

Ajaccio

Zicavo

Monte
Incudine
(2136 m)

Solenzara

CORSE DU SUD

Taravo

Zonza

ALTA
ROCCA

Conca

Levie

Propriano

Sartène

Uomo di
Cagna
(1217m)

Porto-Vecchio

Îles Cerbicale

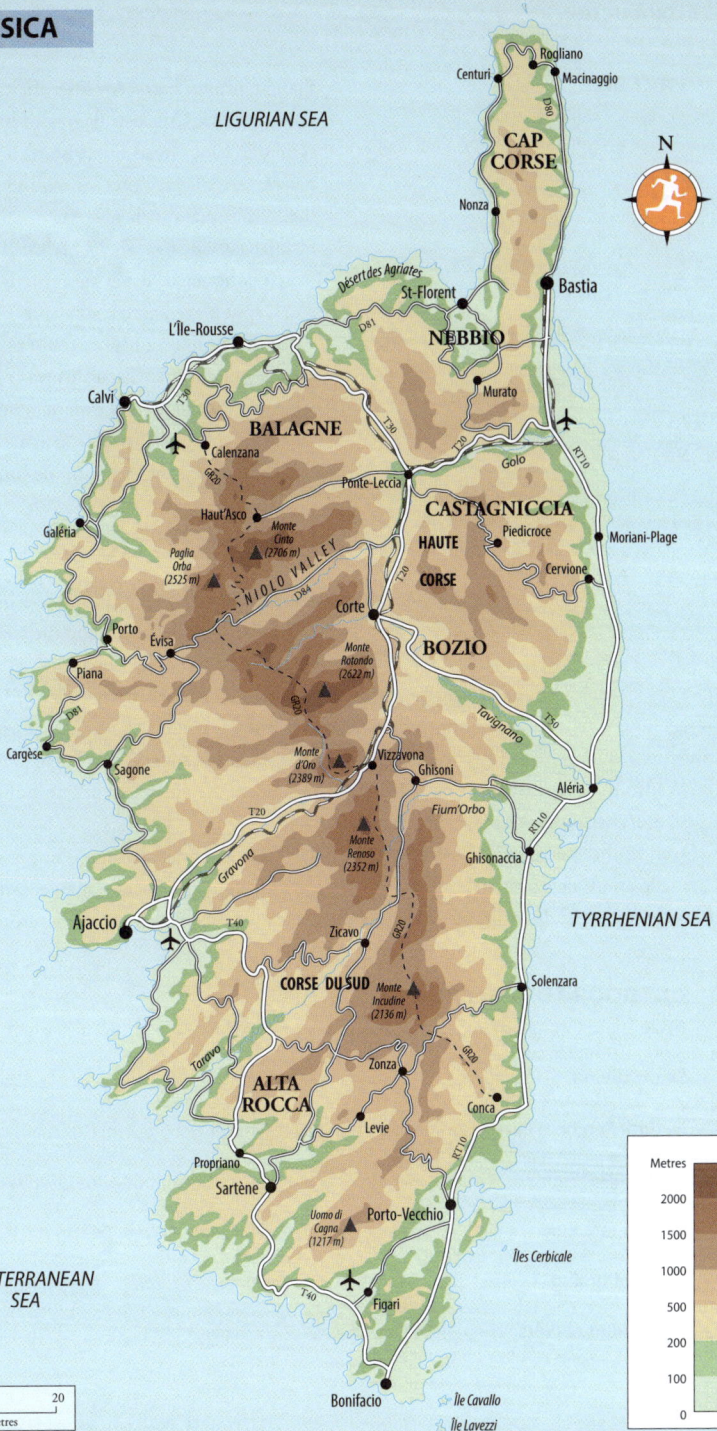

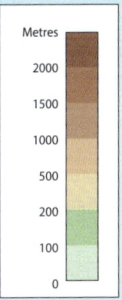

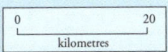

MEDITERRANEAN
SEA

Figari

Metres

2000
1500
1000
500
200
100
0

Bonifacio

Île Cavallo
Île Lavezzi

0    20
kilometres

## FACT FILE

- Corsica is the smallest and least populated region in Metropolitan France, home to just 355,528 people.
- It's the fourth-largest island in the Mediterranean Sea and is closer to Sardinia, Italy, than France.
- Arguably, the most famous Corsican in history is Napoléon Bonaparte, born in Ajaccio.
- French is the official language of Corsica, but locals often speak Corsican (*Corsu*), which is more similar to Italian.
- Corsica has over 1000km of coastline, almost 200 beaches and 20 peaks over 2,000m.
- Coca-Cola may have Corsican roots. The French "wine cola" *Vin Mariani*, invented in 1863 by Corsican entrepreneur Angelo Mariani, is believed to have inspired American inventor John Stith Pemberton.

than anything, locals consider themselves **Corsican**. The Corsican flag, with its symbolic Moor head brandishing a white bandana, is an ever-present reminder of their tenacious spirit, as is the unofficial motto "*souvent conquise, jamais soumise*" (often conquered, never submitted), which you'll spot blazed across souvenirs.

But don't mistake resilience for inhospitality; most Corsicans warmly welcome travellers, and experiencing Corsican culture is just as much a highlight as the island's natural wonders.

# Where to go

**The northern capital of Bastia** sees little tourist activity despite being the island's busiest seaport. Once the principal Genoese stronghold, its fifteenth-century citadelle and Vieux Port have survived almost intact, and recent modernisations hope to entice more travellers to stay. Most head north to explore the sandy coves and fishing villages of the rugged **Cap Corse** peninsula or west to the chic little port of **St-Florent**, from where the vineyards of **Patrimonio** and the **Desert de Agriates** are within easy reach.

Over on the west coast, **L'Île-Rousse** and **Calvi,** the latter graced with an impressive citadelle and long sandy beach, are major targets for holidaymakers. The spectacular **Réserve Naturelle de Scandola** to the southwest is most easily visited by boat from

## OUTDOOR ADVENTURES

**GR20** The 180km GR20 footpath is one of Europe's most demanding long-distance hikes, taking an average of 15 days.

**Scuba diving** Underwater wonders include WWII wrecks, sea canyons, and a sunken American bomber.

**Natural Regional Park** More than half of the island and eight long-distance footpaths lie within the *parc naturel régional de Corse* (PNRC).

**Boat cruises** From the sea caves and islands of the south coast to cruising the island's only UNESCO World Heritage Site.

**Mountain biking** Strong thighs are required for the island's steep climbs and winding mountain passes, but the 550km GT20 is an epic challenge with spectacular views.

**Wild swimming** There are more than 30 natural swimming holes dotted around the island, from gurgling rivers to waterfall pools.

**Adrenaline seekers** Adventurous types can try canyoning, rock climbing, quad biking, horse riding, paragliding and water sports galore.

## CHEESE, CHARCUTERIE & CHESTNUTS

The three Cs are the pillars of local cuisine, and Corsicans are proud of the age-old traditions associated with them. The best **charcuterie** comes from the forested slopes of Castagniccia, where wild *nustrale* (native black pigs) feast on the fallen chestnuts – said to give the meat its flavour – and the pork is dried and cured in the cold cellars of the mountain villages. Three types of charcuterie bear France's prestigious AOC (*Appellation d'Origine Contrôlée*) and AOP (*Appellation d'origine protégée*) labels. *Coppa*, a salted, fat-swirled pork loin, has a rich taste and melt-in-the-mouth texture; *Lonzu*, salted tenderloin with a thick strip of fat, is similar in texture with a stronger, smokier taste; and *Prisuttu*, a slow-matured cured ham, has a sweet, nutty flavour. *Figatellu*, dried pork liver sausage, is most often used in soups and stews.

**AOP Brocciu**, a soft ricotta-like cheese made with ewe's milk, is found everywhere on the island, forming the basis for dishes such as cannelloni and *fiadone* (cheesecake), and you'll also come across various regional cheese varieties, such as the distinctive *corsu vecchiu* or soft, tangy *niulincu*.

The humble chestnut is also a star in its own right and the AOC/AOP Corsican chestnut flour is used in everything from cakes to craft beers. Look out for *fritelli a gaju frescu* (chestnut fritters) and *pulenta* (chestnut porridge) sprinkled with sugar or eau de vie.

the tiny resort of **Porto**, from where hikers can also strike out into the wild **Gorges de Spelunca** and explore the coast of the **Calanques de Piana**. **Corte**, at the heart of Corsica, is the best base for exploring the interior's mountains and gorges, which form part of the **Parc Naturel Régional** that runs almost the entire length of the island.

Sandy beaches and rocky headlands punctuate the west coast all the way down to **Ajaccio**, Napoleon's birthplace and the island's capital, where pavement cafés and palm-lined boulevards teem with tourists in summer. Slightly fewer make it to nearby **Filitosa**, the greatest of the many prehistoric sites scattered across the south. **Propriano**, the principal resort of the southwest coast, lies close to stern **Sartène**, the quintessential Corsican town and former seat of the unruly feudal lords who once ruled this region.

**Bonifacio**, a comb of ancient buildings perched atop furrowed white cliffs at the southern tip of the island, and **Porto-Vecchio** provide a springboard for the beautiful beaches of the south. The eastern plain has less to boast of, but the Roman site at **Aléria** is worth a visit, and the wooded hills of **Castagniccia**, Pascale Paoli's homeland, yield much of Corsica's chestnut and charcuterie supply.

# When to go

With some 2,800 sunshine hours a year, Corsica is a close rival to the French Riviera when it comes to France's sunniest spot. However, it's the crowds, rather than the weather, that should dictate when you choose to visit. Corsica's annual visitor influx exceeds the island's population almost ten times over, and more than a third come in August alone. While **July** and **August** are the hottest and driest months, they are also by far the busiest and most expensive.

## AVERAGE DAILY TEMPERATURES AND RAINFALL

| | Jan | Feb | Mar | April | May | June | July | Aug | Sept | Oct | Nov | Dec |
|---|---|---|---|---|---|---|---|---|---|---|---|---|
| Max/min(°C) | 14/5 | 14/5 | 16/6 | 19/9 | 22/12 | 27/16 | 30/19 | 30/19 | 27/16 | 23/13 | 18/9 | 15/6 |
| Max/min(°F) | 57/41 | 57/41 | 61/43 | 66/48 | 72/54 | 81/61 | 86/66 | 86/66 | 81/61 | 73/55 | 64/48 | 59/43 |
| Rainfall(mm) | 60 | 65 | 62 | 52 | 62 | 26 | 12 | 16 | 49 | 92 | 120 | 77 |

Travel in June or September to dodge the crowds while still enjoying the balmy Mediterranean climate, and don't write off the **shoulder seasons**. It's often warm enough for beach days in late May and early October, and the mild spring and autumn weather is ideal for walking, cycling and exploring the sights without the swathes of people.

A lot of Corsica's activities, accommodation, and international flights are seasonal, which is worth taking into consideration if planning a winter visit. Nonetheless, this is an affordable time to enjoy some coastal sightseeing, and there are seasonal draws such as **Christmas Markets** and the island's short but notable **ski season** (Dec–Mar). Note that Corsica really has two climates, and the mountainous heartlands can often be wet and windy even if the lowland coastal regions stay warm and dry. Be sure to pack plenty of wet weather clothes and some sensible shoes if you decide to explore the interior of the island.

BOCCA PALMENTE ON THE GR 20 TRAIL

# Author picks

Our author has journeyed to all corners of Corsica, traversing dizzying mountain passes and wild coastline, tracking down local artisans and far-flung viewpoints, and seeking out the island's most unique sights and unforgettable activities. Here are some of her favourite things to see, do, and taste.

**Hilltop ghost town** The haunting ruins of Occi (see page 67), a medieval village abandoned since the nineteenth century, sit perched on a hilltop above the Balagne village of Lumio.

**Wreck diving** Just 200m off the shore of Calvi, diving the wreck of an American WWII B-17 bomber (see page 71) is a rare thrill – look closely and you can still spot the bullet holes.

**Hidden beach** The wild and windswept Ostriconi beach (see page 59) boasts a crescent of white sands and a satisfyingly secluded, hike-in-only location.

**Glamping getaway** For a magical place to stay, the Cocoon Village (see page 125) is a certified eco-hotel with glamping domes suspended in a forest canopy overlooking Lake Ospédale.

**Road trip** Rent a car – or better yet, a motorbike – and tackle the serpentine roads of Scala di Santa Regina (see page 148), twisting through ever more spectacular rock formations. Pack hiking shoes and a swimsuit so you can explore the canyon and cool off with a swim in the Golo River along the way.

**Corsican curiosities** Balagne local and history buff Guy Savelli's home museum (see page 67) is a trove of quirky artefacts, Corsican memorabilia and curiosities. If you're lucky, he'll wind up the century-old gramophones and play you some original shellac recordings.

**Polyphonic concerts** Look out for traditional Corsican polyphonic concerts advertised around the island or ask at the local tourist office.

**Chestnut treats** Visit the Castagniccia region to learn how the native nuts get their delicious smoky flavour (see page 138) and taste chestnut cakes, ice cream, and beer.

OCCI RUINS

OSTRICONI BEACH

Our author recommendations don't end here. We've flagged up our favourite places – a perfectly sited hotel, an atmospheric café, a special restaurant – throughout the Guide, highlighted with the ★ symbol.

# 20

# things not to miss

It's not possible to see everything that Corsica has to offer in one trip – and we don't suggest you try. What follows, in no particular order, is a selective and subjective taste of the island's highlights, ranging from mesmerizing natural landscapes and epic hikes to characterful Corsican villages. Highlights are colour-coded by chapter and have a page reference to take you straight into the Guide, where you can find out more.

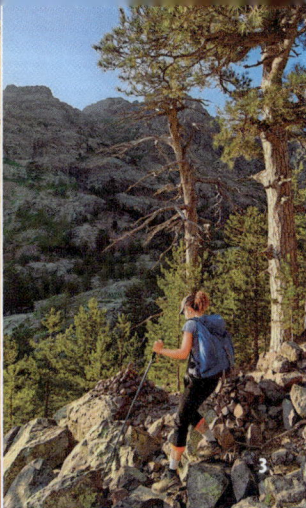

### 1 CAP CORSE
See page 50
Corsica's quintessential coastal road trip serves up ocean views, idyllic sandy coves, and vertiginous sea cliffs at every twist and turn.

### 2 RÉSERVE NATURELLE DE SCANDOLA
See page 78
Only reachable by boat, the island's sole UNESCO World Heritage Site is a wild frontier with sky-scraping red cliffs and incredible biodiversity.

### 3 GR20
See page 74
The challenging 180km footpath is renowned as one of Europe's toughest. A feat best left to the fittest, it's packed with spectacular mountain scenery.

### 4 PLAGE DE SALECCIA
See page 59
On the cusp of the Desert de Agriates, this idyllic beach has soft white shell sand, turquoise water and barely a building in sight.

### 5 CLIFFS OF BONIFACIO
See page 120
Framed by dramatic white limestone cliffs, the southern resort town of Bonifacio is a scenic spot for a sunset hike or boat cruise.

6

7

8

### 6 CORTE
See page 149
A nationalist stronghold, brimming with eighteenth-century charm and the gateway to the mountainous heartlands.

### 7 CANYONING
See page 128
Navigate rugged gorges, waterfalls and natural pools with a mix of abseiling, hiking and swimming that's guaranteed to get your adrenaline pumping.

### 8 MAISON BONAPARTE
See page 95
Visit the childhood home of Napolean Bonaparte in Ajaccio for a fascinating peek into the early life of the formidable French Revolution leader.

### 9 CALANQUES DE PIANA
See page 85
A mass of terracotta-red porphyry eroded into dogs' heads, witches and devils that can be conquered by land or sea.

### 10 GORGES DE LA RESTONICA
See page 152
Restonica Valley offers one of the island's most rewarding day hikes, featuring jaw-dropping views and glacial lakes.

9

10

### 11 BALAGNE VILLAGES
See page 67
Wander the cobbled lanes and peek inside artisan's workshops in the traditional hilltop villages of San Antonino, Pigna and Corbara.

### 12 FILITOSA MENHIRS
See page 110
Noteworthy for their unique carved faces, these 6,000-year-old menhirs are among the greatest archaeological treasures of the western Mediterranean.

### 13 GENOESE TOWERS
See page 51
From Cap Corse to Campomoro, dozens of sixteenth-century defence towers still stand along the island's coast; a visit to at least one of the ruins is a must.

### 14 CALVI
See page 68
Corsica's hallmark resort is framed by snowy peaks, golden beaches, and a glittering blue gulf.

### 15 CORSICAN CUISINE
See page 31
Smoky charcuterie, creamy sheep or goat cheese, hearty wild boar (sanglier), and sweet myrtle berries are menu staples throughout Corsica.

### 16 ÎLES LAVEZZI
See page 121
Reached by boat from Bonifacio, this rocky, uninhabited archipelago is peppered with secluded coves where you can swim, snorkel or kayak far from the bustle of the city.

### 17 PORTO-VECCHIO
See page 121
Flanked by long sandy beaches, the largest city in the south has a lively old town brimming with shops, bars, and restaurants.

### 18 AIGUILLES DE BAVELLA
See page 125
Spiky needle-like rock formations rise up along the southeast stretch of the GR20, affording a dramatic backdrop for hiking and swimming.

### 19 PLAGE DE PALOMBAGGIA
See page 124
The south's flagship beach is a veritable slice of paradise with powdery white sands and gleaming turquoise waters hemmed in by umbrella pines and orange-hued rocks.

### 20 LE TRAIN CORSE
See page 27
Chugging between Bastia and Ajaccio at a glacial pace, a ride on Corsica's diminutive train is all about the views – an endless panorama of mountain scenery.

17

18

19

20

# Itineraries

The following itineraries will lead you to all corners of Corsica, directing you to the most sensational viewpoints, epic landscapes, and characterful coastal towns. The trips below give a taste of what the French island has to offer and what we can plan and book for you at www.roughguides.com/trips.

## LE GRAND TOUR

Plan about three weeks for the ultimate island road trip, leaving time for day trips, outdoor activities, and a zillion photo stops in between.

❶ **Ajaccio** One or two nights is enough to see the highlights of the Corsican capital, including the Maison Bonaparte and the îles Sanguinaires. See page 92

❷ **Corte** Cut your teeth on the gently winding T20 mountain road from Ajaccio to Corte (about a 1.5-hour drive) in the heart of hiking country. See page 149

❸ **Porto** Steel your nerves for the exhilarating hairpin bends along the D84 to Porto, from where boat cruises visit the Calanques de Piana, Girolata and the Réserve Naturelle de Scandola. See page 81

❹ **Calvi** Zig-zagging coastal roads climb north to Calvi (a 75km but 2-hour drive), where you can enjoy beach-hopping and scuba diving, explore the Balagne villages, then ride the train to Île-Rousse. See page 68

❺ **Bastia** It's an easy 2.5-hour drive from Calvi to the historic port city of Bastia, perhaps stopping

at the Patrimonio wine region along the way. See page 42

❻ **Cap Corse** From Bastia, driving the serpentine coastal road around Cap Corse takes about 3.5 hours; ideal for a day or overnight trip, but plan to stop for photos around every curve. See page 50

❼ **Porto Vecchio** From Bastia, it's a straight road south to the lively port of Porto Vecchio, home to some of Corsica's best beaches and a great basecamp for hiking, canyoning, and kayaking. See page 121

❽ **Bonifacio** About a 40-minute drive from Porto-Vecchio, Bonifacio's spectacular sea cliffs, beautiful beaches and wild islands are a fitting finale for your island odyssey. See page 115

## INTO THE WILD

Outdoors adventurers won't want to miss Corsica's wild landscapes and UNESCO-listed natural wonders; with ten days or more, you can pack in some unforgettable activities.

❶ **Cap Corse** Drive the island's most famous coastal road anticlockwise from Bastia to

**Create your own itinerary with Rough Guides**. Whether you're after adventure or a family-friendly holiday, we have a trip for you, with all the activities you enjoy doing and the sights you want to see. All our trips are devised by local experts who get the most out of the destination. Visit **www.roughguides.com/trips** to chat with one of our travel agents.

St-Florent; with extra time, spend a night in Port-Centuri or Nonza. See page 50

❷ **Desert de Agriates** Take a boat or 4WD tour from St-Florent to the remote Agriates beaches. Feeling adventurous? Rent a quad bike or hike the coastal footpath instead. See page 58

❸ **Calvi** From St Florent, it's a 2-hour drive to Calvi, where sandy beaches, scuba dive sites, and the start of the GR20 are within easy reach. See page 68

❹ **Scandola & the Calanques** Hop aboard for a full-day boat cruise from Calvi along the UNESCO-listed coastline of the Réserve Naturelle de Scandola and the Calanques de Piana. See pages 78 and 85

❺ **Gorges de la Restonica** From Calvi, drive the scenic mountain road to Corte, your basecamp for hiking the Restonica footpath, an epic full-day trek passing rocky gorges and glacial lakes. See page 152

❻ **Canyoning** Halfway between Corte and Bonifacio, Solenzara is the entry point to the Aiguilles de Bavella; the saw-toothed rocks provide spectacular terrain for canyoning. See page 128

❼ **Îles Lavezzi** Plan a full-day cruise from Bonifacio to visit these small granite islands, where you can swim, snorkel and kayak around pristine reefs and white-sand coves. See page 121

## CLASSIC CORSICA

Savor Corsica's rich cuisine and cultural traditions during two weeks of slow travel, visiting the island's most remarkable historical sites along the way.

❶ **Campomoro** Hike to the oldest of Corsica's many Genoese towers, now a museum with sweeping views across the Golfe du Valinco. See page 112

❷ **Sartène** From Campomoro, it's a winding 40-minute drive to the hilltop medieval city of Sartène, known for its extraordinary polyphonic choir and traditional *U Catenacciu* Easter festival. See page 113

❸ **Filitosa** A further 40-minute drive brings you to the island's pre-eminent prehistoric site; Filitosa's stern-faced stone menhirs have witnessed some 6,000 years of history. See page 110

❹ **Ajaccio** Napoleon's birthplace is the star of the Corsican capital, but Ajaccio is also home to the island's leading art museum and a Genoese citadel. See page 92

❺ **Corte** Corsica's historic heartland brims with traditional restaurants, emblematic buildings and references to nationalist hero Pascal Paoli. See page 149

❻ **Aléria** From Corte, drive 45 minutes to the archaeological site of Aléria, where excavations of Corsica's earliest Roman settlement are ongoing. See page 134

❼ **Castagniccia** Take your time driving the tree-lined lanes of the "*Land of the Chestnuts*", where you can walk beneath the chestnut trees and indulge in myriad Chestnut-flavoured treats. See page 138

❽ **Balagne villages** An hour's drive from Castagniccia, the Balagne is known for its picturesque hilltop villages, where you browse artisan shops and enjoy hearty local cuisine. See page 67

# Sustainable travel

Join the growing number of travellers choosing to prioritise sustainable travel and impact the environment as little as possible during their adventures.

Proud of their time-honoured traditions and extraordinary natural landscapes, eco-tourism was thriving in Corsica long before the term reached buzzword status. With miles of sandy shores, rambling mountains, and fragrant maquis, back-to-nature activities and artisanal trades are the island's lifeblood, and more than 50 percent of the island is protected as a natural regional park. In recent years, the *Agence de Tourisme de la Corse (ATC)* has focussed its efforts on further developing sustainable tourism, tripling the number of Ecolabelled initiatives, and making strides to become one of France's greenest travel destinations. Here are some ways to embrace sustainable travel in Corsica and make as little impact as possible on the environment.

## EMBRACE SLOW TRAVEL

Whether you're traversing rock-hewn mountain valleys with their multitude of hairpin bends or slowing down to dodge wild boar and goats as they meander across rural lanes, you're unlikely to get anywhere quickly in Corsica. All the more reason to embrace slow travel. Ride the train (see page 27) right through the heart of the island, hike one of the three coast-to-coast footpaths (see page 33), or tackle the inimitable GR20 (see page 74). For cyclists, the GT20 bike route (see page 33) runs north to south, but you'll need some strong quads to conquer the steep inclines – if you're unsure, hire an electric bike instead.

## GO ELECTRIC

While footpaths and outdoor activities abound, the reality is that it's still tricky to get around in Corsica without your own wheels. Thankfully, many locals have made the switch to electric vehicles and the vast majority of rental cars (see page 29) are now electric. Going electric has never been easier and distances are generally small in Corsica (the island itself is just 183km long), so you'll get by for a day on a full charge. When it's time to recharge, Chargemap (https://chargemap.com) has a map of charging points, many run by OZECAR (www.ozecar.fr) and E-Motum (https://e-motum.net); many hotels also now offer charging points.

## SAVOUR LOCAL FLAVOURS

Eating locally and seasonally is an easy feat in Corsica, and there's even a dedicated tourist route, the *Routes des Sens Authentiques* (https://gustidicorsica.com; comprehensive French-language brochures available at tourist offices), listing 71 artisanal food producers, traditional craftspeople, and agritourism destinations. You'll spot the blue triangle logo advertised on signs all around the island, pointing the way to chestnut farms, wineries, cheesemakers, and charcutiers, as well as farm-to-table restaurants and hole-in-the-wall artisan workshops.

## SEEK OUT THE ECO LABEL

Corsica leads the way when it comes to eco-friendly stays, with an impressive

LOCAL CRAFTS

51 establishments (among the highest concentration in France) bearing the sought-after **Écolabel Européen** (https://eu-ecolabel.eu). The list (https://bit.ly/4eU7C0H) includes everything from campsites and glamping to rural gîtes, luxurious eco-hotels, and Best Western's Ajaccio and Bastia branches. Certified accommodation is subject to rigorous assessments on energy and water consumption, waste management, food waste, and environmental optimisation before being awarded the green stamp of approval.

## SIP FROM THE SPRINGS

Corsica abounds in mineral-rich natural springs, and much of the island's bottled water (including notable brands like Orezza, Zilia, and St-George) is locally sourced. It's safe to fill up your bottles with tap water (unless marked "non-potable"), but eco-savvy hikers can also make the most of natural water sources along popular footpaths (maps from the tourist offices detail the locations). Free freshwater fountains (fontaines) are also dotted throughout town and villages, especially in the mountains, and Orezza even has its own from-the-source fountain (see page 139).

## POWERED BY NATURE

The natural landscapes managed by the Parc Naturel Régional de Corse (https://pnr.corsica)

encompass more than 365,000 hectares and include seven additional nature reserves and protected marine areas – providing ample terrain for eco-minded adventurers to explore. Paddle around the Reserve Naturelle Scandola (see page 78) or the Vallée du Fango biosphere reserve (see page 75) in a kayak, cruise out to the Îles Lavezzi (see page 121) from Bonifacio on an electric boat, go wild swimming at one of the many natural water holes, or try eco-approved activities like canyoning, scuba diving or horse riding.

BONIFACIO PORT

# Basics

# Getting there

The quickest way to reach Corsica is by air, and the island has four international airports: Bastia, Calvi, Ajaccio, and Figari. From the United Kingdom, direct flights from London take just over two hours. The only direct flights to Corsica from outside of Europe are from Morocco. Travellers from the US, Canada, and South Africa can fly direct to several European cities, including Paris, London, and Frankfurt, all of which have connecting flights to Corsica. From Australia and New Zealand, the best fares are generally via Asia. Car ferries also connect Corsica to the south of France and northern Italy.

Many flight routes, including those direct from the UK, only operate seasonally; at other times, you'll have to fly via France or another European city. Last-minute fares can shoot up in July and August, so it's best to book well in advance and try to fly to the closest airport, as cross-island transfers can be pricey. Prices quoted below are for July-August and include all taxes and surcharges.

## Flights from the UK and Ireland

There are flights from London directly to two of Corsica's airports. EasyJet (http://easyjet.com) offers seasonal flights from London Gatwick to Bastia (April-September) from £58 and to Figari (June-August) from £51. British Airways (https://britishairways.com) also flies from London Heathrow to Figari (from £223 in August or £56 in October). There are no direct flights to Corsica from Ireland or elsewhere in the UK.

## Flights from the US and Canada

Most major airlines operate scheduled flights to Paris or London from the US and Canada, from where you can fly direct to Corsica during the summer months. Out of season, it's best to fly via a French city. Air France (http://airfrance.co.uk) has the most frequent service

and competitive fares that sometimes undercut US carriers; it also operates a codeshare with Delta. If connecting in Paris, note that while Air France transatlantic flights often terminate at Charles-de-Gaulle, flights to Corsica frequently depart from Orly or Beauvais, entailing an inconvenient transfer between the two airports. Other airlines offering **nonstop** services to Paris from a variety of US cities include: American Airlines from New York, Charlotte, Chicago, Dallas, Philadelphia and Miami; Delta from Boston, Washington, Los Angeles, Seattle, San Francisco and Cincinnati; and United from Chicago, New York, San Francisco and Washington DC. Air Canada offers nonstop services to Paris from Montréal and Toronto, while Air Transat offers good-value nonstop flights to Marseille, Nice, and other destinations from Montréal, Québec or Toronto.

Direct flights to Corsica also depart from several major French cities, including Paris, Marseille, Lyon, Bordeaux and Nice. The largest operators are Air France and Air Corsica (http://aircorsica.com), which fly to Bastia, Ajaccio, Calvi, and Figari year-round. In addition, easyJet (http://easyjet.com), Volotea (http://volotea.com) and Transavia (http://transavia.com) fly to the island from various French and other European cities, so you could also travel via another European destination. A final option is to fly to Nice or Marseille, where you can take the ferry.

## Flights from Australia, New Zealand and South Africa

Most travellers from **Australia** and **New Zealand** choose to fly to Corsica via London, although the majority of airlines can add a Paris leg (or a flight to any other major French city) to an Australia/New Zealand–Europe ticket. Flights via Asia or the Gulf States, with a transfer or overnight stop at the airline's home port, are generally the cheapest option; those routed through the US tend to be slightly pricier.

From **South Africa**, Johannesburg is the best place to start, with Air France flying direct to Paris where there are plenty of options. From Paris, you can find flights to all four of Corsica's airports.

---

### A BETTER KIND OF TRAVEL

At Rough Guides we are passionately committed to travel. We believe it helps us understand the world we live in and the people we share it with – and of course tourism is vital to many developing economies. But the scale of modern tourism has also damaged some places irreparably, and climate change is accelerated by most forms of transport, especially flying. We encourage all our authors to consider the carbon footprint of the journeys they make in the course of researching our guides.

---

### TRAVELLING WITH PETS FROM THE UK

If you wish to take your dog or cat to France, the **Pet Travel Scheme (PETS)** enables you to avoid putting it in quarantine when re-entering the UK as long as certain conditions are met. Current regulations are available on the Department for Environment, Food and Rural Affairs (DEFRA) website http://gov.uk/taking-your-pet-abroad. Note that since Brexit, pets from the UK travelling to the EU will need a valid Animal Health Certificate (AHS) issued by a vet to travel. UK-issued Pet Passports are no longer valid. Travelling by ferry is the most convenient option for pets; if you plan to fly, it's best to contact a pet transport specialist such as Pet Air UK (http://bapetairuk.com).

---

## Ferries

Three companies run services between mainland France and Corsica: Corsica Ferries (http://corsica-ferries.fr; from Nice and Toulon), Corsica Linea (http://corsicalinea.com; from Marseille) and La Méridionale (http://lameridionale.fr; from Marseille), arriving at Ajaccio, Porto Vecchio, Île Rousse, Propriano or Bastia ports. Journeys take between five and twelve hours on either regular ferries or much faster giant hydrofoils ("NGV" or *navire à grande vitesse*), and there is a mix of overnight and day crossings. Corsica Ferries, Corsica Linea, and Moby Moby (http://mobylines.com) also run services to various Italian ports (including to Sardinia from Bonifacio).

Fares fluctuate according to the season, with the lowest between October and May; during July and August, ticket prices sometimes more than treble. In peak season, prices start at around €250 for a family of four with a car and an onboard cabin or around €30 for a foot passenger. Ferry tickets for all companies can be booked via their websites, and reservations are essential for journeys in July and August. Popular cabins and spaces for large vehicles can also fill up quickly.

### AGENTS AND OPERATORS

**Canvas Holidays** http://canvasholidays.co.uk. Tailor-made caravan and camping holidays.
**Corsican Places** http://corsica.co.uk. Corsica specialists.
**Discover France** http://discoverfrance.com. Self-guided cycling and walking holidays throughout France.

---

### ETIAS

By the end of 2026, all non-EU citizens travelling under the 90/180-day rule will need to apply for a €7 ETIAS prior to arrival. Similar to the ESTA system in the US, this travel authorisation requires an online registration and payment before you travel, and it is valid for three years. A new ETIAS is required if you change your passport.

---

**Eurocamp** http://eurocamp.co.uk. Camping holidays with kids' activities and single-parent deals.
**French Side Travel** http://frenchsidetravel.com. Father and son team based in the Dordogne who offer several week-long Corsica packages.
**Headwater** http://headwater.com. UK-based operator offering walking, cycling, and canoeing tours throughout France.
**Just Corsica** http://justcorsica.co.uk. UK company that specialises in Corsica and Sardinia.

# Visas and entry requirements

**Citizens of EU countries can enter France freely on a valid passport or national identity card, while those from many non-EU countries, including Australia, Canada, New Zealand, the United States and the UK since Brexit may spend 90 days in any 180-day period within France and/or the Schengen area without a visa. However, from 2026 they will need to apply for an ETIAS travel authorisation (see box, page 26) prior to travel. Your passport must have an expiry date of more than six months from the date of arrival in the EU or three months from your intended exit date.**

South African citizens require a short-stay visa for up to ninety days, which should be applied for in advance. Any non-EU citizens wishing to spend longer than 90 days in France or the EU must apply for a **long-stay visa** for which you'll have to show proof of – among other things – a regular income or sufficient funds to support yourself and medical insurance (https://france-visas.gouv.fr/en/).

In 2025, all arrivals to France or the Schengen area must pass through the new entry/exit system (EEA), which automatically tracks your 90-day allowance. If you are entering the Schengen area for the first time since the EEA was introduced, your biometric data will be captured. This system doesn't apply to EU citizens or those with a long-stay visa or resident card.

### FRENCH EMBASSIES AND CONSULATES

**Australia** Canberra 02 6216 0100, http://au.ambafrance.org
**Britain** London 020 7073 1000; http://uk.ambafrance.org
**Canada** Montréal 514 878 4385, http://montreal.consulfrance.org; Toronto 416 847 1900, http://toronto.consulfrance.org
**Ireland** Dublin 01 277 5000, http://ie.ambafrance.org
**New Zealand** Wellington 04 384 2555, http://nz.ambafrance.org
**South Africa** Johannesburg 011 77 85 600, http://johannesburg.consulfrance.org
**USA** Washington 202 944 6000, http://franceintheus.org

# Arrival

Corsica's four airports and five main ferry ports are all located in different corners of the island. Taxis to the other side of the island are expensive, so choose your entry point wisely.

## By plane

All airports have taxis and car rentals available, but it's best to book ahead.

**Ajaccio Napoléon Bonaparte Airport (AJA)** is situated 5km (about a 20-minute drive) from the centre of Ajaccio on the west coast of Corsica. Shuttle buses (Line 8) run to Ajaccio city centre and train station approximately every half hour from 5am to 11pm; €8.50 in advance/€10 on board; https://ajaccio-aeroport.cci.corsica/navettes/.

**Bastia Poretta Airport (BIA)** is 17km south of Bastia on the northeast coast. huttle buses run to Bastia city centre/train station (about 25 minutes; €10; http://stib-bastia.com) or Porto-Vecchio (June-Oct only; about 3 hours; €30; http://rapides-bleus.com).

**Calvi Sainte-Catherine Airport (CLY)** is 8km east of Calvi on the northwest coast. No public transport available.

**Figari Sud-Corse Airport (FSC)** is situated around 3km from Figari, 22km from Bonifacio and 25km from Porto Vecchio in south Corsica. Shuttle buses run to Porto Vecchio (June-Sept only; http://corsicabus.org/busPVecchio/PVE_Airport.html; €10).

## By ferry

All ferry ports can be accessed on foot or by car, but taxis aren't always available on arrival, so book transfers in advance.

**Bastia** port is about a 20-minute walk or 5-minute drive from the city centre or train station.

**Ajaccio** port is about a 5-minute walk or 2-minute drive from the city centre or train station.

**L'Ile Rousse** port is about a 15-minute walk or 5-minute drive from the city centre.

**Propriano** port is about a 5-minute walk or 2-minute drive from the city centre.

**Porto Vecchio** port is about a 10-minute walk or 5-minute drive from the city centre or a 5-minute walk from the bus station.

# Getting around

**Having a car will make exploring Corsica much easier; without, it's best to stick to your chosen resort town and take nearby tours to visit the surrounding attractions. Public transport is only really feasible between certain destinations, and you will be unfortunately at the mercy of the limited timetables.**

## By bus

Bus services have massively reduced across the island in recent years, with several lines stopping altogether. Expect a couple of daily services to major destinations out of Bastia and Ajaccio, and along the east coast to Porto-Vecchio and Bonifacio; elsewhere on the island, services tend to peter out in the winter months or are even more infrequent. Bus timetables are typically posted on the door of tourist offices, or check http://corsicabus.org. Some bus tickets can be purchased online in advance; others only accept cash. Prices vary, but for example, the bus from Bastia to Porto Vecchio costs €30 (http://rapides-bleus.com), while the bus from Porto Vecchio to Bonifacio costs €9 (http://bit.ly/3XChztS; €9).

## By train

Corsica's diminutive train, the revamped *Micheline* or *Trinighellu* (https://cf-corse.corsica), travels through the mountains from Ajaccio to Bastia via Corte, with a branch line running northwest to Calvi. Thanks to new trains over the last few years, journeys are now smoother and more comfortable – though unfortunately no quicker. It is, however, an incredibly scenic ride right through the heart of the island. Adult singles from Bastia to Ajaccio costs €21.60 purchased from the train station or onboard. The Pass Liberta (€50; buy online) allows unlimited access to the main

## DRIVING IN CORSICA

Corsica's winding mountain roads make for some thrilling – or hair-raising – driving, depending on your nerves. Plan your route before setting off, especially if you're a nervous driver and avoid driving the mountain roads at night unless absolutely necessary. Stick to the *Routes Territoriales* (T/RT) wherever possible, as these main roads are generally well-maintained and make for smooth driving. The smaller *Routes Départementales* (D) get increasingly narrow and winding as you climb further into the mountains, so prepare yourself for some intimidatingly tight turns and watch out for animals on the road. In July and August, traffic can also be horrendous along popular routes, especially if you find yourself stuck behind a tour bus – set off early to avoid the worst of it.

It's best to plan according to average driving times rather than distance, as you won't cover more than 40km in an hour on the mountain roads. Some popular routes include:

**Bastia to Calvi,** T20/T30: 120km or about 2 hours
**Porto to Corte** D84; 85km or about 2 hours 20 mins
**Bastia – Porto Vecchio**, RT10; 145km or about 2.5 hours
**Bastia – Corte – Ajaccio**, T20: 150km or about 2.5 hours
**Cap Corse circuit,** D80: 118km or about 3.5 hours.

"Grand Ligne" trains only (not the regional "Périurbain" tramways) over a 7-day period.

# By car

With public transport largely inadequate, the most convenient way of getting around Corsica is by rental car, and all the big firms allow you to collect and return vehicles in different places. Even if your budget won't stretch to a week, it's worth renting for a couple of days to explore the interior or drive the Cap Corse.

### Licences, insurance, and breakdown

US, UK, Canadian, Australian, New Zealand, South African and all EU **driving licences** are valid in France for up to twelve months, though an International Driver's Licence makes life easier. The minimum driving age is 18, and you must hold a full licence. Drivers are required to carry their licence, insurance and registration documents with them when driving.

If you are bringing a UK car over to France, you must display a UK sticker (unless your number plate displays the Union Jack flag) and fit headlamp beam deflectors (stickers or otherwise). You must also carry reflective jackets and a warning triangle. Winter tyres or snow chains are mandatory if driving through certain mountainous areas of France between November and March, but the rules don't currently apply to Corsica. **Seat belts** are compulsory and children under ten years must travel in an approved child seat, harness or booster appropriate to their age and size.

There are garages (*garages automobiles*) and breakdown services (*dépannages*) throughout Corsica in case you run into mechanical difficulties; if you have an accident or theft, contact the local police – and keep

a copy of their report in order to file an insurance claim. Within Europe, most car **insurance policies** cover taking your car to France; check with your insurer. It's advisable to take out extra cover for breakdown assistance; rental cars should include breakdown cover. If you have an **accident** while driving, you must fill in and sign a *constat d'accident* (declaration form) or, if another car is also involved, a *constat à l'amiable* (jointly agreed declaration); in the case of a hire car, these forms should be provided with the car's insurance documents.

### Rules of the road

Corsica follows the same rules as mainland France, so you will **drive on the right**. In built-up areas, the law of *priorité à droite* – **giving way** to traffic coming from your right – still sometimes applies. A sign showing a yellow diamond on a white background indicates that you have right of way, while the same sign with a diagonal black slash across it warns you that vehicles emerging from the right have priority. *Cédez le passage* means "Give way"; *vous n'avez pas la priorité* means "You do not have right of way".

Unless otherwise indicated **speed limits** are: 110kph (68mph) on dual carriageways; 80kph (50mph) on regional roads; 50kph (31mph) in built-up areas. In wet weather and for drivers with less than two years' experience, these limits are 110kph (68mph), 100kph (62mph) and 80kph (50mph), respectively, while the town limit remains constant. Many town centres and villages have 30kph limits, and fixed and mobile radars are widely used. The **alcohol limit** is 0.05 per cent (0.5 grams per litre of blood), and random breath tests and saliva tests for drugs are common. There are stiff **penalties** for driving violations, ranging from on-the-spot **fines** for minor infringements to the immediate confiscation of your licence and/or your car for more serious offences. Note that radar detectors and SatNav systems that identify the location of speed traps are illegal in France.

### Car rental

To rent a car in Corsica, as with the rest of France, you must be over 21 (25 with some agencies) and have driven for at least a year. You'll find the big-name international firms – Avis, Hertz and so on – represented at airports and in Bastia and Ajaccio. Unless you specify otherwise (and sometimes even if you do), you will likely be given an electric car – some companies now only have electric fleets available. Prices vary, and longer bookings attract the best rates; expect to pay from €245/week in peak season. Book well in advance for holiday weekends and July-Aug.

### CAR RENTAL AGENCIES

**Avis** http://avis.com
**Alamo** http://alamo.com
**Enterprise** http://enterprise.com
**Europcar** http://europcar.com
**Hertz** http://hertz.com
**Rent a car** http://rentacar.fr

## By scooter and motorbike

**Scooters** are ideal for pottering around locally and the mountain roads, while not for the inexperienced, provide plenty of thrills for motorcyclists. They're easy to rent, and prices start from around €50/day. If you are over 24 years old, you only need a B licence to rent a 50cc moped, but otherwise, you'll need a scooter or motorbike licence. For anything 50cc–125cc, you'll need to have held a driving licence for at least two years regardless of your age and either have the A1 or equivalent licence, and for anything over 125cc, you need a full **motorbike** licence. Crash helmets are compulsory on all bikes, and the headlight must be switched on at all times. For bikes over 125cc it is compulsory to wear reflective clothing at night.

### MOTORBIKE/SCOOTER RENTAL

**Envie2rouler Corsica** https://envie2rouler-moto.com
**Corse Moto Location** https://corse-moto-location.fr/
**Vespa Course Location** https://vespa-corse-location.com
**Moto Corse Evasion** https://corsicamoto.fr

## Taxis

Taxis are not cheap in Corsica, so it's best to treat them as a last resort. However, they are available in most towns; we've listed local firms throughout the guide. Always book in advance. Uber and other ride-share

### ACCOMMODATION ALTERNATIVES

Useful websites that provide alternatives to standard hotel and hostel accommodation.
**AirBnB** http://airbnb.com.
**Abritel** http://abritel.fr
**Gites de France** http://gites-corsica.com
**Chambres d'hôte** http://chambres-hotes.fr
**Refuge Booking** https://pnr-resa.corsica
**Camping France** https://campingfrance.com

apps have yet to take off on the island, so don't rely on these to get around.

# Accommodation

**Corsica has a wide range of hotels, gites, campsites, and Airbnb rentals, most of which are concentrated around the coastal cities and beaches. Most hotels have two or more different price brackets according to the seasons, with mid-July to August always being highest, so being flexible with dates can really pay off. Difficult-to-access roads and patchy wi-fi can be a problem in the mountains, so read the description carefully before booking rural accommodations.**

All **tourist offices** can provide lists of hotels, hostels, campsites and bed-and-breakfast possibilities. As a rule, book as far in advance as possible, especially for peak season; many places book up weeks ahead.

## Hotels

French hotels are graded in five bands, from one up to five, but the rating system doesn't always paint the full picture; some unclassified and single-star hotels can be very good. Note that many of the no-frills chain hotels present throughout France, such as *Formule 1*, *B&B*, and *Campanile*, do not operate in Corsica. However, the cities of Bastia, Ajaccio, and Calvi tend to have a good variety of cheaper establishments; mid-range hotels around Porto Vecchio and Bonifacio are notably pricier. For more upmarket picks, there is also a small selection of Corsican hotels listed with **hotel federations** *Logis de France* (http://logishotels.com) and *Relais & Châteaux* (https://relaischateaux.com). **Breakfast** is optional but will often add between €7 and €30 per person to a bill. Regardless of

## ACCOMMODATION PRICES

You'll be able to find a simple double or studio apartment from €70, even in high season, but expect to pay at least €120 for a reasonable level of comfort and from €150 for a 3-star hotel. Note that you will need to book early to secure these rates; last-minute bookings in July and August can leave you with very slim (and expensive) pickings.

Throughout this book, we use price codes to indicate how much you can expect to pay for a **double/twin room during high season** (July & August) without breakfast. Single rooms, where available, usually cost between 60 and 80 per cent of a double or twin. At **hostels**, we have indicated the price of a dormitory bed and at **campsites**, the cost of two people, a pitch and a vehicle, unless otherwise stated. Prices include the obligatory tourist tax; note that this will be included if using a booking site such as Booking.com or Airbnb. The codes used correspond to the following prices:

**€** = below €100
**€€** = €100–€180
**€€€** = €181–€250
**€€€€** = above €251

the time of year, it's best to book ahead; most hotels will not appreciate you showing up unannounced.

## Bed and breakfast and self-catering

In addition to standard hotels, you will come across chambres d'hôtes (http://chambres-hotes.fr) – bed-and-breakfast accommodation in someone's house or farm. Though the quality varies widely, the best offer more character and greater value for money than an equivalently priced hotel, and many have swimming pools. If you're lucky, the owners may also provide traditional home cooking and a great insight into Corsican life. Prices generally range between €75 and €150 for two people with breakfast; some offer evening meals on request (tables d'hôtes).

If you're planning to stay a week or more, it's worth renting self-catering accommodation. The government-funded agency Gîtes de France has a list of gîtes (http://gites-de-france.com), typically self-contained country cottages or converted barns, mills, or farm outbuildings. Tourist offices will also have lists of gîtes in their area and many now also list on Airbnb.

## Hostels

Budget travellers are probably better off seeking out a cheap Airbnb or campsite, but Corsica does have two youth hostels (auberges de jeunesse) – listed with the Ligue Française (LFAJ: http://auberges-de-jeunesse.com) and the Club Loisirs Action Jeunesse (http://clajsud.com) - both of which require a membership card. Prices start from €30 per night for a **dormitory bed** with breakfast thrown in, and special group rates are available.

## Gîtes d'étape and refuges

Aimed primarily at long-distance hikers and cyclists, Corsica also has several gîtes d'étape or refuges (mountain huts), which provide simple dormitory accommodation, tent rentals and tent pitches. There are more than a dozen of these refuges located along the GR20 and other long-distance footpaths, all managed by the **Parc Naturel Régional de Corse (PNRC)** (https://pnr.corsica). Camping along the trails is prohibited except at these spots.

Costs are typically €9 per pitch, €17 for a dormitory bed, and €31 for two people sleeping in a rental tent (bring your own sleeping bag). A demi-pension option (book ahead), including a hot evening meal and breakfast (around €8 for breakfast and €13 for dinner), is sometimes available. Facilities include toilets and drinking water, but some have showers, and many sell drinks, snacks, and emergency hiking supplies. Refuges are open from May to mid-October, although some do remain open, albeit unstaffed, year-round. Advance bookings are essential; book early to snag a bed.

## Camping

Practically every beach and coastal town in Corsica has at least one **campsite**. Most sites open from around Easter to September or early October and are graded – from one to four stars – by the local authority. One-star sites are basic, with toilets and showers (not necessarily with hot water) but little else, and standards of cleanliness are not always brilliant. Facilities improve with more stars: at the top end of the scale, four-star sites are far more spacious, have hot-water showers and electrical hook-ups; most also have a swimming pool (sometimes heated), washing machines, and a shop or restaurant. A further designation, **Camping Qualité** (http://campingqualite.com), indicates campsites with particularly high standards, while the **Clef Verte** (http://laclefverte.org) label is awarded to sites run along environmentally friendly lines. For those who really like to get away from it all, **camping à la ferme** – on somebody's farm – is a good, simple option.

Lists of sites are available at local tourist offices or from Gîtes de France. The Fédération Française de Camping et de Caravaning also has 21 affiliated sites in Corsica, which can be booked via the Camping France website (http://campingfrance.com). Many big sites also let caravans and chalets.

Most campsites charge per emplacement and per person, usually including a car, with extra charges for electricity. As a rough guide, two people with a tent and car might pay as little as €12 per day at an out-of-the-way rural one-star site, or as much as €70 at a four-star by the beach in July or August.

Lastly, a word of caution: wild camping is prohibited in Corsica, and hefty fines apply, so unless you have permission from the landowner, you should check into an official campsite.

# Food and drink

**With a Mediterranean climate and two gastronomic giants, Italy and France, as neighbours, you can expect to eat well in Corsica. There's a big emphasis on local produce and humble, homecooked cuisine, but Corsica has also upped its gastronomic game in recent years, securing a handful of Michelin stars. You'll find a wealth of farm-to-table restaurants throughout rural areas as well as some excellent world cuisine in the main cities.**

Most restaurants now offer at least one **vegetarian** option on the menu, and a handful of **vegan** restaurants have sprung up in recent years, mostly in Bastia, Ajaccio and the main resorts. However, non-meat dishes are still the exception rather than the rule.

Compared to mainland France, eating out in Corsica tends to be on the pricier side and only select restaurants offer set *menus* – when available these are almost always the best-value option. Note that, as in the rest of France, restaurants tend to adhere to strict serving times, typically 12 to 2pm for lunch and 7 to 9.30pm for dinner. While you may find the odd brasserie that serves food outside of these timeslots, options are usually limited to fast food and snacks.

## EATING OUT PRICE CODES

The **price codes** for Corsica given in this guide are based on the cost of a meat- or fish-based main course; vegetarian options are typically slightly cheaper. *Menus*, when available, often include three courses for just a few euros more than the price of a single dish *à la carte*. Most restaurants include a service charge in the bill. These price codes are:

**€** = below €20
**€€** = €21–€29
**€€€** = €30–€49
**€€€€** = above €50

## Breakfast and lunch

A croissant or *pain au chocolat* in a café or bar, with tea, hot chocolate or coffee, is generally the most economical way to eat breakfast, costing from €6. The standard hotel breakfast comprises bread and/or pastries with butter and jam, served alongside coffee or tea and orange juice, from around €7. Higher-end hotels are likely to offer a breakfast buffet with Corsican cheese, charcuterie, and a selection of homemade pastries, jams and honey, but expect to pay upwards of €15.

At **lunchtime**, you'll find some places offer a *plat du jour* (daily special) or lunchtime *menus* offering a main dish and either a starter (*entrée-plat*) or a dessert (*plat-dessert*) for a set price. If you don't fancy a multi-course affair, *galettes* (savoury buckwheat pancakes) and pizzas, usually *au feu de bois* (baked in wood-fired ovens), are popular options.

For **picnics**, the local food market or supermarket will provide you with everything you need, but for quality produce, head to one of the dedicated *delicatessens* or *epiceries* (grocery stores) that focus on Corsican products. The best cheese and charcuterie is bought directly from the producers – look out for roadside signs when driving in the mountains as you'll never be far from a farm shop (*vente*), and many offer tastings (*degustation*), which can easily serve as a light lunch. You can purchase by weight, or you can ask for *une tranche* (a slice), *une barquette* (a carton) or *une part* (a portion) as appropriate.

## Regional dishes

Corsican cuisine is infused with the fragrant aromas of the *maquis* (see page 165), where thyme, sage, fennel, mint, and rosemary grow in abundance, along with native plants like myrtle, arbutus, and chestnuts. Traditional Corsican dishes include *civet de* sanglier (wild boar stew with red wine and chestnuts), veau aux olives (veal stew with olives and white wine), agneau Corse (slow-roasted lamb) and cannellonis au brocciu (cheese-stuffed cannelloni), while zuppa corsa (meat and bean soup) can be served as either an entrée or a main.

**Sea fish** like red mullet (rouget), bream (loup de mer) and a great variety of shellfish are eaten along the coast, often in the form of an aziminu, the Corsican version of a bouillabaisse (fish soup). The best crayfish (langouste) comes from around the Golfe de St-Florent, whereas oysters (huîtres) and mussels (moules) are a speciality of the eastern plain.

## Drinks

In France, drinking is done at a leisurely pace, whether it's a prelude to food (apéritif) or a sequel (digestif), and café-bars are the standard places to do it. By law, the full price list, including service charges, must be clearly displayed, and you normally pay when you leave.

### Wine, beer and spirits

Corsica produces some excellent, and still little-known, **wines**, mostly from indigenous vine stocks that yield distinctive, herb-tinged aromas. There are two principal AOP wine regions, Ajaccio and Patrimonio. There's also the sweet AOP Muscat du Cap Corse and a general AOP Vin de Corse that encompasses the five other wine regions: Calvi, Sartène, Figari, Porto-Vecchio and Coteaux du Cap Corse.

Names to look out for include: Domaine Torraccia (Porto-Vecchio); Domaine Fiumicicoli (Sartène); Domaine Saparale (Sartène); Domaine Gentille (Patrimonio); Domaine Leccia (Patrimonio); and Venturi-Pieretti (Cap Corse). In addition to the usual whites, reds and rosés, the last of these makes the sweet muscat for which Cap Corse was renowned in previous centuries.

Familiar Belgian, German and French beers can be found at supermarkets, bars and restaurants, but there's a clear preference for local beer brands, many of which are flavoured with chestnuts or native herbs from the maquis. Pietra, Paolina, and Ribella are the most common Corsican beers, and there's a growing craft beer scene (see page 58).

Corsica's most popular aperitif is Cap Corse, a fortified wine flavoured with quinine and herbs, and you'll also find liqueurs made with chestnut cream, Vin d'Orange, cedrat or myrtle.

### Soft drinks, tea and coffee

Standard fruit juices and fizzy drinks are available throughout the island, but look out for artisanal juices or soft drinks made with Corsican clementines, lemons, or agrumes (a mix of citrus fruits).

Bottled mineral **water** (eau minérale) or spring water (eau de source), whether sparkling (gazeuse) or still (plate), is typically local, too – Orezza, Zilia, and Saint George are the most popular brands. You can also ask for tap water (l'eau du robinet) – a jug (une carafe d'eau) will be brought free to your table if you ask for it. The only time you shouldn't drink the tap water is if the tap is labelled eau non potable.

**Coffee** is invariably espresso – small, black and strong. Un café or un express is the regular; un crème is with milk; un grand café or un grand crème are large versions. Un déca is decaffeinated, now widely available. Ordinary **tea** (thé) – Lipton's, nine times out of ten – is normally served black (nature); to have milk with it, ask for un peu de lait frais (some fresh milk). Herbal teas (infusions or tisanes) and chocolat chaud – **hot chocolate** – are also very common in cafés and bars.

# The media

**All the main French newspapers – Le Monde (http://lemonde.fr), Le Figaro (http://lefigaro.fr), Libération (http://liberation.fr) and Le Parisien (https://leparisien.fr) – are available from newsagents (maisons de la presse) or any of the street-side kiosks. Corse Matin (https://corsematin.com) is Corsica's local newspaper, widely available throughout the island and the best source of local news. Some British and US newspapers, including the New York Times and The Guardian, are available in cities.**

French **terrestrial TV** is broadcast throughout Corsica. Of the six channels, TF1 (http://tf1.fr) and France 2 (http://france2.fr) are the most popular channels, while France 3 operates a regional channel, France 3 Corse (https://france3-regions.francetvinfo.fr/corse/).

Radio France (http://radiofrance.fr) and Europe 1 (http://europe1.fr) are the principal radio stations, along with the local Corse Radio (https://corseradio.corsica). Radio France International (RFI, http://rfi.fr) broadcasts in French and English.

# Festivals

**Corsica takes part in nationwide celebrations such as the Fête de la Musique (June 21; http://fetedelamusique.culture.gouv.fr), Bastille Day (Fête Nationale; July 14) and the Assumption of the Virgin Mary**

(Aug 15), all of which are celebrated throughout the island.

## Festival calendar

### APRIL–JUNE

**U Catenacciu**, Sartène (Easter); a centuries-old Good Friday procession and the biggest Easter tradition on the island.
**Fiera di U Casgiu**, Venaco (May; https://www.fromages-corse.org); a weekend celebrating Corsican cheese and cheese-making traditions.
**Musicales de Bastia,** Bastia (June; https://musicalesdebastia. com); music festival with national and international artists.

### JULY

**Calvi on the Rocks**, Calvi (July; https://calviontherocks.com); 4-day electronic music festival on the beach.
**Fiera di l'Alivu**, Montemaggiore (July; https://jazzinaiacciu.com); village fête celebrating the region's olive oil.
**Fiera di U Vinu**, Île Rousse (May; https://fieradiuvinu.corsica); Corsican wine festival, previously held in Luri.
**Festi Lumi**, Bonifacio (July; https://festilumi.fr); 3-day lights festival illuminating Bonifacio's clifftop landmarks.
**Festivoce**, Pigna (July; https://voce.corsica/voce/festivoce); eclectic music festival celebrating vocal traditions from around the world.
**Jazz in Aiaccu**, Ajaccio (June; https://jazzinaiacciu.com); international jazz festival.
**A Notte di a Memoria**, Bastia (Late July; https://agenda.bastia. corsica/agenda/notte-di-a-memoria/); costumed pageant and ceremony to welcome the new governor of Bastia to their post, a spectacular annual tradition dating back to Genoese times.
**Les Nuits de la Guitare**, Patrimonio (July; https://festival-guitare-patrimonio.com); international guitar festival with past performers including Jeff Beck, Patti Smith and Robert Plant.
**Sorru in Musica**, Sartenais-Valinco-Taravo (July; https://sorru-in-musica.corsica); 10-day classical music festival held at churches and chapels across the region.

### AUGUST–SEPTEMBER

**Fiera di U Nuciola**, Cervione (mid-August; https://facebook.com/ nuciola/); village hazelnut festival in Castagniccia.
**Les Journées Napoléoniennes**, Ajaccio (15th August; https://ajaccio-tourisme.com/les-temps-forts/les-journees-napoleoniennes); three days of festivities, costumed parades and firework displays to celebrate Napoleon's birthday.
**Porto Latino**, Saint-Florent (August; https://portolatino.fr); four days of salsa and Latin rhythms.
**Santa di Niolu**, Casamaccioli (around 8th Sept; https://facebook. com/santa.diniolu.77); Corsica's oldest fair honours the birth of the Virgin Mary with three days of traditional foods, artisan markets, and live entertainment, as well as a large procession.
**Rencontre de chants polyphonique,** Calvi (Sept; https:// rencontrespolyphoniques.com); Corsica's leading celebration of polyphonic music featuring local & international acts over five days.

### OCTOBER– DECEMBER

**Fête du Marron**, Evisa (early Dec; https://evisa-corsica.com); village festival devoted to all things chestnut.

# Sports and outdoor activities

**Corsica shares France's passion for sport, but local teams rarely fare well in the national leagues, and national events are seldom held on Corsican soil (although the 2013 Tour de France famously included a Corsica stage). When it comes to outdoor activities, however, Corsica is one of the top destinations in the country.**

## Football

**Football** (soccer) is France's number one team sport, and Corsica is no exception. The island has ten teams, but only two have had any notable success in the national leagues. AC Ajaccio (https://ac-ajaccio. corsica) and rivals SC Bastia (https://sc-bastia.corsica), whose historic successes include reaching the final of the 1977-78 UEFA Cup and winning the Coupe de France. Both currently play in France's Ligue 2, and tickets for matches are available on their websites.

## Motorsports

The once-legendary Tour de Corse was a key fixture of the World Rally Championship, nicknamed the "Rally of 10,000 Corners" for its infamous hairpin bends and sheer drops. Marred by a string of fatal crashes and injuries, the event is no more, but the **Tour de Corse Historique** classic car rally still provides plenty of thrills. Driving the legendary roads in a supercar (www.eventscorsicaracing.com) or by motorbike (see page 29) is a popular choice.

## Walking, running & cycling

With 20 peaks over 2,000m and some 1,500km of marked footpaths leading to wild beaches, glacial lakes and rugged gorges, Corsica is a true paradise for hikers, runners and cyclists. Tourist Offices around the island will give you a list of short footpaths and cycle routes, and popular circuits are mentioned throughout the guide. There are also eight long-distance footpaths that crisscross the island, including the GR20 (see page 74) and three Mare à Mare (coast to coast) routes, plus a 500km north-to-south GT20 cycling route. All are

# LONG-DISTANCE WALKS

Sentier du Douanier

*LIGURIAN SEA*

N

Centuri

Macinaggio

Désert des Agriates Coast Path

L'Île-Rousse

St-Florent

Bastia

Le Sentier Isula-Corti

Vallinca

**HAUTE CORSE**

Calvi

Calenzana

Asco

Moltifao

Galéria

Haut'Asco

*Monte Cinto (2706 m)*

Corscia

Mare a Mare Nord & Variant

Moriani-Plage

Tra Mare e Monti Nord

Porto

Évisa

**Corte**

*Monte Rotondo (2622 m)*

Marignana

Cargèse

Vizzavona

Mare a Mare Nord & Variant

Ghisonaccia

*Bocca Laparo*

Cozzano

Mare a Mare Centre

Ajaccio

Zicavo

*Monte Incudine (2136 m)*

Porticcio

**CORSE DU SUD**

*Col de Bavella*

Tra Mare e Monti Sud

Quenza

Zonza

GR 20

Olmeto

Levie

Conca

Propriano

Ospédale

Campomoro

Mare a Mare Sud

Sartène

Porto Vecchio

*Îles Cerbicale*

Tizzano

Roccapina

*TYRRHENIAN SEA*

*MEDITERRANEAN SEA*

Bonifacio

*Île Cavallo*

0          20
kilometres

managed by the PNRC (https://www.pnr.corsica), and you can view maps, purchase route guides and book refuges via the website. Corsica Adventure (https://www.corsica-aventure.com), Cycling Corsica (https://cycling-corsica.fr), and Discover Corsica (https://corsica-discover.com) offer tours.

### SPORTING CALENDAR

**Ajaccio Marathon**, Ajaccio (April; contact the tourist office for information): full, half, and 10km.

**Bastia Marathon**, Bastia (April; contact the tourist office for information): full, half, and 10km.

**Corsica Raid Adventure**, Lecci (early June; https://corsicaraid.com); 5-day Iron Man competition in the Alta Rocca mountains.

**Corsica Coast Trail** (October; https://corsicacoast.com); five-stage trail running competition from Cap Corse to Bonifacio.

**Tour de Corse Historique** (October; https://tourdecorse-historique.fr); hugely popular classic car rally that takes place over ten days with stages covering most of the island.

## Adventure sports

Thrill-seekers have plenty to get excited about in Corsica. **Canyoning** (see page 128) is a highlight and available all around the island: Corsica Natura (https://corsicanatura-activites.fr), Corsica Forest Canyoning (https://corsica-forest.com) and Corsica Canyon (https://canyoncorse.com/en/) all offer tours, suitable for all levels, including some for children. **Rock climbing** (https://escalade-corse.com/) and via ferratas (https://via-ferrata.fr/corse) are found at several sites around Corsica, and there are also treetop adventure parks offering a variety of activities – Parc Aventure de Solenzara (https://www.corse-canyoning-parc.com) and Parc Aventure Vizzavona (https://corsicanatura-activites.fr) are two of the biggest.

 **Horse riding** is also popular, and almost every town has a riding school (centre equestre) that offers rides on the beach or in the mountains. You can also enjoy **paragliding** and **microlight flights** in the Balagne (https://en.altore.com) or around Ajaccio (http://coccinailes.com), go **skydiving** (https://corse-parachutisme-tandem.fr) or hire a quad bike or buggy in Bonifacio (https://corsicaranger.com). Most activities take place from April through October, and tourist offices can provide recommendations.

## Water sports

The northwest coast of the Balagne gets the most wind for surfing and windsurfing, while sailors tend to head to the islands and lagoons of the south and speed boating and jet skiing are most popular on the east coast. Sea kayaking, stand-up paddleboarding,

and sailing can be enjoyed just about everywhere, but the best scuba diving sites are around Calvi (see page 71), Bonifacio, and Cap Corse.

## Skiing & winter sports

Corsica has three ski resorts: Asco (https://asco.corsica) in the north, Val d'Ese (https://valdese.fr) in the south and Ghisoni Capanelle (https://ghisoni.corsica) in central Corsica, which all have ski schools, ski rentals and snowshoeing excursions (randonnées en raquettes).

# Shopping

**Corsica is known for its local artisans, who produce quality handicrafts and regional delicacies. Traditional crafts use locally sourced materials: handmade knives with olive-wood handles, jewellery set with red Mediterranean coral or musical instruments made from walnut, juniper, and ebony wood. Other products include essential oils and cosmetics made with native flora harvested from the maquis, most notably *immortelle* (see page 133), acclaimed for its healing and anti-ageing properties. Edible specialities include the aforementioned cheeses, charcuterie, and wines, along with a range of jams, spreads and oils made from seasonal fruits, herbs and chestnuts. The ubiquitous *canistrelli* are a popular crunchy biscuit made to a traditional recipe with flavours like lemon, clementine, chestnut, almond or anise.**

 Notable artisan shops are highlighted throughout this guide. You can also look for the island-wide "Routes des Sens" label, which denotes artisanal producers and restaurants in each region, and the Balagne-based "Strada di l'Artigiani" (Artisan's Route), which lists local craftspeople.

# Culture and etiquette

While Corsica has been part of France since the 18th century, most locals prefer to be referred to as Corsican rather than French. Although French is the official language, almost 70 percent of the island speaks Corsican and a "Bonghjornu" (hello) when greeting locals will be much appreciated. The Catholic religion is widely practised, and Corsicans are largely more conservative than their French counterparts, especially in rural areas. That said, topless sunbathing is common on the beach (although naturism is prohibited outside of dedicated nudist beaches) and, as in the rest of France, women won't face any difficulties travelling alone. Smoking is banned in all indoor public places.

# Travel essentials

## Accessible travel

The French authorities have been making a concerted effort to improve facilities for **travellers with disabilities,** and you will find accessible accommodation, parking and public facilities all around the island. That said, Corsica's historic villages, replete with steps and cobblestones, and its steep hills remain serious obstacles for anyone with mobility problems. Hotels, sights and other facilities are inspected under the nationwide "Tourisme & Handicap" scheme and, if they fulfil certain criteria, issued with a certificate and logo.

Local tourist offices should be your first port of call for accessible activities, transport and taxis. You can also filter for accessibility on the Corsica Tourism website (https://www.visit-corsica.com) to find suitable accommodation and tours. Corsica's train offers ramp access and the stations in Ajaccio and Bastia are fully accessible, but not all destination stations are. All of Corsica's main ferry and cruise ports are accessible, but it's best to check ahead for marinas and boat tours.

### USEFUL CONTACTS

**Association des Paralysés de France (APF)** http://apf-francehandicap.org. National association that can answer general enquiries and put you in touch with their departmental offices.
**Irish Wheelchair Association** Ireland http://iwa.ie. Useful information about travelling abroad with a wheelchair.
**Mobility International USA** US http://miusa.org. Information and international exchange programmes.
**Tourism for All** UK http://tourismforall.org.uk. Masses of useful information.

## Costs

Corsica generally ranks among France's more expensive destinations, with prices comparable to that of the French Riviera. For a reasonably comfortable existence – staying in hotels, eating out in restaurants, plus moving around, café stops and museum visits – you need to allow a **budget** of around €130 (£115/$140) a day per person, assuming two people sharing a mid-range room. By counting the pennies – staying at an Airbnb, enjoying hikes and other free activities, and cooking some of your own meals – you could probably manage on €80 (£50/$70) a day per person. Prices receive a considerable bump from mid-July to Aug, so budget travellers should prioritise shoulder season.

Service charges are included at restaurants and additional cash tips are only for exemplary service; rounding up the bill or adding 10% percent is enough.

## Crime and personal safety

While Corsica does have a reputation for mafia-related violent crimes, travellers are highly unlikely to come across any such problems. Corsica, on the whole, is among the safest regions of France and violent crime involving tourists is rare. Opportunist thefts and pickpocketing does occur, especially during peak season, so take the normal **precautions**: don't flash wads of notes around; carry your bag or wallet securely and be careful in crowds; and never leave valuables in your car. It's wise to keep a separate record of cheque and credit card numbers, and make sure you have a good insurance policy.

To **report a theft**, go to the local gendarmerie or Commissariat de Police (addresses are listed for major cities). Remember to take your passport and vehicle documents if relevant.

### Drugs

**Drug use** is just as prevalent in Corsica as anywhere else in Europe – and penalties for use remain harsh by European standards, despite public agitation for a softening of the law. The authorities make no distinction between soft and hard drugs. People caught smuggling or possessing drugs, even just a few grams of marijuana, are liable to find themselves in jail.

### Racism

France might be known for its "liberté, égalité, fraternité", but Corsica, as with the rest of the country,

> **EMERGENCY NUMBERS**
>
> **Police** 17
> **Medical emergencies/ambulance (SAMU)** 15
> **Fire brigade/paramedics** 18
> **Emergency calls from a mobile phone** 112
> **Rape crisis (Viols Femmes Informations)** 0800 05 95 95
> All emergency numbers are toll-free.

still has its share of **racist-related** issues. The rise of nationalism on the island, coupled with the rise in immigrant communities, has led to increasing reports of racist incidents against the Arab community.

If you suffer a **racial assault**, contact the police or your consulate. The **English-speaking helpline** SOS Help (01 46 21 46 46, daily 3–11pm; http://soshelpline. org) is staffed by trained volunteers who can also offer practical advice.

## Road safety

Corsica sadly has some of the highest rates of **road accidents** in France, so both drivers and pedestrians should take great care on the roads. Although the authorities are trying to improve matters, many Corsican drivers pay little heed to speed limits and pedestrian/zebra crossings. Never step out onto a crossing assuming that drivers will stop and be wary on sharp turns, as many locals do not slow down as you might expect.

## Electricity

**Voltage** is 230V, using **plugs** with two round pins. If you need an adapter, it's best to buy one before leaving home, though you can find them in larger supermarkets and electrical stores.

## Health

Visitors to France have little to worry about as far as health is concerned. No vaccinations are required, there are no nasty diseases, and tap water is safe to drink. The worst that's likely to happen to you is a case of sunburn or the effects of high altitude when scaling Corsica's mountains.

Under the French health system, all services, including doctors' consultations, prescribed medicines, hospital stays and ambulance call-outs, incur a charge that you have to pay upfront. **EU and UK citizens** are entitled to a refund (usually 70 percent) of medical expenses, provided you have a European Health Insurance Card (EHIC) or a Global Health Insurance Card (GHIC). Present your EHIC or GHIC card to avoid upfront charges if you're admitted to hospital; you'll generally only have to pay a 20 percent co-payment for treatment you receive there. Note that everyone in the family, including children, must have their own EHIC card, which is free.

For minor complaints, go to a **pharmacie**, signalled by an illuminated green cross. You'll find at least one in every small town, and they keep normal shop hours (roughly 9am–noon & 3–6pm). In larger towns, at least one (known as the *pharmacie de garde*) will stay open 24 hours.

**Condoms** (*préservatifs*) are widely available in pharmacies and supermarkets. The pill (*la pilule*) is available only on prescription but emergency contraception (*la pilule du lendemain*) can be obtained at pharmacies.

For anything more serious you can get the name of a **doctor** (*médecin*) from a pharmacy, police station, tourist office or your hotel. You'll have to pay a consultation fee of €30; ask for a *Feuille de Soins* (Statement of Treatment) for later insurance claims. Any prescriptions will be fulfilled by the pharmacy and must be paid for; little price stickers (*vignettes*) from each medicine will be stuck on the *Feuille de Soins*.

In serious **emergencies** you will always be admitted to the nearest general hospital (*centre hospitalier*). Phone numbers and addresses of hospitals in all the main cities are given in the guide.

## Insurance

EU and UK citizens are entitled to healthcare privileges in France with the abovementioned EHIC/GHIC, but dedicated travel insurance is still recommended if you want full coverage. All **non-EU visitors** should ensure that they have adequate medical insurance coverage. A typical travel insurance policy usually provides cover for theft, cancellation, and the loss of

---

## ROUGH GUIDES TRAVEL INSURANCE

Looking for travel insurance? Rough Guides partners with top providers worldwide to offer you the best coverage. Policies are available to residents of anywhere in the world, with a range of options whether you are looking for single-trip, multi-country or long-stay insurance. There's coverage for a wide range of adventure sports, 24-hour emergency assistance, high levels of medical and evacuation cover and a stream of travel safety information. Even better, roughguides.com users can take advantage of these policies online 24/7, from anywhere in the world – even if you're already travelling. To make the most of your travels and ensure a smoother experience, it's always good to be prepared for when things don't go according to plan. For more information go to http://roughguides.com/bookings/insurance.

baggage, tickets and – up to a certain limit – cash or cheques. Most exclude so-called **dangerous sports** unless an extra premium is paid.

## Internet

Free wireless internet (wi-fi) is the norm in even the cheapest Corsican hotels, but wi-fi and 4G coverage can still be unreliable in remote rural areas.

## Laundry

You'll find self-service **laundries** in most major towns and cities – just ask in your hotel or the tourist office, or search for "*Laveries automatiques*" or "*Laveries en libre-service*".

## LGBTQ+ France

In general, France is as liberal as other Western European countries: the age of consent is 15, and same-sex couples have been able to get married since 2013. However, while LGBTQ+ communities thrive in mainland cities, Corsica is notably behind. Thankfully, this is changing, albeit slowly, with Bastia hosting the island's first official Gay Pride march in 2023 (following a small event in Ajaccio in 2022). L'ARCU (https://www.facebook.com/ArcuCorsica/) offers advice for LGBTQ+ people in Corsica, as well as detailing local events and gatherings.

## Living in Corsica

**EU citizens** are able to work in Corsica on the same basis as French citizens, which means that you won't typically require a residence or work permit. Non-EU citizens (including UK citizens post-Brexit) will need a long-stay visa (see page 26) to stay longer than 90 days in France. A standard visitor long-stay visa does not allow you to work; for that you will need a specific work or business visa. There are few options for foreigners to work in Corsica and most English-speaking expats work in the tourism industry. The University of Corsica also offers a French as a Foreign Language diploma as part of the EU-run Erasmus student programme (https://universita.corsica/en/study/study-in-corsica).

## Mail

**Post offices**, known as La Poste (http://laposte.fr) and identified by bright yellow-and-blue signs, are located all around Corsica. Most open from around 9am to 5pm Monday to Friday, and 9am to noon on Saturday. However, these hours aren't set in stone: smaller branches and those in rural areas are likely to close for lunch, while big city centre branches may stay open longer. You can also buy stamps from *tabacs* and newsagents. To post your letter on the street, look for the bright yellow postboxes.

## Maps

In addition to the **maps** in this guide and the various free town plans you'll be offered along the way, serious hikers should pick up one of the Institut Géographique National (IGN; 1:250,000; http://ign.fr) maps, available for several different regions. If you're relying on GPS, it's a good idea to download the maps before heading into the mountains, as coverage can be patchy.

## Money

France's currency is the euro, which is divided into 100 cents (often still referred to as *centimes*). There are seven notes – in denominations of 5, 10, 20, 50, 100, 200 and 500 euros – and eight different coins – 1, 2, 5, 10, 20 and 50 cents, and 1 and 2 euros. At the time of writing, the **exchange rate** for the euro was around €1.15 to the pound sterling (or £0.85 to €1) and €0.95 to the dollar (or $1.15 to €1). See http://xe.com for current rates.

You can change cash at **banks** and main **post offices**, and travellers' cheques at post offices and some BNP Paribas branches. Rates and commission vary, so it's worth shopping around. There are **money-exchange counters** (*bureaux de change*) at Corsica's airports, though they don't always offer the best exchange rates.

By far the easiest way to access money in Corsica is to use your credit or debit card to withdraw cash from an **ATM** (known as a *distributeur* or *point argent*); most machines give instructions in several European languages.

**Credit and debit cards** are widely accepted, but it's recommended to carry some cash in Corsica – some smaller establishments still don't accept cards or have a minimum charge. Visa (*carte bleue*) and MasterCard are widely accepted; American Express less often.

## Opening hours and public holidays

As in the rest of France, basic **hours of business** are Monday to Saturday, 9am to noon and 2 to 6pm. In big cities and tourist towns, **shops** and other businesses stay open throughout the day, as do most **tourist offices** and museums in July and August. In rural areas, places tend to close for at least a couple of hours at lunchtime. The standard **closing day** is Sunday, but

Corsica's high number of tourists and weekend hikers means that some supermarkets and tourist offices are open Sundays from May to September.

**Banking hours** are typically Monday to Friday 8.30am to 12.30pm and 1.30/2pm to 5 or 6pm. Some branches, especially those in rural areas, close on Monday, while those in big cities may remain open at midday and may also open on Saturday morning. All are closed on Sunday and public holidays.

**Museums** tend to open from 9 or 10am to noon and from 2 or 3pm to 5 or 6pm, though in the big cities some stay open all day and opening hours tend to be longer in summer. Museum closing days are usually Monday. **Churches** are generally open from around 8am to dusk but may close at lunchtime and are reserved for worshippers during services (times of which will be posted on the door).

> ## PUBLIC HOLIDAYS
>
> **January 1** New Year's Day
> **Easter Monday**
> **Ascension Day** (forty days after Easter)
> **Whit Monday** (seventh Monday after Easter)
> **May 1** Labour Day
> **May 8** Victory in Europe (VE) Day 1945
> **July 14** Bastille Day
> **August 15** Assumption of the Virgin Mary
> **November 1** All Saints' Day
> **November 11** Armistice Day
> **December 25** Christmas Day

## Phones

If you want to use your **mobile/cellphone**, contact your phone provider to check whether it will work in France and what the call charges are. EU mobile phones are free from roaming charges, while UK travellers should check the rules with their provider. French mobile phones operate on the GSM standard; if you're travelling from the US your cellphone may not work if it is not tri-band or from a supplier that has switched to GSM. It may be worth buying a pay-as-you-go **French SIM card** from any of the big mobile providers (Orange, SFR, Bouygues Telecom and Free), all of which have high-street outlets and offer low-cost SIM cards, typically around €10; alternatively, various eSIMs are available.

France's country code is +33. Within France, numbers beginning 0800 and 0805 are free-dial numbers; those beginning 081 are charged as a local call; numbers starting 06 and 07 are mobile numbers.

## Time

France is in the Central European Time Zone (GMT+1). Daylight Saving Time (GMT+2) in France lasts from the last Sunday in March to the last Sunday in October.

## Tourist information

The Corsica Tourism Board (https://visit-corsica.com/en) oversees all of the island's tourist offices – **Office du Tourisme** (OT). There are 21 tourist offices, along with regional offices such as Ouest Corsica (https://ouestcorsica.com), covering the Northwest Coast from Porto to Cargèse and La Balagne Corsica (https://balagne-corsica.com), which covers Calvi and Île-Rousse. Addresses, contact details and opening hours are detailed throughout the book.

### GOVERNMENT WEBSITES

**Australian Department of Foreign Affairs** https://dfat.gov.au
**British Foreign & Commonwealth Office** https://gov.uk
**Canadian Department of Foreign Affairs** https://international.gc.ca
**French Ministry of Foreign Affairs** https://diplomatie.gouv.fr/en
**Irish Department of Foreign Affairs** https://he.dfa.ie
**New Zealand Ministry of Foreign Affairs** https://mfat.govt.nz
**US State Department** https://state.gov
**South African Department of Foreign Affairs** https://dirco.gov.za

## Travelling with children

France is an easy country in which to travel with children, and Corsica is no exception. They're generally welcome everywhere, and young children and babies, in particular, will be fussed over. Local **tourist offices** will have details of family-oriented activities and there are masses of kid-friendly hikes, water sports, and boat cruises, along with children's play areas, treetop adventure parks, and donkey rides. In summer, many seaside resorts and campsites organise clubs for children, with programmes of activities and entertainment.

Children under four years travel free on ferries and public transport, while under-12s pay half-fare. **Hotels** charge by the room, with a small supplement for an additional bed or cot, and many offer family rooms. Nearly all **restaurants** offer children's menus at a reduced price. Disposable **nappies/diapers** (*couches jetables*) are available at most pharmacies and supermarkets, alongside a vast range of **baby foods**, though many have added sugar and salt. **Milk powders** also tend to be sweet, so bring your own if this is likely to be a concern. You can **breastfeed** in public.

# Bastia and Northern Corsica

THE VIEUX PORT AT SUNRISE

**1**

# Bastia and Northern Corsica

With Bastia at its helm, Northern Corsica is a rough-hewn jigsaw of windswept coastline and maquis-clad valleys jutting out into the Ligurian Sea. From the rocky finger-shaped peninsula of Cap Corse that extends up to the island's northernmost point to the arid seaside desert of the Agriates, there's an air of the undiscovered that lingers despite the region boasting one of the island's most famous road trips. Perhaps it's the exhilaratingly twisty roads that cut into the sea cliffs and valleys, ensuring every panorama is a slow reveal or the fact that even the shortest distances pack in the full gamut of beach-to-mountain landscapes. If the top corner is, as it's often nicknamed, "Corsica in miniature", then it's an enticing prelude for what's to come.

The north, more than anywhere, has been shaped by Genoese rule and traces of their centuries-long occupation – marred by frequent clashes with both local rebels and foreign opponents – remain around every turn. **Bastia**, capital of the north, was the principal Genoese stronghold, and its fifteenth-century citadelle has survived almost intact. The highest concentration of Genoese towers dot the coast of the **Cap Corse**, where the sandy coves and fishing villages like **Macinaggio, Centuri-Port and Nonza** were once prime targets for barbary pirates sailing the Mediterranean. The coastal road hugs the cliffs at every turn, providing spectacular scenery for a road trip, but you'll have to get out and hike along the **Sentier des Douaniers** to reach the secluded **Plage de Barcaggio** and the island's northernmost tip.

South of Bastia, the fertile region of **the Nebbio** contains a scattering of churches built by Pisan stoneworkers, the prime example being the **Église Saint-Michel de Murato**. Olive groves and vineyards, most notably those of the AOC **Patrimonio wine region**, blanket the hillsides on the descent to **St-Florent**. Nestled in the crook of the **Cap Corse peninsula**, the chic little port is the closest that the north has to a fully-fledged beach resort. From here, boat trips and 4WD excursions set out for the **Désert des Agriates**, where serene bays with fine sands and glassy waters are cut off from civilisation by a vast and largely untraversable expanse of rocky scrubland.

# Bastia

The dominant tone of Corsica's most successful commercial town, **BASTIA**, is one of charismatic discord, its historic districts haphazardly sewn together over the centuries. The result is a tapestry of architectural styles and increasingly flamboyant Baroque churches, as the Corsicans, Genoese and French each stamped their identity across the *centre ville*. The city's industrial zone spreads onto the lowlands to the south, leaving the centre of town with plenty of aged charm, from the tightly packed streets of the Terra Vecchia to the weathered ramparts of the Terra Nova, all set against a backdrop of maquis-covered hills.

The centre of Bastia is not especially large, and all its sights can easily be seen in a day without the use of a car. The spacious **place St-Nicolas** is the obvious place to get your bearings: open towards the sea and lined with shady trees and cafés, it's the main focus of town life. Running parallel to it on the landward side are Boulevard Paoli and rue César-Campinchi, the two main shopping streets, but all Bastia's historic sights lie within **Terra Vecchia**, the old quarter immediately south

# Highlights

❶ **Vieux Port** Bastia's historic heart is abuzz at sunset, whether sipping an apéritif with a view of the citadelle or haggling over fresh-off-the-boat fish. See page 47

❷ **Cap Corse** Chiseled cliffs, wind-ravaged ruins, and coral-smudged sands provide spectacular visuals on the island's most popular road trip. See page 50

❸ **Plage de Barcaggio** A crescent of white sand where you'll share the scenery with sunbathing cows. See page 53

❹ **Nonza** This village clings to a cliff along the Cap Corse, crowned by a tower that looks down over a black sand beach. See page 54

❺ **St-Florent** This lively beach town, bordered by vineyards, beaches, and mountains, is a starting point for boat cruises. See page 56

❻ **Église Saint-Michel de Murato** A dazzling mosaic of green and white stone, this Pisan church is one of the island's oldest – and most unusual. See page 58

❼ **Wine tasting** The sun-blushed vineyards of Patrimonio make up Corsica's first AOC-classified wine region. See page 58

❽ **Désert des Agriates** This untamed stretch of rocky, arid desert hides some glorious sandy beaches, reachable only by boat, 4x4, or on foot. See page 58

**HIGHLIGHTS ARE MARKED ON THE MAP ON PAGE 47**

# BASTIA AND NORTHERN CORSICA

## HIGHLIGHTS

1. Vieux Port
2. Cap Corse
3. Plage de Barcaggio
4. Nonza
5. St-Florent
6. Église Saint-Michel de Murato
7. Wine tasting
8. Désert des Agriates

N

0 ————— 5
kilometres

**LIGURIAN SEA**

Île de la Giraglia

Tollare
Barcaggio ③
Îles Finocchiarola
SITE NATUREL DE LA CAPANDULA
Ersa
Rogliano
Centuri-Port
Macinaggio
Meria
Pino
Luri
Tour de Sénèque
Santa Severa
Marine de Porticciolo
Canari
**CAP CORSE** ②
Punta di Canelle
Cima di e Folicce (1324 m)
Marine de Pietracorbara
Sisco
Marine de Sisco
Monte Stello (1307 m)
Nonza ④
Castello
Erbalunga
Lavasina
Figarella
Miomo
San Martino di Lota

Plage de Guignu
Plage de Saleccia
Punta di Curza
Plage de Loto
Tour de Mortella
Golfe de Saint-Florent
⑧ DÉSERT DES AGRIATES
Lisciu
Patrimonio ⑦
Ostriconi
Mte Genova
Mte Revincu
Saint-Florent ⑤
① Bastia
Casta
Bocca di Vezzu
**NEBBIO**
Oletta
Biguglia
Mte Ambrica (1063 m)
Olmeta-di-Tuda
Défilé de Lancône
Bevincu
Santo-Pietro-di-Tenda
Rapale
Sorio
Pieve
⑥ Saint-Michel
Mte Asto (1535 m)
Murato
Bastia-Poretta Airport
La Canonica
Pineto
San Parteo
Étang de Biguglia
Mariana
La Marana

L'Île Rousse & Calvi
Marseille, Nice, Toulon & Italian Ports
ROUTE DE LA CORNICHE
Golo

Ponte-Leccia & Corte
Ponte-Leccia & Corte
Aléria

of place St-Nicolas, and the **Terra Nova**, the hillside area surrounding the Genoese citadelle. Tucked away below the imposing, honey-coloured bastion is the much-photographed **Vieux Port**, with its boat-choked marina encircled by crumbling eighteenth-century tenement buildings.

### Brief history

The city dates from Roman times, when a base was set up at Biguglia to the south, beside a freshwater lagoon. Little remains of the former colony, but the site merits a day trip for the well-preserved pair of Pisan churches at Mariana, rising from the southern fringes of Poretta airport. Through the eleventh and twelfth centuries, wine was exported to the Italian mainland from Porto Cardo, forerunner of the Vieux Port, but Bastia itself wasn't established until 1378 when the Genoese moved in. The Terra Nova was built on the hill above the port, which then became known as the Terra Vecchia.

Despite the fact that, in 1811, Napoleon appointed Ajaccio capital of the island, initiating a rivalry between the two towns which exists to this day, Bastia soon established a stronger trading position with mainland France. The Nouveau Port, created in 1862 to cope with the increasing traffic with France and Italy, became the mainstay of the local economy, exporting chiefly agricultural products from Cap Corse, Balagne and the eastern plain.

## Place St-Nicolas

The enormous palm-fringed **Place St-Nicolas**, laid out by the French in the nineteenth century and presided over by a towering statue of Napoleon Bonaparte depicted as a Roman god, is the strategic starting point of any city tour. Elegant bourgeois buildings rise up along its south and western flanks, fronted by a string of terrace cafés, while to the east, you can see glimpses of the ferry port. On Sunday mornings, it's taken over by a sprawling *brocante* (antiques market).

## Terra Vecchia

From place St-Nicolas, the main route into Terra Vecchia is **rue Napoléon**, a narrow, pedestrianised (from 11am onwards) street lined with small shops, lively cafés and a pair of sumptuously decorated chapels on its east side. The first of these, the **Oratoire de St-Roch**, is a Genoese Baroque extravagance built in 1604, with walls of finely carved wooden panelling and a magnificent gilt organ.

### Oratoire de L'Immaculée Conception

The **Oratoire de L'Immaculée Conception** was completed in 1609 as the showplace of the Genoese in Corsica, who used it for state occasions. The austere white-marble facade belies a flamboyant interior of gilt and velvet, whose centrepiece (behind the High Altar) is a copy of Bartolomé Esteban Murillo's celebrated depiction of the Immaculate Conception (the original hangs in Madrid's El Prado Museum). During the British rule of the island in 1795, the chapel was used as the seat of the regional parliament.

### Place du Marché

The **place de l'Hôtel-de-Ville**, to the rear of the Oratoire de L'Immaculée Conception, is commonly known as **place du Marché** after the lively farmers' market that takes place here each morning, from around 7am until 2pm. Dominating the south end of the square is the **church of St-Jean-Baptiste,** an immense ochre edifice that dominates the Vieux Port. Its twin campaniles are iconic of the city, but the interior – a Rococo overkill of multicoloured marble – is less impressive.

1

▲ Cap Corse

# BASTIA

0    100
metres

North Ferry
Terminal

AVENUE EMILE SARI

RUE DU COMMANDUCE DE CASABIANCA

VIALE PASCAL LOTA

RUE CHANOINE LESCHI

Préfecture

BLVD GÉNÉRAL GRAZIANI

RUE CÉSAR CAMPINCHI

SQ
ST-VICTOR

RUE DU NOUVEAU PORT

Nouveau
Port

Jetée St-Nicolas

Airport
Bus Stop

St-Florent

Gare
Routière

ROND-
POINT
LECLERC

Hôtel de Ville

AV. MAL SÉBASTIANI

South Ferry
Terminal

Gare
SNCF

AV. F. PIETRI

RUE G. PÉRI

RUE CONVENTIONNEL
SALICETI

PLACE
SAINT-
NICOLAS

VOIE RAPIDE

PROMENADE DES QUAIS

RUE CÉSAR CAMPINCHI

BOULEVARD SÉN DE GAULLE

BOULEVARD PAOLI

RUE MIOT

RUE NAPOLEON

Oratoire de
St-Roch

CHEMIN DE L'HÔPITAL MILITAIRE

RUE CÉSAR CAMPINCHI

TERRA
VECCHIA

QUAI DES MARTYRS DE LA LIBÉRATION

Oratoire de
l'Immaculée
Conception

Theatre

BOULEVARD GÉNÉRAL GIRAUD

RUE FAVALELLI

RUE DES TERRASSES

PLACE DU
MARCHÉ

RUE PINO

St-Jean-Baptiste

BOULEVARD PAOLI

Vieux
Port

VOIE RAPIDE

QUAI DU SUD

RUE GÉN CARBACCIA

St-
Charles

RUE DU COLLE

Tunnel

Jetée
du Dragon

Palais
de Justice

Oratoire de Monserato

BOULEVARD AUGUSTE GAUDIN

Jardin
Romieu

Porte Louis-XVI

CHEMIN DES FILLIPINES

Palais des
Gouverneurs
(Bastia Museum)

PLACE DU
DONJON

TERRA
NOVA

PLACE
GUASCO

Lift/elevator

Oratoire
Ste-Croix

PLACE
D'ARMES

Ste-Marie

Citadelle

VOIE RAPIDE

Aldilonda

N

| ● SHOPPING | |
|---|---|
| Chez Mireille | 4 |
| Mattei | 1 |
| U Muntagnolu | 2 |
| U Paese | 3 |

| ■ ACCOMMODATION | |
|---|---|
| Bonaparte | 1 |
| Central | 5 |
| Monsieur Miot | 4 |
| Napoléon | 3 |
| Les Sables Rouges | 6 |
| Camping | |
| Les Voyageurs | 2 |

| ● EATING | |
|---|---|
| A Tana | 6 |
| Café Casale | 5 |
| Café des Gourmets | 4 |
| Glacier Raugi | 2 |
| Le Petit Vincent | 8 |
| Le Conti | 3 |
| VG | 1 |
| Volontiers | 7 |

| ■ DRINKING & NIGHTLIFE | |
|---|---|
| Le Coude à Coude | 4 |
| L'Ombrage | 3 |
| La Rhumerie | 2 |
| Vintage Club | 1 |

## Vieux Port

The oldest and most photogenic part of Bastia is the **Vieux Port** – a secretive zone of dark alleys, vaulted passageways and seven-storey houses packed around the base of the church of St-Jean-Baptiste. Site of the original Roman settlement of Porto Cardo, the harbour later bustled with Genoese traders, but since the building of the ferry terminal and commercial docks to the north, it has become a backwater. The harbourside café-restaurants are nonetheless a scenic spot for a sundowner, and when the fishing boats come in (about 7pm), you can purchase the day's catch fresh off the boat.

## Terra Nova

The military and administrative core of old Bastia, **Terra Nova** (or "the Citadelle"), is focused on **place du Donjon**, which gets its name from the squat round tower that formed the nucleus of Bastia's fortifications: it was used by the Genoese to incarcerate Corsican patriots, among them the nationalist rebel Sampiero Corso in 1657, who was held in the dungeon for four years. If you're in Bastia in late July, don't miss the annual **changing of the Governor**, which takes place here to much pomp and ceremony.

Large parts of the Terra Nova have now been renovated, facilitating access to the old ramparts – an elevator links Quai Albert Gillio with the upper city – and a freshly paved promenade, the **Aldilonda**, now runs around the base of the Citadelle, cutting through the sea cliffs. You can follow this seafront promenade on foot or by bike along the seashore all the way to the **plage de l'Arinella**, Bastia's closest beach, about 3km south.

### Palais des Gouverneurs

**Musée de Bastia** Charge • https://musee.bastia.corsica

Facing the place du Donjon is the impressive fourteenth-century **Palais des Gouverneurs**, a building with a distinctly Moorish feel originally built for the Genoese governor and bishop. It became a prison after the French transferred the capital to Ajaccio and was then destroyed during a British attack of 1794 (in which an ambitious young captain named Horatio Nelson played a decisive part). The subsequent rebuilding was not the last, as parts of it were mistakenly blown up by American B-52s in the bungled attack of 1943, which devastated the city centre on the day after the island's liberation. Today, the Palais hosts the state-of-the-art **Musée de Bastia**, which charts the city's evolution as a trade and artistic centre. Its collection includes part of Cardinal Fesch's famous hoard of Renaissance art, and it affords magnificent views across the Vieux Port from its hanging gardens.

### Église Ste-Marie and Oratoire Sainte-Croix

If you cross the place du Donjon and follow rue Notre-Dame, you come out at the **Église Ste-Marie**. Built in 1458 and overhauled in the seventeenth century, the church was the cathedral of Bastia until 1801, when the bishopric was transferred to Ajaccio. Inside, its principal treasure is a small silver statue of the Virgin (housed in a glass case on the right wall as you face the altar), which is carried through Terra Nova and Terra Vecchia on August 15, the Festival of the Assumption. Immediately behind Ste-Maire in rue de l'Évêché stands the **Oratoire Sainte-Croix**, a sixteenth-century chapel decorated in Louis XV style, with lashings of rich blue paint and gilt scrollwork. It houses another holy item, the *Christ des Miracles*, a blackened oak crucifix much venerated by Bastia's fishermen.

## L'Oratoire de Monserato

One of Bastia's most extraordinary monuments, the **Oratoire de Monserato** or **Chapelle de la Scala Santa**, lies a pleasant two-kilometre uphill walk from the town centre. The

**1**

building itself looks unremarkable from the outside, but its interior houses the much-revered **Scala Santa**, a replica of the Holy Steps of the Basilica of Saint John of Lateran in Rome. Penitents who ascend it on their knees as far as its high altar may be cleansed, or so it is believed, of all sins, without the intercession of a priest.

## ARRIVAL AND DEPARTURE                                                                                        BASTIA

### BY FERRY
**Nouveau Port** All ferries arrive and depart from the Nouveau Port, just a five-minute walk from place St-Nicolas and the centre of town. Toilet facilities are inside the South Terminal, where there's a left luggage counter (*consigne*). Taxis queue outside at disembarkation times.
**Ferry offices** Corsica Ferries, av Pascal Lota, http://corsica ferries.com; Corsica Linea, Nouveau Port http://corsicalinea. com; Moby, 4 rue du Commandant Luce-de-Casabianca http://mobylines.com; La Méridionale, Port de Commerce http://lameridionale.fr.

### BY PLANE
Bastia's Poretta airport (http://bastia.aeroport.fr) is 16km south of town, just off the route nationale (N193). Shuttle buses to and from the centre coincide with flights and arrive on the north side of place du Maréchal-Leclerc, across the square from the train station.

### BY TRAIN
Trains run to Ajaccio year-round, several times daily in high season or twice a day in winter; you can also connect to Calvi by changing trains in Ponte Leccia. Timetables are updated

regularly and available at tourist offices and online (https://cf-corse.corsica).

### BY BUS
Services to local destinations (like Cap Corse) operate out of the *gare routière*, at the north end of place St-Nicolas behind the *hôtel de ville*. Buses for Bonifacio, Porto-Vecchio and services to the east coast can be picked up outside the Rapides Bleus office, opposite the main post office on av du Maréchal-Sébastiani. Services for Calvi via L'Île Rousse depart from outside the train station. Departure points and timetables may vary, so check in advance at the tourist office.
Destinations Aléria/Cateraggio (2–3 daily; 1hr 20min); Calvi (1–2 daily; 2hr); Erbalunga (daily; 30–50min); L'Île Rousse (1–2 daily; 1hr 30min); Porto-Vecchio (2 daily; 2hr 50min); St-Florent (2–3 daily; 45min).

### BY CAR
Traffic can be horrendous during rush hour (7–9am & 5–7pm), so avoid entering or exiting the city at these times if possible. Bastia has plenty of paid parking, but there's also the large, free parking de Tova by the port if you're lucky enough to get a spot.

## GETTING AROUND AND INFORMATION

**Taxis** There are ranks outside the *gare routière*, train station and Nouveau Port.
**Bike & Motorbike rental** Bike-Rental-Corsica (http://bike-rental-corsica.com) hires out e-bikes, mountain bikes, and scooters and delivers to your hotel; Corse Moto Location (https://corse-moto-location.fr) hires motorbikes, scooters and gear.
**Car rental** Avis, Bastia airport, https://www.avis.fr;

Europcar, Bastia airport http://europcar.fr; Hertz, av Pierre-Giudicelli http://hertz.fr.
**Petit train** (https://lepetittrainbastia.corsica) Multiple departures daily in season; 50-minute tour plus 20-minute guided walk around the Citadelle.
**Tourist office** At the north end of place St-Nicolas (http://bastia-tourisme.com); offers free maps of the city and Cap Corse, bus timetables and other essentials.

## ACCOMMODATION                                                                                   SEE MAP PAGE 46

**Bonaparte** 45 Bd du Général Graziani; http://hotel-bonaparte-bastia.com/hotel-bastia. Modern, muted décor makes this 3-star hotel a safe bet and rooms, while a bit on the small side, are spotless and well-equipped. It's worth paying extra for a superior room, which are substantially more spacious and have balconies. €€
**Central** 3 rue Miot; http://centralhotel.fr. Eighteen stylishly furnished rooms (plus a handful of larger studios), with art-splashed walls and sparkling bathrooms, just off the southwest corner of place St-Nicolas. By far the most pleasant and best-value place to stay in the centre. Advance reservation essential. €€

★ **Monsieur Miot** 2 rue Miot; http://monsieurmiot.com. Hidden down a leafy side street off place St-Nicholas, slip behind the ornate wooden doors and into an oasis of calm at this central boutique hotel. Housed in an elegant bourgeois townhouse, the seven rooms are a masterclass in clean lines and creative minimalism with gorgeous dark parquet floors. The same team run the deservedly popular *Café du Centre* next door. €€
**Napoléon** 43 bd Paoli; http://hotel-napoleon-bastia. fr. Smart, if a little basic, two-star in a central location. The rooms have small fridges and effective a/c, staff are friendly and welcoming, and breakfast (extra charge) is

served directly to your room. €€

**Les Sables Rouges Camping** Plage de l'Arinella, 2km south of the city; http://lessablesrouges.com. Bastia's closest and cheapest campsite has a beachside location and easy access to the city and port by car and train (you can also walk or cycle the seafront promenade). Facilities are basic, and hygiene standards sometimes questionable; for a longer stay, head to one of the Cap Corse campsites instead. €

**Les Voyageurs** 9 av du Maréchal-Sébastiani; http://hotel-lesvoyageurs-bastia.com. Established in 1910, this long-running three-star hotel is located near the train station, with friendly staff, on-site parking (charge) and a/c throughout. The surprisingly quirky décor of the rooms is somewhat at odds with the decidedly more drab public areas but adds a touch of fun. €€

## EATING

SEE MAP PAGE 46

Lined with smart café-restaurants, place St-Nicolas is the place to be during the day, but the best restaurants are hidden away in the **Terra Vecchia**. The atmospheric eateries lining the Vieux Port are generally substandard and overpriced; better suited to sunset cocktails with a view than fine dining.

**A Tana** 2 Bis Rue Posta vecchia; https://www.facebook.com/A-Tana-458973884525517/. Just west of the quai des Martyrs, this unpretentious Italian restaurant serves up excellent and reasonably priced dishes in a convivial atmosphere. The seafood pasta dishes deserve a special mention, inspired by the catch of the day. €

**Café Casale** 3 rue Jean Casale. Frequented by locals at lunchtime, this lively café executes simple dishes to perfection, from deliciously fresh salads with *jambon truffé* (truffled ham) or spicy ginger duck to the tasty sea bass *à la Bastiaise* (with a tomato, garlic and saffron relish). Prices are reasonable too. €

**Café des Gourmets** 23 Bv Paoli; https://instagram.com/cafe_des_gourmets. If you're craving an American-style brunch, this bustling cafe fits the bill. Bacon-maple pancakes, avocado toast, eggs Benedict, and all the usual brunch suspects hit the spot, or you can stick to a buttery *pain au chocolat*. €

**Glacier Raugi** 2 bis rue du Chanoine-Colombani. Corsica's greatest ice-cream maker, from an illustrious line of local *glaciers*. They also serve pizzas, but skip the savoury food and head straight to the ice cream counter, where you'll find

local specialities like *canistrelli de Zilia* (Corsican biscuit), *marron glacé* (candied chestnut), and *noisette de Cervioni* (hazelnut) among the two-dozen flavours. €

★ **Le Petit Vincent** Rue du Dragon; https://instagram.com/lepetitvincent1. In an elevated position in the Terra Nova, with a glorious terrace overlooking the sea, this little restaurant is a delight. Expect a mix of Provençal and Asian flavours on the menu, such as *pissaladière*, or beef fillet in satay sauce. €€

**Le Conti** Place St-Nicolas. One of the few dependable restaurants on the main square, this perennially popular restaurant is frequented as much by Bastiais as visitors. There's a varied menu that hits all bases, from pizzas and burgers to generous platters of *charcuterie corse*. €€

**VG** 7 Rue du Commandant; https://commande-vg.corsica. A welcome addition to Bastia's restaurant repertoire is this small and exceedingly friendly haven for wandering vegans, celiacs, and health-conscious foodies. Everything on the menu is vegetarian, and most dishes have vegan and gluten-free options, from poke bowls and focaccia to homemade dishes like coconut chickpea curry. The only downside is it's closed at weekends. Lunch only. €

**Volontiers** 13 rue du Général de Carbuccia; https://www.pizzeriavolontiers.com. Ask any local and they'll assure you that this elegant pizzeria, within ambling distance of the Vieux Port, serves the best pizzas in town. The *calzone* is a highlight, as are the towering wedges of tiramisu. €

## DRINKING AND NIGHTLIFE

SEE MAP PAGE 46

**Le Coude à Coude** 6 Rue du Dragon. On the corner of place Guasco in the heart of the Citadelle, this wine and tapas bar turns up the atmosphere – and the music – after dark. They organise live music evenings and wine tastings on the square during the summer.

**L'Ombrage** 13 Bd Auguste Gaudin; https://facebook.com/barombrage/. This cosy cave-like bar doubles up as an intimate live music venue showcasing local jazz, blues, and rock artists. There's something going off most Saturday nights in summer.

**La Rhumerie** 9 rue Monseigneur Rigo; http://larhumerie

bastia.unblog.fr/. Rum gets its moment in the spotlight at this lively spot, tucked away in a courtyard just off the Vieux Port. Live DJs often play on Saturday nights, and the (excellent) mojitos will be easier on your wallet than those along the waterfront.

**Vintage Club** 5 Rue du Chanoine Leschi. This is really the only *boîte* (nightclub) of note in the city, open on Friday and Saturday nights from midnight. It attracts a fairly young crowd, and its theme nights draw a large crowd intent on dancing the night away.

## SHOPPING

SEE MAP PAGE 46

**Chez Mireille** 5 rue des Terrasses. A Bastiais institution for decades, this small family-run deli sells a selection of

1

wonderful Castagniccian specialities, such as traditional *canistrelli* biscuits baked with lemon and white wine, and perfect *fiadone*.

**Mattei** Bd du Général-de-Gaulle. The wonderful Art Deco facade of this established wine merchant hints at the institution that it is. In addition to wine, they sell liqueurs from all over the island, including the famous local quinine-based aperitif, Cap Corse, which they bottle themselves.

**U Muntagnolu** 15 Rue Cesar Campinchi; https:// umuntagnolu.com. Beneath the stone arches of this long-standing *epicerie*, established in 1982, the shelves are overflowing with specialities from the region's artisan farmers and winemakers. Don't be afraid to ask for recommendations – the owner is a well of local knowledge.

**U Paese** 4 Rue Napoléon; https://upaese.corsica. A one-stop-shop for regional products, from chestnut jam to fresh *boutargue*, the "caviar of the Mediterranean". A selection of cheeses and charcuterie are available to taste at the counter.

## DIRECTORY

**Hospital** Centre Hospitalier de Bastia, Furiani; 04 95 59 11 11.

**Left luggage** The Nouveau Port terminal has a small consigne.

**Police** 10 bis rue Luce-de-Casabianca; 04 95 55 22 22; open 24/7.

# South of Bastia

Fed by the rivers Bevinco and Golo, the **ÉTANG DE BIGUGLIA**, to the south of the city, is the largest lagoon in Corsica, and one of its best sites for rare migrant birds. The Roman town of **MARIANA**, on the southern shore of the *étang*, can be approached by taking the turning for Poretta airport, 16km along the N193, or the more scenic coastal route through **LA MARANA**. Mariana was founded in 93 BC as a military colony, but today's houses, baths and basilica are too ruined to be of great interest. It's only the square baptistry, with its remarkable mosaic floor decorated with dancing dolphins and fish looped around bearded figures representing the four rivers of paradise, that warrants a detour.

Adjacent to Mariana stands the **church of Santa Maria Assunta**, known as **La Canonica**. Built in 1119 close to the old capital of Biguglia, it's the finest of around three hundred churches built by the Pisans in their effort to evangelise the island. Modelled on a Roman basilica, the perfectly proportioned edifice is decorated outside with Corinthian capitals plundered from the main Mariana site and with plates of Cap Corse marble. Another ancient church, **San Parteo**, built in the eleventh and twelfth centuries, stands 300m further south.

# Cap Corse

Until Napoléon III had a coach road built around **Cap Corse** in the nineteenth century, the northern promontory was effectively cut off from the rest of the island and relied on Italian maritime traffic for its income – hence its distinctive Tuscan dialect. Many Capicursini later left to seek their fortunes in the colonies of the Caribbean, which explains the distinctly ostentatious mansions, or *palazzi*, built by the successful émigrés (nicknamed "les Américains") on their return. For all the changes brought by the modern world, Cap Corse still feels like a separate country, with wildflowers in profusion, backcountry vineyards and quiet, traditional fishing villages.

Forty kilometres long and only fifteen across, the peninsula is divided by a spine of mountains called the Serra, which peaks at **Cima di e Folicce**, 1324m above sea level. The coast on the east side of this divide is characterised by tiny ports, or *marines*, tucked into gently sloping river-mouths, alongside coves which become sandier as you go further north. As you follow the road round to the western coast, you'll find yourself skirting the high sea cliffs, gazing out over the rough sea and rocky inlets below. Driving the entire peninsula takes about three and a half hours from Bastia – doable on a day trip, although you'll wish you had longer – and it's one of Corsica's most rewarding, if formidable, drives.

## GENOESE TOWERS

One of the most predominant features of Corsica's rugged coastline is its many **defence towers**, more commonly referred to as *tours génoises* or "Genoese towers". Perched on rocky promontories with a view out to sea or standing guard at the mouth of the island's coastal villages and natural harbours, there are 67 towers left standing, in various states of ruin, dotted all around the island. More than a third of these towers – 29 in total - are found along the Cap Corse, and they frame some of the peninsula's most dramatic viewpoints, whether clinging to the cliffside or marooned on an island.

The Genoese built at least 86 towers (some reports list more than a hundred) between the mid-sixteenth century and the late eighteenth century to protect the island from the increasingly frequent attacks by Barbary pirates. The towers vary in style but are traditionally three-storey round towers between 12 and 15 metres tall and constructed from local materials. Around the Cap Corse, most towers are built from schist stone, whereas those in the south tend to be fashioned from granite. Only a handful of square towers were built, the most notable of which are the Tour de Porto (see page 82) on the west coast and the Nonza and Giraglia towers along the Cap Corse.

Visiting the Genoese Towers is a quintessential part of any Cap Corse trip, and some of the most photographed include the Tour de l'Osse, right on the roadside along the east coast; the beautifully sited ruins of the Tour d'Agnello, reached by hiking along the **Le Sentier des Douaniers** (see page 53); and the Tour de Giraglia, the northernmost tower, which sits on a tiny island off the north coast.

Other famous towers around the island include the Tour de Parata on the Îles Sanguinaires in Ajaccio (see page 100), the Tour de Campomuro, the largest on the island at 15 metres high (see page 112), and the restored Tour d'Omigna near Cargèse (see page 88). Some towers are open to the public and house small museums, while others form the focal point of scenic coastal walks. You can even spend a night at the Tour de Micalona in Olmeto (see page 112).

---

### GETTING AROUND                                    CAP CORSE

**By bus** Buses to Macinaggio depart from Bastia's *gare routière*, with two departures a day (in both directions; Mon-Sat); from September to June, this drops to just twice a week. Check timings before departure via the Bastia tourist office or online (http://corsicabus.org).

**By car/motorbike** Car and motorbike rentals are available in Bastia (see page 48). The classic route around Cap Corse goes anticlockwise, benefitting from the early-morning and late-evening light as you drive from east to west; nervous drivers might prefer the clockwise route, putting you on the inside lane. Fill up in Bastia before heading out; there are petrol stations in Erbalunga and Macinaggio, but none along the west coast.

## Erbalunga

Built along a rocky promontory 10km north of Bastia, the small port of **ERBALUNGA** is the highlight of the east coast, with its aged, pale buildings stacked like crooked boxes behind a small harbour and ruined Genoese watchtower. A little colony of French artists lived here in the 1920s, and the village has drawn a steady stream of admirers ever since. Come summer, it's transformed into something of a cultural enclave, with concerts and art events adding a spark to local nightlife. The town is most famous, however, for its Good Friday procession, known as the **Cerca** (Search), which evolved from an ancient fertility rite. Hooded penitents, recruited from the ranks of a local religious brotherhood, form a spiral known as a *Granitola*, or snail, which unwinds as the candlelit procession moves into the village square.

### ACCOMMODATION                                    ERBALUNGA

★**Castel Brando** On the main square; http://castel brando.com. Shaded by a curtain of mature date palms, this elegant, stone-floored *palazzu* is like a *belle époque* backdrop to a classic Visconti movie. The rooms have

unfussy period furnishings, with the welcome addition of air conditioning, a lovely pool, spa and ample parking. €€€
**Camping A Casaiola** Lieu-dit Mortola, La Marine, Sisco; https://www.camping-acasaiola.com. A 10-minute drive north of Erbalunga and a 5-minute walk to the beach, this quiet campsite has been serving road-trippers since the 1960s and is still going strong. Sites are spacious, facilities are spotless, and there's a large swimming pool. No reservations, but you can call and check availability in the morning. €̄

## EATING

**A Piazzetta** In the tiny square behind the harbour. The village's budget option, serving quality pizzas, veal in Cap Corse liqueur, excellent *moules-frites* and refreshingly tangy sorbets. €€
★ **Le Pirate** On the harbourside; http://restaurant lepirate.com. Well-heeled Bastiais flock year-round to this restaurant on the waterfront for its famous *haute gastronomie*. Local seafood and meat delicacies dominate their set *menus*, which are exquisitely presented and peppered with surprising combinations. If you really want to splash out, the seasonal lobster and champagne *menu* is a true showstopper. €€€

# Macinaggio

A port since Roman times, well-sheltered **MACINAGGIO**, 20km north of Erbalunga, was developed by the Genoese in 1620 for the export of olive oil and wine to the Italian peninsula. The Corsican independence leader, Pascal Paoli, landed here in 1790 after his exile in England, whereupon he kissed the ground and uttered the words *"O ma patrie, je t'ai quitté esclave, je te retrouve libre"* ("Oh my country, I left you as a slave, I rediscover you a free man"). There's not much of a historic patina to the place nowadays, but with its packed **marina** and line of colourful seafront awnings, Macinaggio has a certain appeal, made all the stronger by its proximity to some of the wildest landscapes on the Corsican coast.

Another reason to linger is to sample the superb **Clos Nicrosi** wines, grown in the terraces above the village and aged in the cellars of the **Palazzu Nicrosi** (see page 52), which you can taste at the *domaine*'s little shop on the north side of the Rogliano road.

## Site Naturel de la Capandula

North of the town lie some beautiful stretches of sand and clear sea – an area demarcated as the **Site Naturel de la Capandula**. A marked footpath, known as **Le Sentier des Douaniers** (see page 53) because it used to be patrolled by customs officials, threads its way across the hills and coves of the reserve, giving access to an area that cannot be reached by road. The **Baie de Tamarone**, 2km along this path, is a good place for diving and snorkelling. Just behind the beach, the *piste* forks: follow the left-hand track for twenty minutes and you'll come to a stunning arc of turquoise sea known as the **rade de Santa Maria**, site of the isolated Romanesque **Chapelle Santa-Maria**. The bay's other principal landmark is the huge **Tour Chiapelle**, a ruined three-storeyed watchtower dramatically cleft in half and entirely surrounded by water.

## INFORMATION                                                    MACINAGGIO

**Tourist office** At the port (http://macinaggiorogliano-capcorse.fr).
**Boat trips** San Paulu (http://sanpaulu.fr) runs a shuttle service for walkers between Macinaggio, Barcaggio and Centuri-Port (Apr–Oct, three times daily in July & Aug; by reservation only; charge), as well as half-day excursions to outlying beauty spots (charge).

## ACCOMMODATION

**Palazzu Nicrosi** Lieu-dit Vignale; http://www.palazzu-nicrosi.com/. Crowning a wooded hilltop 6km west of Macinaggio, this nineteenth-century bourgeois mansion is one of the Cap's illustrious *Maison d'américains*, built by Corsican entrepreneur Pierre-Marie Nicrosi, who made his fortune in America. Two centuries later, it's still owned by his descendants and welcomes guests to share this slice of history in one of its five rooms, three of which are suites. €€€
**U Libecciu** Rte de la Plage; http://u-libecciu.com. The best option in Macinaggio is this welcoming, modern three-star located down the lane leading from the marina to the Plage de Tamarone. Smallish rooms without balconies or larger

ones with terraces. There's also a pleasant swimming pool and a basic bar. €€

**U Stazzu** 1km north of the harbour, signposted off the Rogliano road; http://camping-u-stazzu.jimdo.com. Basic site on the edge of the village. The ground slopes and is rock hard, but it's cheap, there's ample shade and easy access to the nearby beach; the site's little café serves particularly good breakfasts and pizzas. There's also a number of bungalows that sleep up to four people, available by the

week. No reservations for tents/caravans. €

**Le Tomino** lieu-dit a Girasca; https://hotelletomino.fr. Soothing pebble tones and sweeping ocean views keep up the air of serenity afforded this fashionable boutique hotel, nestled on the hillside overlooking Macinaggio Beach. The bright, airy rooms come with spacious terraces that look out over the leafy garden or the seaward-pointing infinity pool, and with just a handful of guests, everyone gets the special treatment. €€€€

## EATING

Macinaggio's best cuisine is served in its 4-star hotels, but you'll find more affordable options lining the harbour.

**Le Vela d'Oro** Down a narrow alleyway running off the little square opposite the port. Capcorsin seafood specialities – such as local crayfish in homemade spaghetti – served in a cosy dining room decorated with old nautical maps. €€

# Centuri-Port

When Dr Johnson's biographer, James Boswell, arrived here from England in 1765, the former Roman settlement of **CENTURI-PORT** was a tiny fishing village, recommended to him for its peaceful detachment from the dangerous turmoil of the rest of Corsica. Not much has changed since Boswell's time: Centuri-Port exudes tranquillity despite

## LE SENTIER DES DOUANIERS

The roadless northern tip of Cap Corse is among the few stretches of coastline on the island crossed by a waymarked path, **Le Sentier des Douaniers**. Following the yellow splashes of paint, it's possible to trace it all the way from Macinaggio to Centuri-Port (or vice versa) in seven to eight hours (about 19km).

The first leg from Macinaggio to **Barcaggio** takes about three hours and is arguably the most picturesque, passing pebble-strewn beaches, bays blanketed in thick cushions of dried posidonia algae, and the tiny *Îles du Cap Corse*, a natural reserve where Audouin Seagulls nest. Just north of here, the haunting ruins of the Tour Santa Maria stand half-submerged at high tide.

Rounding the Pointe d'Agnello is one of the walk's most emblematic views – the crumbling ruins of the Tour d'Agnello looking out towards the offshore Île de la Giraglia with its tower and lighthouse. Nearby, the Plage de Barcaggio is one of the few sandy stretches and perfect for a swim, although you'll likely share it with a herd of unfazed wild cows sunbathing on the shore.

From the port of Barcaggio, it's a further 45 minutes to reach Tollare, the last town before you venture out into the wilds, cutting through the craggy, maquis-clad west coast for four hours until you reach Centuri-port.

### INFORMATION

The **tourist office** in Macinaggio will furnish you with a free **map**. Being mostly flat, the route presents no great physical challenges, although you should be aware of the force of the sun and wind along this stretch of coast. In July and August, set off at dawn and aim to rest up in the shade (of which there's precious little) between 11.30am and 4pm. Bring plenty of water, as there are no springs.

### EATING

★ **Paillote les Tamaris** 3 Foce, Barcaggio https://www.facebook.com/tamarisbarcaggio/. A warm and cheery welcome awaits as you reach the halfway point at this traditional *paillote* (fishing hut). A beloved hangout of the intrepid hikers and road-trippers that make it this far north, it's situated right on the beach and shaded beneath Aleppo pines. Gracing the menu are staples of the burger and salad kind, alongside seafood dishes like tuna carpaccio, octopus and *moules à la boutarde*, but the real star of the show is the view. €€

**1**

a serious influx of summer residents, many of them artists who come to paint the fishing boats in the slightly prettified harbour, where the grey-stone wall is highlighted by the green serpentine roofs of the encircling cottages, restaurants and bars. The only drawback is the beach, which is disappointingly muddy and not ideal for sunbathing.

**ACCOMMODATION AND EATING** **CENTURI-PORT**

**L'Antonino** On the hillside as you walk out of the village. This family-run restaurant pays attention to the details, whether it's the cosy fairy-light strewn garden terrace, the attentive service or the carefully curated daily menus with local specialities like lobster or *brocciu* lasagne. Tables are limited, so book ahead and let yourself be tempted by the truly indulgent homemade desserts – you'll regret skipping it. €

**De la Jetée** At the entrance to the port; http://hotel-de-la-jetee-centuri.fr. The *Jetée* has 14 spacious, airy rooms, most with balconies overlooking the harbour. Furnishings are bland but adequate, and there's a busy, good-value terrace restaurant tacked on the back. Half-board is also available. €

**Vieux Moulin** At the entrance to the village; http://le-vieux-moulin.net. Centuri's most stylish option: a converted *maison d'Américain* with a wonderful terrace and attractively furnished en-suite rooms. There's also a restaurant with a lovely terrace overlooking the sea. €€

## Nonza

Set high on a black rocky pinnacle that plunges vertically into the sea, the village of **NONZA**, 18km south of Centuri, is one of the highlights of the Cap Corse shoreline. It was formerly the main stronghold of the da Gentile family, and the remains of their **fortress** are still standing on the overhanging cliff. Reached by a flight of six hundred steps, Nonza's long grey **beach** is discoloured as a result of serpentine residue from the now-disused asbestos mine up the coast. This may not inspire confidence, but the locals insist it's safe (they take their own kids there in summer), and from the bottom, you get the best view of the tower, which looks as if it's about to topple into the sea.

**ACCOMMODATION AND EATING** **NONZA**

**Casa Lisa** At the bottom of the village; http://casalisa.fr. Lovely rooms with exposed beams, original tiled floors and shuttered windows looking across the gulf to the Désert des Agriates. Cards not accepted. €

**Casa Maria** Chemin de la Tour; http://casamaria-corse. com. Four pleasantly furnished rooms (and one pricier family suite) housed in a restored schist building above the square. Breakfast is served on a delightful outdoor terrace with lovely views. There's also an apartment that sleeps up to six people and can be hired by the week. €

★ **La Sassa** Near the Tour Génoise; http://lasassa.com. One of the loveliest café-restaurants on the island, *La Sassa* occupies a plum location on a craggy spur below the *tour*, with a to-die-for view over the beach from its teak deck. A chilled young crew serve succulent charcoal-grilled meat, pasta and salads at restrained prices, as well as artisanal ice creams and craft beers and ciders, to a soundtrack of Corsican lounge grooves – particularly atmospheric at sunset time when the surrounding rocks are floodlit. €€

# The Nebbio

Taking its name from the thick mists that sweep over the region in winter, the **Nebbio** (U Nebbiu) has for centuries been one of the most fertile parts of the island, producing honey, chestnuts and some of the island's finest wine. An amphitheatre of rippled chalk hills, vineyards and cultivated valleys surrounds the area's main town, **St-Florent**, half an hour's drive west over the mountain from Bastia at the base of Cap Corse. Aside from EU subsidies, the major money earner here is viticulture: the village of **Patrimonio** is the wine-growing hub, with *caves* offering *dégustations* lined up along its main street.

**St-Florent** is the obvious base for day trips to the beautifully preserved Pisan church of Santa Maria Assunta, just outside the town, and the **Désert des Agriates**, a wilderness of parched maquis-covered hills across the bay whose rugged coastline harbours one of Corsica's least accessible, but most picturesque, beaches.

**1**

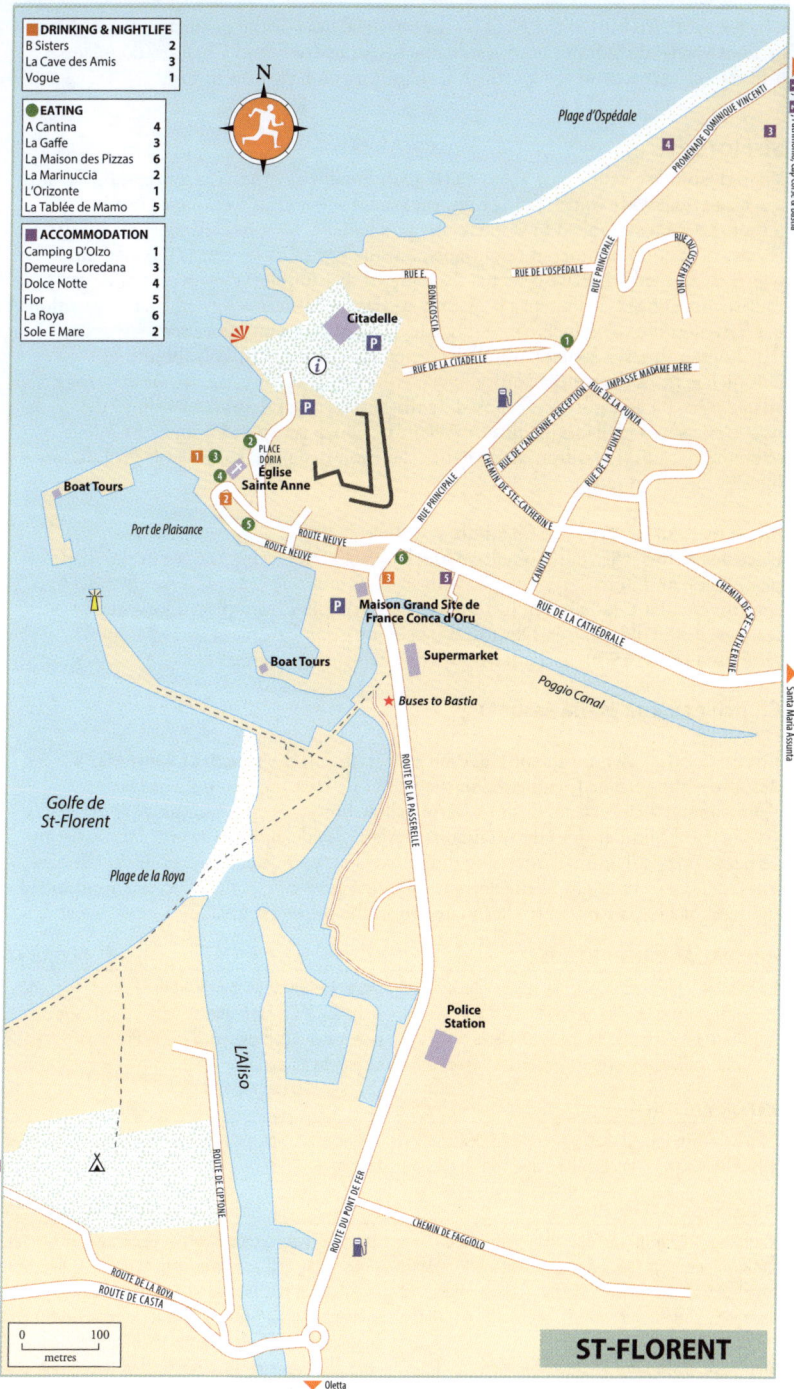

N

Plage d'Ospédale

Citadelle

RUE DE L'OSPÉDALE

RUE PRINCIPALE

RUE E. BONACORSCIA

RUE DE LA CITADELLE

IMPASSE MADAME MÈRE

RUE DE L'ANCIENNE PERCEPTION

RUE DE LA PUNTA

PLACE DORIA
Église Sainte Anne

Boat Tours

Port de Plaisance

ROUTE NEUVE

RUE PRINCIPALE

CHEMIN DE STE-CATHERIN E

CANUTTA

RUE DE LA CATHÉDRALE

CHEMIN DE STE-CATHERINE

Maison Grand Site de France Conca d'Oru

Boat Tours

Supermarket

★ Buses to Bastia

Poggio Canal

Santa Maria Assunta

Golfe de St-Florent

Plage de la Roya

ROUTE DE LA PASSERELLE

Police Station

L'Aliso

ROUTE DE CIPTONE

ROUTE DU PONT DE FER

CHEMIN DE FAGGIOLO

Casta & Calvi

& Punta Mortella

ROUTE DE LA ROYA
ROUTE DE CASTA

0    100
metres

**ST-FLORENT**

Oletta

**1**

In the southern hills of the Nebbio, the only real draw is the distinctive Pisan church of **Saint Michel de Murato**, but it's still a picturesque drive, and Corsica Zoo (charge; https://corsicazoo.com) is a worthwhile detour if you have kids in tow.

# St-Florent

Viewed from across the bay, **ST-FLORENT** (San Fiurenzu) appears as a bright line against the black tidal wave of the Tenda hills, the pale stone houses seeming to rise straight out of the sea, overlooked by a squat circular citadelle. It's a relaxed town with a decent beach and a good number of restaurants, but the key to its success is the **marina**, which is jammed with lavish yachts throughout the summer. However, neither the tourists nor indeed St-Florent's proximity to Bastia, entirely eclipse the air of isolation conferred on the town by its brooding backdrop of mountains and scrubby desert.

In Roman times, a settlement called Cersunam – referred to as Nebbium by chroniclers from the ninth century onwards – existed a kilometre east of the present village. The ancient port was eclipsed by the harbour that developed around the new Genoese citadelle in the fifteenth century, which prospered as one of Genoa's strongholds, and it was from here that Pascal Paoli (see page 161) set off for London in 1796, never to return.

## Place des Portes and the Citadelle

**Place des Portes**, the centre of village life, has café tables facing the sea in the shade of plane trees, and in the evening, fills with strollers and *pétanque* players. The fifteenth-century circular **Citadelle** can be reached on foot, uphill from place Doria at the seafront in the old quarter. Destroyed by Nelson's bombardment in 1794, it was renovated in the 1990s and affords superb views from its terrace.

## Church of Santa Maria Assunta

6 Piani • Charge

Just east of the town on the original site of Cersanum, the **church of Santa Maria Assunta** – the so-called "cathedral of the Nebbio" – is a fine example of Pisan Romanesque architecture. Built in warm yellow limestone, the building has gracefully symmetrical blind arcades decorating its western facade and, at the entrance, twisting serpents and wild animals adorning the pilasters on each side of the door. In the nave, immediately to the right of the entrance stands a glass case containing the mummified figure of St Flor, a Roman soldier martyred in the third century.

### ARRIVAL AND DEPARTURE

**ST-FLORENT**

**By bus** The former twice-daily bus service from Bastia to St-Florent stopped in 2024, although it's worth checking with the tourist office whether there's a replacement service. Otherwise, you'll need your own transport or to rely on taxis.

**By car** If you don't mind walking, there's ample free parking at the top of the hill by the citadelle, but get there early in peak season; otherwise, you'll usually find a spot in the paid car park by the port.

### INFORMATION

**Tourist office** On the road up to the citadelle (http://corsica-saintflorent.com), they have free maps of the town and Nebbio region, plus plenty of info on tours and wine tasting.

### ACCOMMODATION

**SEE MAP PAGE 55**

**Camping D'Olzo** Off the D81, 2km northeast of town; https://campingolzo.com. A small but well-designed campsite with shaded plots, electric hookups, and a pool. The cabins, chalets, and eco-huts, rented with no bedding, are also surprisingly affordable. €

**Demeure Loredana** Promenade Vincenti; http://

demeureloredana.com. Five-star opulence with glorious views of the gulf and decor straight out of Architectural Digest. From the 450-year-old Maharaja balcony to the sumptuous period-style sitting room, every room is a showpiece. Rooms are spacious and beautifully furnished with contemporary art pieces dotted throughout, plus there's a large, heated pool. €€€€

**Dolce Notte** Route de bastia; https://hotel-dolce-notte. com. This beachfront hotel is excellent value for money, especially if you snag one of the standard rooms. The older rooms are a little faded in comparison to those at the higher end of the price scale, so you get what you pay for, but all have a/c and balconies with a sea view. The ready-to-please staff are a bonus. €€

**Flor** Chemin de la Cathédrale, just off place des Portes; http://hotel-flor.com. Bright, modern hotel in the centre, but tucked down a quiet side street away from the noise. Rooms to the rear of the building have French windows and little balconies overhanging the canal. Open April to Nov. €€

**La Roya** Rte de la Roya; http://hoteldelaroya.com. Stunning 4-star hotel with a garden terrace that sweeps down to a private beach, a heated outdoor pool, and a gastronomic restaurant with ocean views. Plush linens and gleaming bathtubs await in the rooms, most of which have sea view balconies, plus there's a spa, gym, and wellness area. €€€€

**Sole E Mare** Lieu dit tettola, off the D81; https://solemare-stflorent.com. Good-value hotel with free parking in a handy location just north of town. Rooms are basic but comfy, some with garden terraces, and there are also some studio apartments with a kitchenette. €€

## EATING SEE MAP PAGE 55

**A Cantina** Port de St Florent; https://instagram.com/ acantina_saintflorent. Tasty home cooking at a convivial spot with a lush, leafy terrace by the port. The *menu corse* is a great way to try local dishes like *soupe corse*, *sanglier* (wild boar) and *fiadone*. €€

**La Gaffe** St-Florent marina; http://restaurant-lagaffe.com. One of the town's top seafood restaurants, where you can order pasta with spider crab or sea bass carpaccio. Prepare to fork out for the privilege, though. €€€

**La Maison des Pizzas** At the corner of La Porta and rte de la Cathedrale. No prizes for guessing what's on the menu here. There's a huge selection of pizzas on offer, including some special Corsican toppings, all baked to perfection in the wood-fired pizza oven. The fact that it's always rammed with locals is a good sign. €

**La Marinuccia** Place de l'Ancienne Poste; http:// marinuccia.com. You can't get closer to the seafront than

this water-lapped terrace, but this long-established restaurant is more than just a pretty view. Seafood is their speciality, and while it's not cheap, you'd be hard-pressed to find better grilled octopus tentacles or *brocciu*-stuffed sardines in town. €€€

**L'Orizonte** Parc de l'hotel Bellevue; https://fb.com/profile. php?id=100063798750042. In the garden of the Hôtel Bellevue on the hilltop overlooking the golfe, this grillhouse has arguably the best view in town. Juicy steaks (Argentine, not Corse) are cooked up on the barbecue, and the tasting platters to share are a meat lover's dream. Diners can also use the hotel pool. €€

**La Tablée de Mamo** St-Florent marina. A cosy restaurant along the marina where simple dishes are given a little extra pizzazz. The gnocchi dishes are particularly scrumptious, and portions are restrained enough to save space for dessert. €€

## DRINKING AND NIGHTLIFE SEE MAP PAGE 55

**B Sisters** St-Florent marina. The lively seafront terrace buzzes with activity at sundown and there are few better places for a cocktail. Try a Corsican Spritz made with Cap Corse Mattei or a Frenchy mule.

**La Cave des Amis** Immeuble le Glacier, by the riverside. With the Patrimonio wine region right on the doorstep, this wine cellar makes a perfect pitstop to brush up on your local

wine knowledge and sample a selection by the glass.

**Vogue** Marinaccio; https://facebook.com/levogue.coffee. If pumping music and cocktails sounds like your idea of a good night, this is the place. It's more of a bar than a nightclub, but it's the closest you'll get to dancing the night away in St Florent.

# Patrimonio

As you leave St-Florent by the Bastia Road, the next village you come to, after 6km, is **PATRIMONIO** (Patrimoniu), centre of the first Corsican wine region to gain *appellation contrôlée* status. Apart from the renowned local muscat, which can be sampled in the village or at one of the *caves* along the route from St-Florent, Patrimonio's chief asset is the sixteenth-century **church of St-Martin**, occupying its own little hillock and visible for kilometres around. The colour of burnt sienna, it stands out vividly against the rich green vineyards and chalk hills. In a garden 200m south of the church stands a limestone **statue-menhir** known as U Nativu, a late megalithic piece dating from 900–800 BC. A carved T-shape on its front represents a breastbone, and two eyebrows and a chin can also be made out.

1

The U Nativu menhir takes pride of place next to the stage at Patrimonio's annual open-air guitar festival (http://festival-guitare-patrimonio.com), held in the last week of July next to the church, when performers and music aficionados from all over Europe converge on the village.

### EATING AND DRINKING
### PATRIMONIO

**Brasserie Ribella** Rte de St-Florent; http://biereribella. com. A refuge for beer lovers in the depths of wine country, this brewery is home to one of Corsica's most prized craft beers. 100% Corsican, the often-surprising beers are infused with the flavours of the island, from maquis herbs like rosemary and immortelle to chestnut flour. This flagship brewery has a well-stocked shop, more than half a dozen brews on tap, plus the entire catalogue of bottled beers, and staff will passionately talk you through them.

★ **Libertalia Bistro Tropical** Rue d'Eglise, Patrimonio; https://fb.com/restaurant.patrimonio. Founder of the Ribella brewery (above), Pierre François Maestracci, is the driving force behind Corsica's growing slow food scene, and this is his pioneering restaurant. Set in a stunning nineteenth-century *palazzu* with a leafy garden terrace, you'll dine on 100 percent Corsican dishes paired with regional wines and beers. It's delicious, farm-fresh, unpretentious, and above all, an experience to be savoured slowly. €€

## Église de Saint Michel de Murato

Along the D5, about a 3-minute drive northeast of Murato village • Charge • https://sanmichele.corsica

Built by angels, if you believe the legend, or – more probable – the Pisans, the **Église de Saint Michel de Murato** is one of the most remarkable examples of Pisan Romanesque architecture on the island. Dating back to the 12th century, the church stands out for its elaborate chequered stone façade, alternating between grey-green serpentine and white limestone to dramatic effect. Restored in the 18th century when its central bell tower was added, its interiors are adorned with 15th-century frescoes and, if you look closely, you can still see the original carvings of the Garden of Eden and other religious symbols. It's open from May to mid-September but closed on Mondays.

## Désert des Agriates

Extending westwards from the Golfe de St-Florent to the mouth of the Ostriconi River, the **Désert des Agriates** is a vast area of uninhabited land, dotted with clumps

---

### THE PATRIMONIO WINE REGION

Switchback lanes climb up into the verdant hills northeast of St-Florent, where the sloping vineyards of the Patrimonio wine region are backlit by the glittering aquamarine of the Gulf of Saint Florent below. The first of Corsica's wine appellations has been producing some of the island's most celebrated wines since 1968, earning acclaim for its full-bodied red wines and fruity, floral whites, as well as the odd rosé. Covering some 425 hectares, the wine region also encompasses the Nebbio villages of Farinole, Oletta, Poggio d'Oletta, and Casta to the south – all of it protected as a "Grand Site de France" since 2017.

It's the region's sheltered microclimate and mixed soils, a blend of schist, granite, and clay-limestone, that result in its renowned terroir, while strictly controlled grape varieties guarantee its distinctive character. A Patrimonio white must be made with 100 percent Vermentino grapes, while reds must include 90 percent Nielluccio grapes, typically blended with Sciacarello and Grenache, or 75 percent for rosés.

**Domaine Lazzarini** (https://domainelazzarini.com) and **Domaine Orenga de Gaffory** (https://orengadegaffory.com) both offer guided tastings (advance booking recommended, while **Corsica Wine Tours** (https://corsicawinetours.com) offer bespoke wine tasting tours from Bastia or St-Florent. The **Maison Grand Site de France Conca d'Oru** (https://grand-site-concadoru.fr/maison-grand-site/; charge) in St-Florent operates a museum devoted to the wine region and can provide details of winery tours and tastings.

**TRIPS TO THE DESERT**

Excursion boats run out of St-Florent marina to the superb beaches – Lotu and Saleccia – across the bay in the Désert des Agriates. The *Popeye* (http://lepopeye.com) leaves at regular intervals throughout the day from 9am, the last service returning around 4pm (or later in July & Aug).

From Lotu, an all-terrain 4WD runs via a rough track inland to Saleccia. The firm **Saleccia Off Road** (http://saleccia-off-road.com) offers packages that could include the outward and return trips by boat.

If you want to go it alone, **Agriates Kayak** (https://agriateskayak.com) rent kayaks by the half- or full-day, **Corsica Nautic** (https://corsica-nautic.com) rent RIB and open-hull boats, and **Corse Horizon** (https://corse-horizon.com) rent RIBs, as well as buggies.

of cacti and scrub-covered hills. It may appear inhospitable now, but during the time of the Genoese, this rocky moonscape was, as its name implies, a veritable breadbasket (*agriates* means "cultivated fields"). In fact, so much wheat was grown here that the Italian overlords levied a special tax on grain to prevent any build-up of funds that might have financed an insurrection. Fires and soil erosion eventually took their toll, however, and by the 1970s the area had become a total wilderness.

Numerous crackpot schemes to redevelop the Désert have been mooted over the years – from atomic weapon test zones to concrete Club-Med-style resorts – but during the past few decades the government has gradually bought up the land from its various owners (among them the Rothschild family) and designated it as a protected nature reserve.

### The beaches

A couple of rough *pistes* wind into the desert, but without a 4WD vehicle, the only feasible way to explore the area and its rugged coastline, which includes two of the island's most beautiful **beaches**, is on foot or by boat. From St-Florent, a pathway winds northwest to **plage de l'Ostriconi**, just off the main Calvi highway (T30), in three easy stages. The first takes around 5hr30min, and leads past the famous **Martello tower** and much-photographed **plage du Lotu** to **plage de Saleccia**, a huge sweep of soft white sand and turquoise sea.

From plage de Saleccia, it takes around three hours to reach the second night halt, **plage de Ghignu**, where a simple *gîte d'étape* provides basic facilities. The last stretch to l'Ostriconi can be covered in under six hours. Note that the only water sources along the route are at Saleccia and Ghignu, so take plenty with you.

For a taste of the desert without hiking the entire coastline, the southwesternmost beach at Ostriconi is the most accessible. From the Parking de l'Ostriconi, just off the T30, it's about a 20-minute walk – there's some scrambling and wading (depending on the tide) involved to reach the beach, so wear your walking shoes and prepare to get wet.

### GETTING THERE             DÉSERT DES AGRIATES

Excursion boats leave at regular intervals throughout the day from the jetty in St-Florent marina, ferrying passengers across the gulf to and from plages du Lotu and Saleccia.

### ACCOMMODATION

**Paillers du Ghignu** Plage de Ghignu; ghignu@haute-corse.fr. This superbly remote *gîte d'étape* offers the most far-flung accommodation in coastal Corsica. Housed in a converted shepherd's hut close to the shoreline, its only facilities are basic bunks (no mattresses), hot showers and toilets – you'll need to bring a sleeping bag, food and drink. Reservations essential. €

**U Paradisu** Plage de Saleccia; http://camping-uparadisu. com. Well set-up campsite with pitches for tents in shady scrub behind the dunes, plus a scattering of delightful dry-stone cottages with comfortable bunks that can be rented nightly by coast walkers (outside of high season only; no linen provided) and more luxurious cabins (with a higher price tag). Cash only. €

# The Balagne

STUNNING COASTLINE AT L'ÎLE-ROUSSE

# The Balagne

The sun-kissed shores of the Balagne, the region stretching west from the Ostriconi valley as far as the red-cliffed wilderness of Scandola, has been renowned since Roman times as "Le Pays de l'Huile et Froment" (Land of Oil and Wheat). Backdropped by a wall of imposing, pale grey mountains, the characteristic outcrops of orange granite punctuating the coast shelter a string of idyllic beaches, many of them sporting ritzy marinas and holiday complexes. Beautiful beaches are just the beginning. Inland, a staggered skyline of mountain peaks beckons you into its folds, where you'll find artisan villages perched high on the hilltops and highland valleys cocooned in evergreen woodlands.

The region's two honeypot towns, **L'Île Rousse** and **Calvi**, get swamped in summer, but the scenery more than compensates. The seafront stroll along Île Rousse's namesake promontory affords knockout views, and Calvi, with its cream-coloured citadelle and immaculate white-sand bay, should not be missed. Most visitors make one of the two their base, from where there are countless opportunities for day trips into the mountains. Follow the serpentine lanes into the mountains to wander the overgrown ruins of **Occi**, abandoned since the early twentieth century, and explore the **hilltop villages** of **Sant'Antonino**, **Pigna**, and **Corbara**, where dozens of artisans are keeping the region's age-old traditions alive. Just south of Calvi, the clifftop **Notre Dame de la Serra** is a spectacular spot to watch the Balagne's blazing sunsets, which bathe the coast in hues of molten orange.

Relics of the past can be found underwater, too, and **scuba divers** can take the plunge at various wreck dives right off the coast of Calvi, among them a **WWII bomber**. Further adventures await in the rambling forests of **Bonifato** and the **Vallée de Fango** to the south, while the holy grail of hiking trails, the **GR20**, sets out from the mountain town of **Calenzana**. On the southern cusp of the Balagne, the fishing village of **Galéria** is the less-frequented gateway to the Réserve Naturelle de Scandola.

**GETTING THERE AND AROUND** **THE BALAGNE**

While you can get around Calvi and Île Rousse on foot, and there are bus tours in the summer season, it's far easier to explore the Balagne with your own vehicle.

**BY TRAIN**

Trains run from Bastia and Ajaccio to Calvi via Île Rousse year-round, several times daily in high season, petering out to just twice a day in winter. Timetables are updated regularly and available at tourist offices and online (https:// cf-corse.corsica). Note that the main "Grand Ligne" train services don't always stop at the smaller stations between Calvi and Île Rousse; check the timetable carefully.

## L'Île Rousse and around

Developed by Pascal Paoli in the 1760s as a "gallows to hang Calvi", the port of **L'ÎLE ROUSSE** (L'Isula Rossa) simply doesn't convince as a Corsican town, its palm trees, smart shops, neat flower gardens and colossal pink seafront hotel creating an atmosphere that has more in common with the French Riviera. Pascal Paoli had great plans for his new town on the Haute-Balagne coast, which was laid out from scratch in 1758 as a port to export the olive oil produced in the region. A large part of it was built

COLOURFUL CALVI PORT

# Highlights

❶ **Île Rousse** Walk the red-rock promontory that gives the town its name, and you'll be rewarded with sweeping views from the 19th-century lighthouse. See page 62

❷ **Balagne villages** The perched villages of Balagne of Sant'Antonino, Pigna, and Corbara are replete with picturesque churches and artisan workshops. See page 67

❸ **Occi** Scramble up to this hilltop ghost town to wander through the hauntingly beautiful ruins of an early twentieth-century village. See page 67

❹ **Calvi** One of Corsica's most atmospheric beach towns, framed by a medieval citadel and miles of golden beaches. See page 68

❺ **Scuba diving** Plunge to 28m to see the bullet-riddled wreck of a WWII B17 bomber, dive along thrilling drop-offs and spot large schools of fish. See page 71

❻ **Notre Dame de la Serra** Built on a granite crag a magnificent mountain-to-ocean panorama; this is Calvi's go-to sunset spot. See page 73

❼ **GR20** Only the hardiest adventurers complete the ultimate hike: 180km of jagged peaks and steep gorges, traversing the entire island from Calenzana to Conca. See page 74

❽ **Vallée de Fango** Bathe in natural pools and walk along lush riverside trails in this UNESCO Biosphere Reserve. See page 75

**HIGHLIGHTS ARE MARKED ON THE MAP ON PAGE 64**

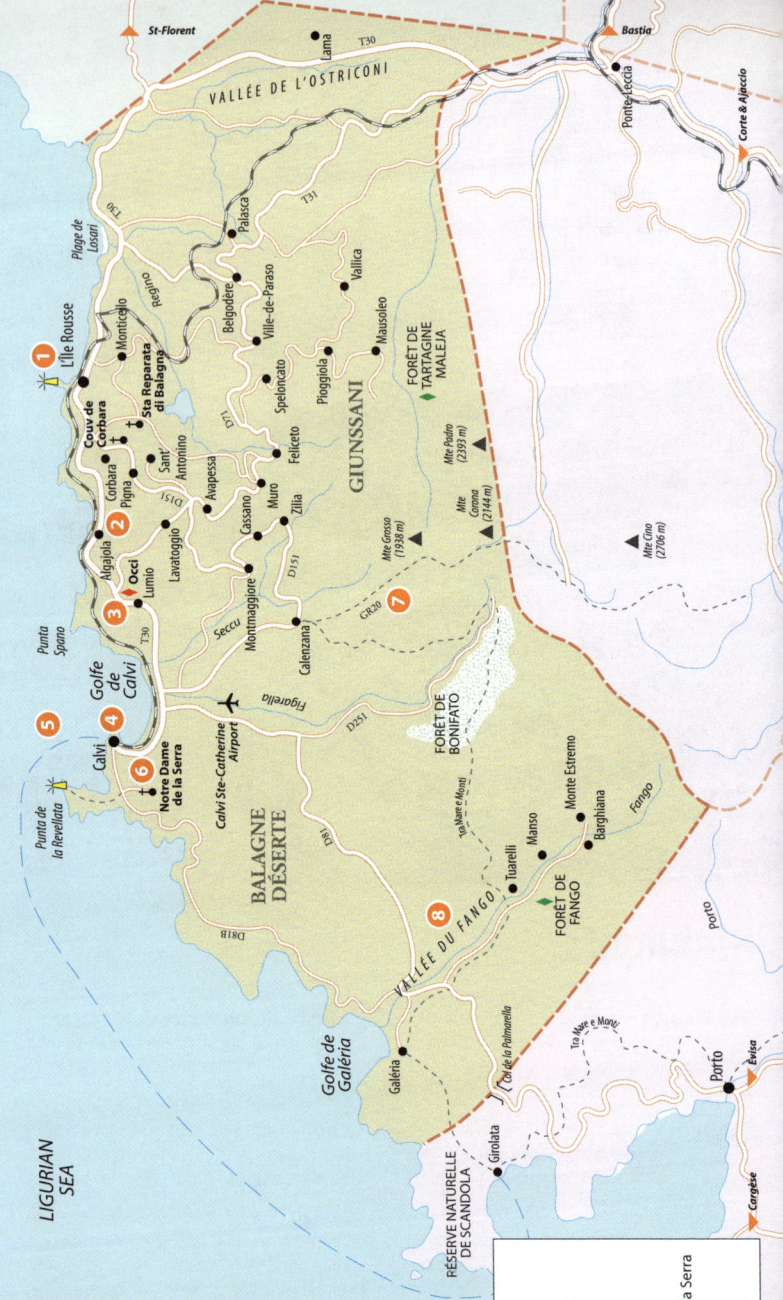

# THE BALAGNE

## LIGURIAN SEA

**N**

## VALLÉE DE L'OSTRICONI

St-Florent

Bastia

Lama

T30

Ponte-Leccia

Corte & Ajaccio

Plage de Losari

Palasca

L'Île Rousse ①

Monticello

Belgodère

Ville-de-Paraso

Vallica

Sta Reparata di Balagne

Couv de Corbara

⚓

Regino

D71

Speloncato

Pioggiola

GIUNSSANI

FORÊT DE TARTAGINE MALEJA

Mausoleo

Corbara

Pigna

Sant' Antonino

Avapessa

Feliceto

Mte Padro (2393 m)

Aregno

D151

Muro

Zilia

Mte Corona (2144 m)

Occi

Algajola

Lumio

Cassano

Mte Grosso (1938 m)

Mte Cino (2706 m)

② 

③ 

Lavatoggio

Montemaggiore

GR20 ⑦

Punta Spano

Golfe de Calvi

Seccu

Calenzana

FORÊT DE BONIFATO

④ 

⑤ Calvi

⑥ Notre Dame de la Serra

Calvi Ste-Catherine Airport

Figarella

D251

Monte Estremo

Fango

Punta de la Revellata

⚓

BALAGNE DÉSERTE

D81

Tra Mare e Monti

Tuarelli

Manso

Barghiana

FORÊT DE FANGO

⑧ 

VALLÉE DU FANGO

Col de la Palmarella

Porto

Golfe de Galéria

Galéria

Tra Mare e Monti

Porto

Evisa

RÉSERVE NATURELLE DE SCANDOLA

Girolata

Cargèse

D18B

## HIGHLIGHTS

① Île Rousse
② Balagne villages
③ Occi
④ Calvi
⑤ Scuba diving
⑥ Notre Dame de la Serra
⑦ GR20
⑧ Vallée de Fango

kilometres 0 5

on a grid system, quite at odds with the higgledy-piggledy nature of most Corsican villages and towns. Thanks to the busy trading of wine and oil, it soon began to prosper and, two and a half centuries later, still thrives as a successful port. These days, however, the main traffic consists of holiday-makers, lured here by brochure shots of the nearby beaches. This is officially the hottest corner of the island, and the town is deluged by sun-worshippers in July and August. It's undoubtedly an attractive place, but given the proximity of Calvi, and so much unspoilt countryside on its doorstep, you may prefer to stop here for little more than lunch or a coffee on the square.

## Place Paoli

All roads in L'Île Rousse lead to **place Paoli**, a shady but traffic-clogged square that's open to the sea and has as its focal point a fountain surmounted by a bust of "U Babbu di u Patria" ("Father of the Nation"), one of many local tributes to Pascal Paoli. There's a Frenchified covered **market** at the entrance to the square, which is home to a daily fresh produce market and a popular artisan-cum-antiques sale on Saturday mornings. On the west side rises the imposing facade of the **church of the Immaculate Conception**, while the pedestrianised Rue Notre Dame and Rue Napoléon are packed with shops and restaurants. From here, you can also catch the Petit Train to the Île de la Pietra (April-Oct).

## Île de la Pietra

To reach the **Île de la Pietra**, the islet that gives the town its name, continue north from the top of the promenade, passing the station on your left. Once over the causeway, you can walk through the crumbling mass of red granite as far as the lighthouse at the far end, from where the view of the town is spectacular, especially at sundown, when you get the full effect of the red glow of the rocks. From the centre of town, it's about a 30-minute, gently climbing walk to the lighthouse along purpose-built footpaths (no bikes); additional short trails loop around the peninsula, offering plenty of options for walking or running.

## The town beach

The recently extended **Promenade de la Marinella** runs along the **town beach**, a crowded Côte d'Azur-style strand blocked by ranks of sun loungers and parasols belonging to the row of lookalike café-restaurants behind it. Two much more enticing beaches, **Bodri** and **Ghjunchitu**, lie a couple of kilometres around the headland to the west; you can get there by train (alight at "Botri").

### ARRIVAL

L'ÎLE ROUSSE AND AROUND

**By train** The train station is en route du Port, 500m south of where the ferries arrive. Two services run daily to Bastia, and to Calvi via the beaches and villages en route.

**By bus** The Bastia–Calvi bus, operated by Corsicar (twice daily in July & Aug, daily the rest of the year; https://corsicar.com), stops just south of place Paoli.

**By ferry** Passenger ferries from Nice, Marseille and Toulon, and the Italian port of Savona, dock at the quayside on the northwest side of the centre, a 10min walk from the town centre.

**By car** There's a large but unpaved free car park up the hill from the train station and several paid car parks around town. Get there early in summer to snag a spot.

### GETTING AROUND AND INFORMATION

Île Rousse is easily navigated on foot, but you'll need your own wheels to explore the surrounding villages.

**By taxi:** Transport Corse (24/7 by reservation only; http://transports-corse.fr); Taxi Guidicelli (https://guidicelli-voyages.com).

**Bike rental:** B-bikes rent mountain bikes and e-bikes by the day (https://balagnebikes.fr)

**Car rental:** Utile in Monticello (https://ulocation.com)

**2**

Île de la Pietra

Ferry Terminal

# L'ÎLE ROUSSE

Marseille & Nice

RUE ISULA GRANDE

Port

IMPASSE DES ÎLES

AVENUE DAVID DARY

Boat & jet ski rentals

AVENUE DAVID DARY

RUE PONTE COLLE

Hôtel de Ville

BOULEVARD SOTTO MARE

RUE NOTRE DAME

RUE DE NUIT

RUE PASCAL PAOLI

RUE JEAN BEPETTI

RUE DOMINIQUE FIORAVANTI

RUE LOUIS PHILIPPE

Promenade de la Marinella

BOULEVARD PIERRE PASQUINI

PLACE PASCAL PAOLI

BOULEVARD CHARLES MARIE SAVELLI

Église de l'Immaculée Conception

RUE GÉNÉRAL GRAZIANI

AVENUE JOSEPH CALIZI

PICCIONI

AVENUE COMTE VALERY

RUE DU COLONEL ALLEGRINI

RUE DE BANDOL

RUE BLASINI

AVENUE PAUL DOUMER

Bastia, Corte & Saint-Florent

ROUTE DE CALVI

ROUTE DE MONTICELLO

& Plage de Bodri

RUE J. ALBERTINI ANDRÉ & V. VANNI

0    100
metres

Giunchetu, Corbara, Monticello & Calvi

| ACCOMMODATION | |
|---|---|
| Camping Le Bodri | 5 |
| Casa Rossa | 3 |
| Cala di L'Oru | 4 |
| Le Grillon | 2 |
| Santa Maria | 1 |
| Villa Josephine | 6 |

| EATING | |
|---|---|
| La Bodega | 1 |
| L'Escale | 2 |
| L'Ostéria | 3 |
| Terra D'Amore | 4 |
| U Spuntinu | 5 |

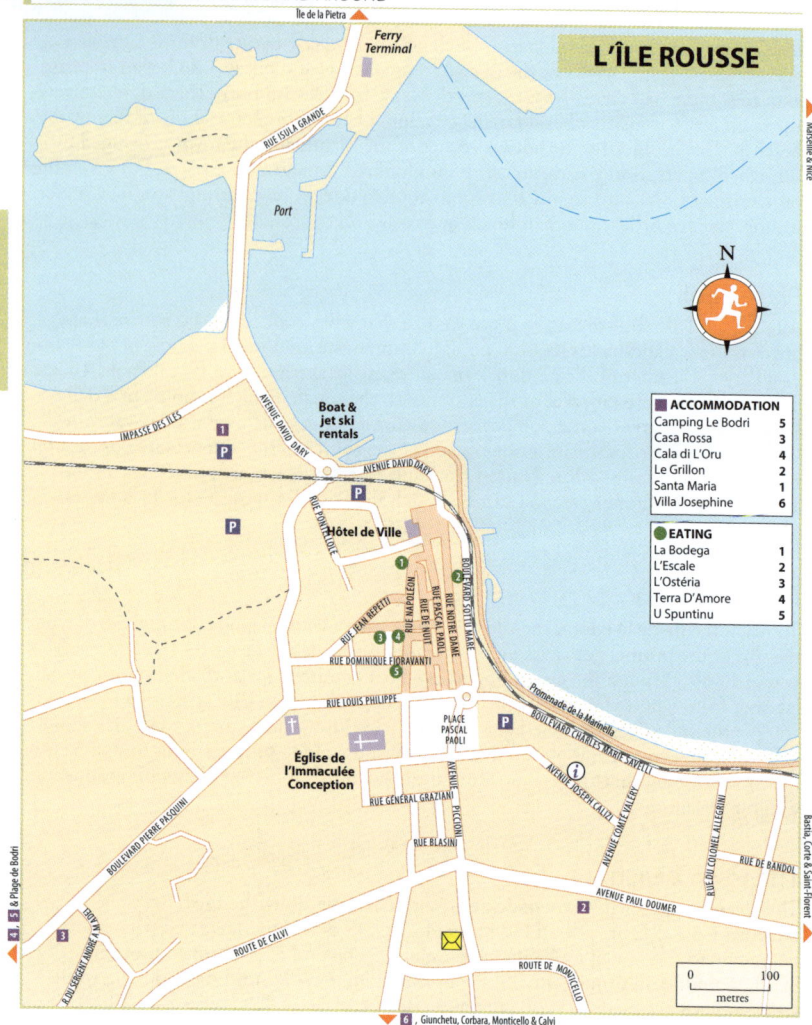

offers some of the best-value rentals.

**Tourist office** Av de Calizi (http://balagne-corsica.com) has detailed maps of the region's bike and footpaths, and plenty of recommendations for tours and transport.

## ACCOMMODATION                                    SEE MAP PAGE 66

**Camping Le Bodri** 3km west off the main Calvi rd; http://campinglebodri.com. Just 200m from the beach, and set among extensive grounds of eucalyptus and pine trees, this very pleasant campsite does get rammed in summer, though it's pleasantly quiet outside the *grandes vacances*. It's possible to reach it by train – alight at "Botri". €̄

**Casa Rossa** Bd Pierre Pasquini; https://hotel-casarossa. com. This gorgeous old stone complex offers spacious modern rooms with huge beds and patio seating. There's also a large, heated pool, a small gym, and a spa with a sauna, jacuzzi and massages. €̄€̄€̄

**Cala di L'Oru** Bd Pierre-Pasquini; http://hotel-caladiloru. com. Relaxed three-star hotel, swathed in greenery, on the outskirts of town. The rooms are functional without being bland, and a good-sized pool is a welcome bonus. Generous discounts low- and mid-season. €̄€̄

**Le Grillon** 10 av Paul-Doumer; http://hotelgrillon.com. The best cheap hotel in town, just 1km from the centre on the St-Florent/Bastia road. Nothing special, but quiet and immaculate. Half-board available. €̄

**Santa Maria** Rte du Port; http://hotelsantamaria.com. At the base of the promontory, this four-star complex has sweeping views and exclusive access to a tiny pebble beach. Affiliated with the Best Western chain, it's one of the larger and better-value four-star places and the closest to town. Prices plummet in off-season. €€€€

**Villa Josephine** Rue Bisgambiglia; http://villajosephine. corsica. Set back in the hills a 10-minute walk from town, this luxurious four-star hotel is a peaceful sanctuary with plant-filled gardens and breezy, pared-down décor. The *piece de resistance* is the glittering infinity pool that looks out over verdant swathes of maquis. €€€€

## HILLTOP VILLAGES OF THE BALAGNE

**2**

Fig, olive, and citrus trees shade the country lanes as you climb up into the granite hills above the Haute-Balagne coast and hopping between the hinterland villages is one of the most rewarding side trips from Calvi or Île Rousse. The mountains lie just a half-hour drive from the coast, making it easy to visit three or more villages in a day; there are also abundant walking and cycling trails (ask at the tourist office for a map). Many of the villages are home to artisan shops and workshops, making them a great place to shop for traditional handicrafts – look out for those awarded the *Rencontres Balanines* label (a brochure is available from the tourist office).

Leaving from Île Rousse, **Monticello** is the first village you'll come across, known for its seventeenth-century churches, Saturday morning market, and lively Saint Roch Celebrations (Aug 16th). Nearby **Corbara** is a tangled web of cobbled lanes, vaulted passageways, and elegant old churches, but the highlight is, hands-down, the **Musée Guy Savelli** (mid-April to September; Place de l'église; free), a truly mind-boggling private collection of historical artefacts and curiosities housed in the home of local collector Guy Savelli – ring the doorbell to enter!

Climbing higher into the hills, **Pigna** is a charming sight with its jumble of terracotta-roofed houses, all with blue-painted shutters. A town known for its music and annual Festivoce music festival (July), you can peek inside a traditional luthier atelier (https://casa-liutaiu.com), visit a museum of Corsican musical instruments (MuseuMusica; charge; https://voce.corsica/voce/museumusica) or watch a concert at the Casa Musicale auditorium.

Arguably the most famous of all the Balagne villages, **Sant'Antonino** is also the region's oldest and highest (at 521m). Scrambling through the narrow stairwells, covered alleyways, and labyrinth sidestreets of this hilltop town will make you feel like you've travelled back to medieval times – and the views from the top are worth the steep climb.

Along the T30 just east of Calvi, **Lumio** is the "Village of Light" – stick around until sunset and you'll see why – thanks to its characteristic pink granite buildings and striking Baroque church tower. Take a detour to the Clos Culombu vineyard (tours & tastings by reservation only; https://closculombu.fr), then hike up to the hilltop ghost town of **Occi** (a 1-hour there-and-back from the roadside or follow the 2-hour circular footpath from the village).

### ACCOMMODATION & EATING

**Casa Musicale** Fondu di u Paese, Pigna; https://casamusicale.corsica. Pigna's most charming 2-star hotel-restaurant has fourteen individually decorated rooms in a characterful old house at the heart of the village. At the restaurant, the chef's passion for his region shines through in Balanine dishes crafted from local, seasonal ingredients, more often than not grown in their own gardens. Hotel € Restaurant €€

**U Furnellu Di Davia** 306 Vla Di Mezzo, Corbara; https://instagram.com/furnellu_di_davia. This restaurant terrace affords one of the best views in the Balagne, to be savoured over doughy slices of wood-fired pizza. Pair it with a Capo Spritz for the perfect sundowner. €

**I Scalini** Sant'Antonino. Reaching this restaurant is all part of the fun as you follow the tiny signs up the labyrinth alleyways and uneven steps right to the very top of the village. The reward is a magnificent rooftop terrace and a menu packed with delicious regional delicacies. €€

★ **La Table di Mà** Rte de Calvi, Lumio; https://acasadima.com. Awarded a Michelin star for its visionary dishes and sleek presentation, this glamorous restaurant is the Balagne's ultimate foodie destination. Corsican flavours pop up in unexpected places, whether its blue crab sprinkled with *immortelle* flowers, scallops seared in *figatellu* drippings or a *brocciu* panna cotta sweetened with *miel du maquis*. €€€€

## EATING AND DRINKING SEE MAP PAGE 66

**La Bodega** 7 Rue Napoléon; https://www.facebook.com/p/Bodega-Ile-Rousse-Restaurant-Cocktails-100062988263656. With tables spilling out across the street and under the arch, this trendy restaurant does it all. Come to dine on delicious Thai-inspired dishes or share tapas with friends, then stick around until late when the music picks up and the cocktail bar keeps the drinks flowing. €€

**L'Escale** 20 Rue Notre-Dame; https://lescaleilerousse.fr. Giant fresh mussels, prawns and crayfish from the east coast *étangs* are the thing here, served in various *menus* on a spacious terrace looking across the tramway line to the bay. Brisk, courteous service, copious portions and the house white (by the glass or *pichet*) is decent. €€

**L'Ostéria** Pl. Santelli. You can depend on this swanky restaurant to nail all the classics, whether it's a *cannelloni au brocciu* seasoned with fresh mint or local delicacy, *poulpe*

*grillé* (grilled octopus). All the meat and fish is sourced locally. €€€

★ **Terra D'Amore** Rue Napoléon; https://instagram.com/terradamorestaurant. Latino-inspired fusion food is the name of the game at this cool, classy eatery, which marries quality Corsican ingredients with international flavours. Try the tacos, which are tangy, zesty, and bursting with caramelised pulled (Corsican) pork or the deliciously spicy *ceviche* made with the *pêche du jour*. Everything's 100 percent homemade and presented with care. €€

**U Spuntinu** 1 Rue Napoléon. Painted bright orange and decked out with cheery, multi-coloured chairs, you can't miss this tourist favourite along the main drag. Its popularity is deserved, though; the hearty *tianu de corse* (stews) are rich, filling and almost enough to make you pass on the delicious *fiadone* desserts. €€€

## Haute-Balagne coast

The beaches of the Haute-Balagne coast are some of the most stunning in Corsica, if not the Mediterranean, with champagne-coloured sands lapped by a glittering expanse of aquamarine. The string of beaches between Île Rousse and Calvi are the most visited, with the **plage de Bodri**, **plage d'Algajola** and **plage de l'Arinella** attracting the most attention. All three offer water sports, including jet skiing, windsurfing and kayak and SUP rentals, while the latter is renowned for its snorkelling.

The Balagne beaches are known for their high winds and big waves, so for calmer swimming waters, head to the sheltered **plage de Sant Ambroggio,** the rocky coves of **Punta Spano**, or the gently sloping **plage de Sainte Restitude**. East of Île Rousse, the less-developed **plage de Losari** is also worth a shout-out, fringed by wild maquis.

## Parc de Saleccia

Route de Bastia • April to October • Charge • https://parc-saleccia.fr • Bus Ligne 1 runs from Algajola in season; https://abalanina.corsica

This seven-hectare botanical garden draws nature lovers in their droves in summer. The leafy paths promise a taste of the maquis, and many of the island's native shrubs (myrtle, lavender, juniper, immortelle) are on display, punctuated by olive groves, oleander and rose gardens, and a lake filled with water lilies. Visit in spring for the most vibrant colours; by the end of summer, it's a sea of green. The farmyard animals, playground and aviary provide plenty of distractions for children, plus there's a pleasant café serving farm-to-table dishes.

## GETTING AROUND HAUTE-BALAGNE COAST

**By train** Regional trains – dubbed the "tramway" or, officially, the *desserte périurbaine* – run between Calvi and Île Rousse, stopping at most of the beaches and small towns along the coast. Timetables vary throughout the year, so check at the tourist office or online (https://cf-corse.corsica).

**By car** Many of the beaches offer free parking, but it can fill up quickly in summer, so arrive early.

# Calvi and around

Seen from the water, **CALVI** is a beautiful spectacle, with its three immense bastions topped by a crest of ochre buildings, sharply defined against a hazy backdrop of mountains. Located twenty kilometres west along the coast from L'Île Rousse, the town began as a fishing port on the site of the present-day *ville basse* below the citadelle, and remained just a cluster of houses and fishing shacks until the Pisans conquered the island in the tenth century. Not until the arrival of the Genoese, however, did the town become a stronghold when, in 1268, Giovaninello de Loreto, a Corsican nobleman, built a huge citadelle on the windswept rock overlooking the port and named it Calvi. A fleet commanded by Nelson launched a brutal two-month attack on the town in 1794; he left saying he hoped never to see the place again, and very nearly didn't see anywhere else again, having sustained the wound that cost him his sight in one eye.

The French concentrated on developing Ajaccio and Bastia during the nineteenth century, and Calvi became primarily a military base. A hangout for European glitterati in the 1950s, the town these days has the ambience of a slightly kitsch Côte d'Azur resort, whose glamorous marina, souvenir shops and fussy boutiques jar with the down-to-earth villages of its rural hinterland. It's also an important base for the French Foreign Legion's parachute regiment, the 2ème REP, and immaculately uniformed legionnaires are a common sight around the bars lining Avenue de la République.

## Quai Landry

Social life in Calvi focuses on the restaurants and cafés of the **quai Landry**, a spacious seafront walkway linking the marina and the port is the best place to get the feel of the town, although the majority of Calvi's sights are found within the walls of the **citadelle**. Scuba diving excursions (see page 71) and boat tours leave from here to Scandola and the calanques de Piana. Parallel to the quay, the pedestrianised Rue Georges Clemenceau is brimming with shops, restaurants and bars.

## The citadelle

Free • Audio guide tours available from the Tourist Information point; charge

"Civitas Calvis Semper Fidelis" – always faithful – reads the inscription of the town's motto, carved over the ancient gateway into the fortress. The best way of seeing the citadelle is to follow the ramparts connecting the three immense bastions, the views from which extend out to sea and inland to Monte Cinto. Within the walls, the houses are tightly packed along tortuous stairways and narrow passages that converge on the place d'Armes. Dominating the square is the **Cathédrale St-Jean-Baptiste**, set at the highest point of the promontory. This chunky ochre edifice was founded in the thirteenth century but was partly destroyed during the Turkish siege of 1553 and then suffered extensive damage twelve years later, when the powder magazine in the governor's palace exploded. It was rebuilt in the form of a Greek cross. The church's great treasure is the **Christ des Miracles**, which is housed in the chapel on the right of the choir; this crucifix was brandished at marauding Turks during the 1553 siege, an act which reputedly saved the day.

### La Maison Colomb

To the north of place d'Armes in rue de Fil stands **La Maison Colomb**, the shell of a building which Calvi believes – as the plaque on the wall states – was Christopher Columbus's birthplace, though the claim rests on pretty tenuous, circumstantial evidence. The house itself was destroyed by Nelson's troops during the siege of 1794; more interesting is the Christopher Columbus monument located along the outside walls of the Citadelle.

## The beach

Calvi's **beach** sweeps round the bay from the end of quai Landry, but most of the first kilometre or so is owned by bars which rent out sun loungers for a hefty price. To avoid these, follow the track behind the sand, which will bring you to the start of a more

**2**

# CALVI

ST-FRANÇOIS

Anse de
Fontanaccia

La Maison
Colomb

CITADELLE

Cathédrale
St-Jean-
Baptiste

Oratoire
St-Antoine

AVE SAINT-FRANÇOIS

RUE DE L'URUGUAY

PLACE DE
L'OMBRE

Caserne
Sampiero

PLACE
CHRISTOPHE
COLOMB

Christopher
Columbus

Port

Maison de
la Presse

AVENUE GÉRARD MARCHE

VILLAS ST-ANTOINE

R. RASCE LORRAINE

RUE CLEMENCEAU

Quai Landry

Tour
du Sel

Port de
Commerce

Hôtel de
Ville

AVENUE NAPOLÉON

BOULEVARD WILSON

Église Ste-Marie-Majeure

PLACE ST-
CHARLES

RUE CLEMENCEAU

QUAI LANDRY

AVENUE SANTA MARIA

Buses to Bastia,
Calenzana &
Galéria

RUE OFFRE

LA
PORTEUSE
D'EAU

Boat excursions
to Girolata

Gare CFC

LE PICCHETTO

Marina

Galéria & Punta de la Revellata

AVENUE SANTA MARIA

SAN FRANCESCO

SAN FRANCESCO

AVENUE DE LA RÉPUBLIQUE

| ◼ **ACCOMMODATION** | |
|---|---|
| Camping Bella Vista | 6 |
| La Caravelle | 3 |
| Cyrnea | 4 |
| Il Tramonto | 1 |
| Le Magnolia | 2 |
| Le Home | 7 |
| Relais International de la Jeunesse "U Carabellu" | 8 |
| La Villa Calvi | 5 |

ROUTE DU STADE

Plage de Calvi

AVENUE CHRISTOPHE COLOMB

Super-U

Calvi Talle
Train Station

| ● **EATING** | |
|---|---|
| A Casetta | 5 |
| A Punta | 1 |
| Aux Bons Amis | 3 |
| Les Boucaniers | 8 |
| Casa Bella Storia | 6 |
| Kelly's Pastry | 7 |
| Le Tire Bouchon | 2 |
| U Fanale | 4 |

| ● **SHOPPING** | |
|---|---|
| Annie Traiteur | 2 |
| Maes Bijoux | 1 |

| ◼ **DRINKING & NIGHTLIFE** | |
|---|---|
| Bar de la Tour | 1 |
| La Licorne | 3 |
| Loch Ness Pub | 2 |

VILLA

ROUTE DE SANTORE

VILLA

VILLA

ROUTE DE LA PIETRA-MAGGIORE

STAGNONE

Ste-Catherine Airport & L'Île Rousse

0        100
metres

N

secluded stretch. The sea might not be as sparklingly clear as at many other Corsican beaches, but it's warm, shallow and free of rocks.

## ARRIVAL AND DEPARTURE

**CALVI AND AROUND**

**By plane** Ste-Catherine airport, served by domestic and international flights, lies 7km south of Calvi (http://calvi. aeroport.fr); the only public transport into town is by taxi.

**By train** The train station on Av de la République is the terminus for regular long-distance trains to Bastia and Ajaccio, as well as villages and resorts along the route of the seasonal tramway between Calvi and Île Rousse. There

are several departures daily in summer, but limited winter services and timetables change frequently, so check online (https://cf-corse.corsica).

**By bus** Buses to and from Bastia and towns along the north coast (twice daily in July and Aug, daily the rest of the year; https://www.corsicar.com), stop outside the train station on place de la Porteuse d'Eau.

## GETTING AROUND AND INFORMATION

**By taxi:** Transport Corse (1 Bd Wilson; http://transports-corse.fr); Eco Limousine (Lieu-dit Val al Legno; http://ecolimousine.fr).

**Bike rental:** Wild Machja (Av Christophe Colomb; http://wildmachja.com) rents and repairs mountain and road bikes.

**Car rental:** Hertz (Calvi airport; http://hertzcorse.com).

**Tourist office** Chemin de la plage (http://balagne-corsica.com); this regional office covers the Balagne and has a souvenir shop and tour booking service. They also sell detailed guides to the region's walking and cycling routes (charge).

## ACCOMMODATION

**Camping Bella Vista** Rte de Pietramaggiore, 1km southeast of the centre (700m inland from the beach); http://camping-bellavista.com. The best option for campers as it's much closer to the centre of town than the competition – though you pay a couple of euros per night extra for the privilege. Plenty of shade, nice soft ground and clean toilet blocks, plus an on-site pizzeria. €

**La Caravelle** Marco Plage, 1km south of centre; http://hotel-la-caravelle.com. An impeccably clean, modern hotel virtually on the beach, with ground-floor rooms set around a garden; those on the first floor are more luxurious. Buffet breakfasts are served on a sunny patio, and there's a nice bar-restaurant. Good value in this bracket considering the location, quality of the property and service. €€€

**Cyrnea** Rte de Bastia; http://hotel-cyrnea.fr. Large budget hotel, a twenty-minute walk south of town, and 300m from the beach. Good-sized rooms for the price, all with bathrooms and balconies (ask for one with "vue sur les montagnes" to the rear), and there's even a pleasant outdoor pool. Outstanding value for money, especially in high season. €€

**Il Tramonto** Rte de Porto; http://hoteliltramonto.com. Excellent little hotel, with clean, comfortable and light rooms on the far north side of town. Definitely worth splashing out on one with "vue sur la mer", which have little terraces and a superb panorama over Punta de la Revellata. €€

**Le Magnolia** Rue d'Alsace-Lorraine; http://hotel-le-

---

## SCUBA DIVING AROUND CALVI

The sunken wreck of a bullet-ridden B-17 bomber, its propeller still intact, is one of the most unique dive sites in the Mediterranean, and its story – a heroic emergency water landing that somehow saw pilot and crew escape unscathed – is just as remarkable. Diving the wreck at 28 metres is reserved for certified divers only (PADI advanced/deep dive or equivalent), but the coast of Calvi has plenty of other dive sites suitable for all levels, including first-time divers.

Most dives take place around **La Revellata**, the peninsula west of Calvi, where you can spot large grouper, barracudas, seabream, and damselfish, along with octopus, moray eels, and starfish. For certified divers, there's also the opportunity to explore "The Canyon", where steep drop-offs plummet to depths of 38 metres, and you can see red coral colonies, purple sea fans, and several species of nudibranchs (dalmatian, hervia and flabellina). Fluorescence night diving and several wreck dives are also open to certified divers.

**Hippocampe Plongée** (at the south end of the marina; https://plongee-calvi-corse.com) offer excursions to all dive sites and cater for both beginner and certified divers. They also offer scuba diving classes

and courses.

**Incantu** (https://incantu.com) in Galéria, 30km south of Calvi, offer scuba dives for all levels on the edge of the Réserve Naturelle de Scandola.

2

magnolia.com. Nineteenth-century townhouse with *belle époque* decor and the atmosphere of an elegantly old-fashioned *pension*, set behind high walls in the heart of the historic quarter. The eponymous magnolia tree shades a lovely terrace restaurant where breakfast is served in the mornings. Welcoming management. €€

★ **Le Home** Rte de Pietramaggiore; http://residence-lehome.com. Comfortable, a/c chalet studios and apartments set in beautiful gardens a five-minute walk from the beach and old town. Impeccably clean, they're equipped with hobs, coffee makers, toasters and microwaves for basic self-catering, and have balconies. Friendly management. €€

**Relais International de la Jeunesse "U Carabellu"** 4km from the centre of town on rte Pietramaggiore; http://clajsud.fr. Follow the N197 for 2km, turn right at the sign for Pietramaggiore, and the hostel – two little houses with spacious, clean dormitories, family and double rooms, looking out over the gulf – is in the village another 2km further up the lane. Book in advance. €

**La Villa Calvi** Chemin Notre Dame de la Serra; https://lavilla.fr. Lavish five-star paradise set on the hillside with views across to the citadelle and beach. Everything about la villa oozes luxury, from the manicured gardens to the quartet of swimming pools and the marbled bathrooms. There's also a gym, spa, two restaurants and a pool bar. €€€€

## EATING

★ **A Casetta** 16 rue Clemenceau; http://www.acasetta.net. This fabulous deli has just a handful of tables on a lovely harbour view from which you can enjoy sharing plates of Corsican specialities – from cheese to *saucisse* to terrines – all beautifully presented. €

**A Punta** Av. Napoléon; https://m.facebook.com/profile.php?id=792144457618981. If you've got a craving for pizza, then this reliably packed pizzeria is a safe bet. There's a huge choice of toppings and you can even double up and have Nutella-filled pizza for dessert. €

**Aux Bons Amis** 9 rue Clemenceau. Cosy restaurant decorated with fishing paraphernalia serving up surprisingly sophisticated dishes. The focus is – unsurprisingly – on fish, with menus including dishes like carpaccio of red tuna. €€

★ **Les Boucaniers** Lieu dit Padula, Calvi beach. Set back from the beach amid the trees, this relaxed and friendly steakhouse has a shady terrace where you can dangle your toes in the sand. Naturally, meat dominates the menu, and it's served to your liking on wooden boards with a choice of sauces and thick-cut homemade fries. €€

**Casa Bella Storia** 8 Quai Adolphe Landry; https://casabellastoria.com. Gastronomic cuisine without an air of pretension or an astronomical price tag. Tuck into beef tartare, calamari with chorizo, or butternut risotto, then treat yourself to one of the sensational desserts. €€

**Kelly's Pastry** 9 Rue Maréchal Joffre; https://www.instagram.com/kelly_s_pastry. The Barbie pink façade and cutesy flower-filled bicycles out front are all part of the tea party aesthetic at this decadent bakery. Come for strong coffee and pastries in the morning or mid-afternoon for a homemade cheesecake or *tarte aux figures*. €€

**Le Tire Bouchon** 15 Rue Georges Clemenceau. Wholesome Corsican specialities served in a cosy family restaurant with red chequered tablecloths and book-stuffed shelves. It's good value, with menu staples including lasagne, cannelloni, and wild boar stew. €€

**U Fanale** Rte de Porto, just outside the centre of town on the way to Punta de la Revellata. Worth the walk out here for their delicious, beautifully presented Corsican specialities – mussels or lamb simmered in ewe's cheese and white wine, a fine *soupe corse*, and melt-in-the-mouth *fiadone* (traditional flan). You can dine outside in the garden or inside their *salle panoramique*, with views across the bay to Punta de la Revellata. €€

## DRINKING & NIGHTLIFE

**Bar de la Tour** Quai Adolphe Landry. Right on the waterfront at the foot of the citadelle with a prime view for sunset. There's a decent range of beers, aperitifs, and cocktails, and in summer, musicians often play outside by the harbour.

**La Licorne** Plage de Calvi. By day, this chic rattan-adorned beach bar is the place to hire a sun lounger and tuck into platters of seafood; by night, it's a bar serving signature cocktails into the early hours.

**Loch Ness Pub** 11 Rue Georges Clemenceau. Calvi's coolest and quirkiest bar pays homage to its namesake with an elaborate beer bottle mosaic. Inside, the décor is just as wacky, with purple lighting and a vintage car suspended from the roof. There's also a pool table, a well-stocked bar, and a huge selection of world craft beers to enjoy while head-banging to blaring rock and metal.

## SHOPPING

**Annie Traiteur** 5 rue Clemenceau. Recommended for local specialities and other authentic souvenirs, including a huge range of wines, olive oil, honey, charcuterie, liqueurs and *canistrelli* biscuits. They also prepare fresh *bastelles* (pasties) with spinach and local *brocciu*.

**Maes Bijoux** At the entrance to the citadelle. This tiny shop hides the workshop of local artist and jeweller Marjorie, whose schtick is repurposing old silverware and metals into necklaces, earrings, bangles and other jewellery. Her creations are striking, innovative and eco-friendly.

## La Revellata

West of Calvi, the rocky, maquis-clad Revellata peninsula is one of the wildest stretches of the Balagne Coast and, at its tip, the closest point to mainland France. You can explore parts of the peninsula in a 4x4, by mountain bike, or on a boat cruise around the coast, but most alluring is the rugged **Sentier des Douaniers** footpath, which cuts along the top of the sea cliffs all the way to the Revellata lighthouse. Part of the fun is venturing off-piste; rough trails lead down to tiny coves, some with slivers of white sand, others sheltered by the rocks and providing calm waters for swimming. From Calvi, it takes about 1.5 hours to reach the lighthouse; bring plenty of water as the entire trail is exposed to the sun.

### Notre Dame de la Serra
About 5km south of Calvi, off the D81, or a 50-minute walk from Calvi • Free

At the southern end of the Revellata peninsula, the 15th-century **Notre Dame de la Serra** church sits on a hilltop perch with panoramic views of the mountains, coast and citadelle. Rebuilt in the 19th century and recently restored, the church is an important site of pilgrimage, renowned for the gleaming white statue of the Virgin Mary that towers atop a huge rock outside the chapel. For locals, it's a sacred site where the annual Notre Dame de la Serra festival is celebrated each September; for the non-religious, it's Calvi's most magical sunset spot. The chapel is open from May to September only, but you can visit the viewpoint at any time.

## Calenzana

About 12km southeast of Calvi, the sleepy mountain town of Calenzana sits at the trailhead of two of the island's flagship long-distance hikes, the 15-day GR20 (see page 74) and the 10-day Mare è Monti (Coast to Mountain). There's little in the town itself aside from a few restaurants, reliably full of hungry hikers, and a handful of bakeries where you can stock up on freshly baked snacks for the road. If you do spend an extra day in town, the nearby Domaine 'Alzipratu (https://domaine-alzipratu.com) winery offers tours and tastings by reservation only.

### ARRIVAL AND DEPARTURE
CALENZANA

**By bus** Corsicar (https://corsicar.com) runs twice daily buses to and from Calvi from July 1st to the first week of September. The rest of the year, the service operates once a day from Calvi on weekdays only; to return from Calenzana, you'll need to take a taxi.

**By taxi** Taxi Calenzana (by reservation only; www.taxi-calenzana-calvi.fr) offers taxis from Calvi airport, train station or hotels year-round.

### ACCOMMODATION & EATING

**A Casa di Jo** 9 Rte de Moncale. One of the smarter options in town, with a swimming pool, mountain views, and private parking. Book early; like all of Calenzana's hotels, it fills up fast for peak season. €€

**A Stazzona** Rue du Fond. Fill up on steaming stews – *civet de sanglier* or *sauté de veau aux olives* – served with fresh gnocchi, capped off with a chestnut cream tiramisu for a satiating pre-hike dinner. Cash only. €€

## Forêt de Bonifato

The Forêt de Bonifato – literally, the "blessed forest" – was awarded its name for its fresh mountain air and mineral-rich waters of the Figarella River. Just a half-hour drive south of Calvi, it's still the mountain escape of choice for day-trippers and wildlife enthusiasts, laced with forested footpaths. Take your pick from eight walks (Calvi tourist office will talk you through your options), ranging from 30-minute child-friendly trails to half-day

2

## HIKING THE GR20

Winding some 180km from Calenzana (12km from Calvi) to Conca (22km from Porto-Vecchio), the **GR20** is Corsica's most demanding long-distance footpath. Only one-third of the 18,000 to 20,000 hikers who start it each season complete all sixteen stages, which can be covered in ten to twelve days if you're in good physical shape – if you're not, don't even think about attempting this route. Marked with red-and-white splashes of paint, it comprises a series of harsh ascents and descents, sections of which exceed 2000m and become more of a scramble than a walk, with stanchions, cables and ladders driven into the rock as essential aids. The going is made tougher by the necessity of carrying a sleeping bag, all-weather kit and two- or three-days' food with you. That said, the rewards more than compensate. The GR20 takes in the most spectacular mountain terrain in Corsica and along the way you can spot the elusive mouflon (mountain sheep), glimpse lammergeier (a rare vulture) wheeling around the crags, and swim in ice-cold torrents and waterfalls.

The first thing to do before setting off is get hold of the Cicerone Trekking the GR20 Corsica guidebook (http://cicerone.co.uk), by far the most detailed and up to date book in English on the trail.

The route can be undertaken in either **direction**, but most hikers start in the north at Calenzana, tackling the most demanding *étapes* early on. The hardship is alleviated by extraordinary mountainscapes as you round the Cinto massif, skirt the Asco, Niolo, Tavignano and Restonica valleys, and scale the sides of Monte d'Oro and Rotondo. At Vizzavona on the main Bastia–Corte–Ajaccio Road, roughly the halfway mark, you can call it a day and catch a bus or train back to the coast, or press on south across two more ranges to the needle peaks of Bavella.

**Accommodation** along the route is provided by **refuges,** where you can take a hot shower, use an equipped kitchen and bunk down on mattresses. Usually converted *bergeries*, these places are staffed by wardens during the peak period (June–Sept). Advance reservations, made online via the PNRC website (https://pnr-resa.corsica), are essential.

The **weather** in the high mountains is notoriously fickle. A sunny morning doesn't necessarily mean a sunny day, and during July and August, violent storms can envelop the route without warning. It's therefore essential to take good wet-weather gear with you, as well as a hat, sunblock and shades. In addition, make sure you set off on each stage with adequate **food** and **water**. At the height of the season, most *refuges* sell basic supplies (*alimentation* or *ravitaillement*), but you shouldn't rely on this service; ask hikers coming from the opposite direction where their last supply stop was and plan accordingly (basic provisions are always available at the main passes of Col de Vergio, Col de Vizzavona, Col de Bavella and Col de Verde). The *refuge* wardens (*gardiens*) will be able to advise you on how much water to carry at each stage.

Finally, a word of **warning**: each year, injured hikers have to be air-lifted to safety off remote sections of the GR20, normally because they strayed from the marked route and got lost. Occasionally, fatal accidents also occur for the same reason, so always keep the paint splashes in sight, especially if the weather closes in – don't rely purely on the many cairns that punctuate the route, as these sometimes mark more hazardous paths to high peaks.

treks that join parts of the GR20 or Mare è Monti. Park by the Auberge de la Forest off the D251 (charge) and bring your swimsuit so you can cool off at the natural pools nearby. Wildlife is prolific here, so look out for wild boar and mouflon grazing the forest floor or golden eagles and bearded vultures swooping overhead.

## Galéria

The southernmost town in the Balagne and one of few coastal towns within the Parc Naturel Régional de Corse, **Galéria** makes a tranquil basecamp for boat cruises to the soaring rouge cliffs of Scandola or wildlife walks in the Vallée de Fango. The town's pebble beach manages to dodge the summer crowds that plague the Haute-Balagne coast; instead, you'll share the shore with local fishermen and the odd wandering cow.

## Vallée de Fango

Follow the D351 inland from Galéria and park at one of the roadside parking bays • Free; some car parks charge in July & Aug

From the mouth of the Fango River, just north of Galéria, the wildlife-filled wetlands of the Fango Delta mark the start of the Vallée de Fango, a UNESCO Biosphere Reserve which runs for some 15km before disappearing into the granite peaks of Corsica's central massifs. Canoeing excursions along the Fango river delta, where wildlife sightings include turtles and waterfowl, are an easy way to dip into the valley. Further up, footpaths curl down to the riverside, where you can bathe beneath waterfalls and plunge into swim in glassy pools framed by multi-coloured rocks or crumbling stone bridges. There are few wild swimming spots as breathtaking.

2

### GETTING AROUND      GALÉRIA

**By boat** Galéria Marina (https://visite-scandola.com) offer short cruises to Scandola (2hr 15mins) and full-day cruises to Scandola, Piana, and Girolata.

**By canoe** Delta du Fangu (https://delta-du-fangu.com) offer canoeing tours from June to September.

### ACCOMMODATION & EATING

**Hotel L'Alivu** Route du bord de mer; https://hotel-lalivu.com. Within strolling distance of the beach, this small, friendly hotel is great value. Rooms are spacious with air-con and garden view balconies, plus there's a heated pool and restaurant. €

**La Cabane du Pêcheur** Route de borde de mer; https://facebook.com/lacabanedupecheurgaleria/. Rustic *cabane* serving fresh-from-the-boat seafood cooked by the fishermen themselves. Come here for simple dishes like fish 'n' chips and lobster rolls done to perfection, albeit with a rather hefty price tag. It's worth it to support a 100 percent local and sustainable business. €€

# The Northwest

GIROLATA BAY

# The Northwest

Nowhere have Corsica's rewilding efforts paid off so spectacularly than the riotously rocky Northwest coast. The flame-red porphyry cliffs of Scandola crown the northern brow of the Golfe de Porto, swaddled in a vast quilt of uncharted maquis where wildlife is left to roam. On the southern shore, the lava-forged Calanques de Piana are equally showstopping, with golden rocks eroded into teetering spindles and steep scarps that envelop both the clifftop coastal road and the coves and sea caves below. When you've finished cruising the coast – an unmissable experience for any first timer – follow the zigzagging lanes east into the wooded hills or south to lounge on the sandy beaches of the Golfe de Sagone.

Straddling the river of the same name at the heart of the **Golfe de Porto**, the bijou fishing village of **Porto** enjoys a glorious setting, clasped between forest-clad mountains and tangerine sea cliffs on the brink of the shimmering gulf. Porto is the main departure point for boat cruises to the **Réserve Naturelle de Scandola** and the **Calanques de Piana**, which make up the island's only **UNESCO World Heritage Site**. Pint-sized **Girolata** is the last inhabited village amid the Scandola wilderness and the starting point for one of the few hiking trails that skirt the protected coastline.

From Porto, the D84 curls east through thick forest and craggy mountains, climbing past the mountain villages of **Ota** and **Évisa**, where lush walking trails set out through the **Gorges de la Spelunca** and the **Forêt d'Aïtone**.

More jaw-dropping scenery unfolds along the coast of the calanques to the south, where rockfalls and meandering livestock remind you that this is a drive to be savoured at a slow pace. The pink-hued village of **Piana** has views aplenty, and you can also sneak a peek at the picturesque **Ficajola cove**, reached by a thrilling descent through the calanques.

South of Piana, well-heeled **Cargèse** marks the point where the soaring cliffs give way to sandy bays, but you can still enjoy rugged coastal hikes, the most rewarding of which leads to the **Tour d'Omigna**, one of the few Genoese towers open to visitors. The road finally smoothes out as it leaves the glides around the **Gulfe de Sagone** with its handsome sandy bays and lively seaside resorts.

---

**GETTING THERE AND AROUND**                                   **THE NORTHWEST**

While there are infrequent buses from Ajaccio to Porto year-round (see https://corsicabus.org), it's far more enjoyable to explore the northwest coast with your own vehicle.

## The Réserve Naturelle de Scandola

The extraordinary **Réserve Naturelle de Scandola** takes up the promontory dividing the Balagne from the Golfe de Porto. Composed of striking red porphyry granite, its sheer cliffs and gnarled claw-like outcrops were formed by Monte Cinto's volcanic eruptions 250 million years ago, and subsequent erosion has fashioned shadowy caves, grottoes and gashes in the rock. Scandola's colours are as remarkable as the shapes, the hues varying from the charcoal grey of granite to incandescent rusty purple, and the tallest cliffs reach heights of 900m.

The headland and its surrounding water were declared a nature reserve in 1975 and a UNESCO World Heritage Site (along with the adjoining coastline of the Gulfe de Porto and the Calanques de Piana) in 1983. Since then, conservation efforts have been

# Highlights

**❶ Scandola boat cruises** Steady your sea legs and ride the crashing waves beneath the rust-red scarps of Corsica's only UNESCO World Heritage Site. See page 80

**❷ Girolata** The last fishing village on the island still inaccessible by road, set against a backdrop of red cliffs and dense maquis. See page 80

**❸ Porto** Nuzzled between tree-cloaked bluffs at the mouth of its namesake river with a still-intact defence tower, this is arguably Corsica's prettiest port. See page 81

**❹ Forêt d'Aïtone** East of the village of Evisa; walk, cycle or drive through the verdant forest canopy. See page 85

**❺ The Calanques** Sun-baked porphyry cliffs and rock formations moulded by nature over millennia and set against an expanse of aquamarine ocean. See page 85

**❻ Anse de Ficajola** Smuggled away on the cusp of the calanques, this tiny fishing cove has just enough sand to lay out your towel. See page 86

**❼ Tour d'Omigna** With two hours to spare, this painstakingly restored tower is the grand finale of an easy but nonetheless impressive walk. See page 88

**HIGHLIGHTS ARE MARKED ON THE MAP ON PAGE 80**

made to protect and reintroduce wildlife to the region, including rare Audouin's gull and osprey (*balbuzard pêcheur*), who build their nests high on the rocks. Aside from the boat tours that shuttle tourists to see the mighty cliffs, the entire reserve is off-limits to human activity.

**GETTING THERE**                                    **RÉSERVE NATURELLE DE SCANDOLA**

**By boat** Scandola is off-limits to hikers and can be   excursions from Porto (see page 83).
viewed only by boat, which means taking one of the daily

# Girolata

The **Sentier du Facteur** (Postman's trail), so-called as this was the route the village's postman used to take, connects the tiny fishing haven of **GIROLATA** to the rest of the

**THE NORTHWEST**

**HIGHLIGHTS**
1. Scandola boat cruises
2. Girolata
3. Porto
4. Forêt d'Aïtone
5. The Calanques
6. Anse de Ficajola
7. Tour d'Omigna

island. Located immediately east of Scandola, it's now the only village on Corsica without road access. Girolata has a dreamlike quality highlighted by the vivid red of the surrounding rocks and its short stretch of stony beach and few houses are dominated by a stately watchtower, built by the Genoese in the seventeenth century on a bluff overlooking the cove.

For much of the year, this is one of the most idyllic spots on the island, with only the odd yacht and party of hikers to threaten the settlement's tranquillity. In July and August, though, daily boat trips from Porto and Calvi ensure the village is swamped during the middle of the day, so if you want to make the most of the scenery and peace and quiet, walk here and stay a night in one of the *gîtes*.

The head of the Girolata trail is at **Bocca à Crocce** (Col de la Croix), on the Calvi–Porto road just north of the village of Osani. From here, a clear path plunges downhill through dense maquis and forest to a flotsam-covered cove known as **Cala di Tuara** (30min). The more rewarding of the two tracks that wind onwards to Girolata is the gentler one running left around the headland, but if you feel like stretching your legs, follow the second, more direct route uphill to a pass. It's about 1hr 30min on foot.

**3**

### GETTING THERE
**GIROLATA**

**By boat** If you don't fancy hiking, boats run from Porto to Girolate daily from April to September (https://transport- girolata.com/); in winter, they peter out to just once a week.

### ACCOMMODATION & EATING

Girolata's smattering of restaurants are on the pricey side, but there's also a stall by the beach that sells tasty Corsican pasties (*bastelles*) filled with spinach, onions and *brocciu*.
**Le Bon Espoir** Along the promontory, below the fort. http://restaurant-girolata.com. Specialising in fish and seafood, this long-established restaurant has a beautiful view over the bay. A proper family restaurant, the fish comes straight off the patron's own boat, while his son is the chef. Open April-Sept. €€€
**Café Gobi** On the beach. With a large, shaded deck that's a tempting proposition on a hot day, this café has ice-cold drinks, ice cream sundaes, and *spuntinu* – platters of Corsican cheese and charcuterie to share. €€

**Gîte E Casarelle** On the beachfront; https://ecasarelle. wixsite.com/ecasarelle. Basic *gîte d'étape* offering a choice of accommodation in dorms or small wood cabins in the garden behind (these accommodate two people); you can also put your tent up here. Meals are served in their quirky wood-carved bar, but the food isn't up to much. No card payments. Dorms €; bungalows €€
**Le Cormoran** Clean, well-maintained *gîte d'étape* with dorm beds. The half-board option is highly recommended as the attached restaurant is one of the better ones, serving pasta dishes with homemade pesto and tomatoes from their garden. Try the *casarecci aux chataignes*, gnocchi made with chestnut flour. Dorms €; restaurant €

# Porto

The overwhelming proximity of the mountains, combined with the pervasive eucalyptus and spicy scent of the maquis, give **PORTO**, 30km south of Calvi, a uniquely intense atmosphere that makes it one of the most atmospheric places to stay on the west coast. Except for a watchtower erected here by the Genoese in the second half of the sixteenth century, the site was only built upon with the onset of tourism since the 1950s; today, the village is still so small that it can become claustrophobic in July and August when overcrowding is no joke. Off-season, the place becomes eerily deserted, so you'd do well to choose your times carefully; the best months are May, June and September.

## Vaïta and the marina

The eucalyptus-bordered **route de la Marine** links the two parts of the resort. The village proper, known as **Vaïta**, comprises a strip of supermarkets, shops and hotels 1km from the sea, but the main focus of activity is the small **Marine de Porto**, located at the avenue's end and presided over by the **Tour Génoese de Porto**. Restaurants look out across the gulf to the north of the tower or the River Porto to the south, affording plenty of options for dining with a view, while boats line the riverside marina.

## Tour Génoese de Porto

Charge; includes museum entry

Overlooking the entrance to the harbour is the much-photographed **Genoese Tower**, a square chimney-shaped structure that was cracked by an explosion in the seventeenth century, when it was used as an arsenal. It's one of just four square towers on the island; most are round. An awe-inspiring view of the crashing sea and maquis-shrouded mountains makes it worth the short climb. There's also a tiny museum hidden away in the rocks with exhibitions on Porto's fortifications and abundant local shrub, heather.

## The beach

Porto's **beach** consists of a broad stretch of sand and pebbles, hidden from view beyond the looming rocks that mark the south shore of the River Porto. To reach it from the marina, cross the wooden footbridge which spans the River Porto, then walk through the car park and follow the trees around to the right. Although it's rather rocky and exposed, and the sea very deep, the great crags overshadowing the shore give the place a vivid, wild atmosphere. There are far better beaches for bathing, but it's a glorious spot to watch the sunset.

### ARRIVAL AND INFORMATION

PORTO

**By car** There's plenty of paid parking around the marina, but it's chockful in summer; better to park in the large, free car parks by the beach and walk over the footbridge.

**By bus** Buses from Ajaccio, via Cargèse and Piana (https://autocars-iledebeaute-ajaccio-20.fr/services-reguliers), pull into the junction at the end of route de la Marine, opposite the Banco supermarket, en route to the marina. They run twice a day year-round and three times daily in July & August; timetables are posted at the tourist office.

**Tourist office** Porto's tourist office is down by the harbour (http://ouestcorsica.com), a source of Topo-guides and brochures for hikes in the area. The building also hosts an

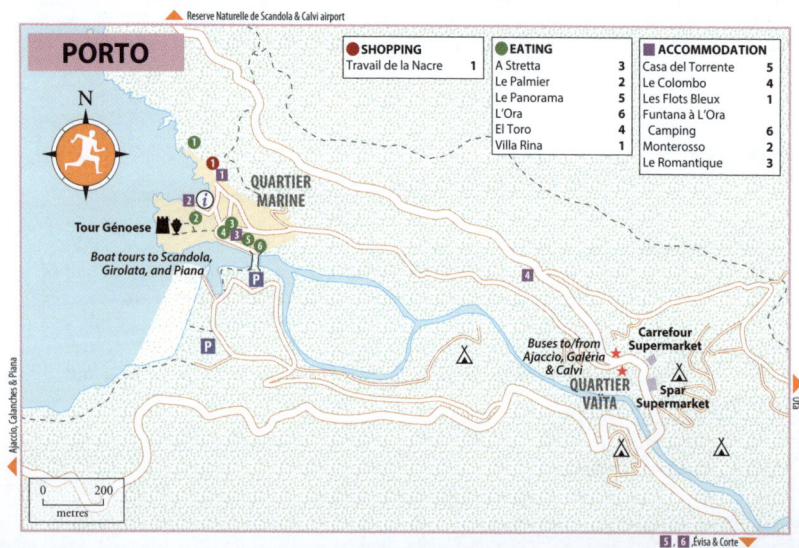

**PORTO**

N

| ● SHOPPING | |
|---|---|
| Travail de la Nacre | 1 |

| ● EATING | |
|---|---|
| A Stretta | 3 |
| Le Palmier | 2 |
| Le Panorama | 5 |
| L'Ora | 6 |
| El Toro | 4 |
| Villa Rina | 1 |

| ■ ACCOMMODATION | |
|---|---|
| Casa del Torrente | 5 |
| Le Colombo | 4 |
| Les Flots Bleux | 1 |
| Funtana à L'Ora Camping | 6 |
| Monterosso | 2 |
| Le Romantique | 3 |

Reserve Naturelle de Scandola & Calvi airport

QUARTIER MARINE

Tour Génoese

Boat tours to Scandola, Girolata, and Piana

Ajaccio, Calanches & Piana

Buses to/from Ajaccio, Galéria & Calvi

Carrefour Supermarket

Spar Supermarket

QUARTIER VAÏTA

Ota

0    200
metres

5 , 6  Évisa & Corte

## BOAT TRIPS FROM PORTO

A number of firms run **boat excursions** out of Porto harbour between April and October. Most follow comparable itineraries around the Gulf, combining a tour of the **Réserve Naturelle de Scandola** headland with a stop at **Girolata** and a cruise around the Calanques de Piana, a huge mass of weirdly eroded pink rock just southwest of Porto. It's worth taking the longer itinerary that combines all three – each one is a highlight.

The main difference between them is the kind of vessels they use, which vary from converted fishing boats to superfast inflatables. Tickets should be booked in advance direct from the operators, who have stalls around the marina, and prices can vary slightly according to demand and time of year. Reduced tariffs for **children** apply to all of the following.

**Nave Va** Place de la Marine; http://naveva.com. The largest firm, with 11 boats running tours around the island, including one that accommodates up to 150 people.

**Corse Adrénaline** Place de la Marine, Porto; http://corseadrenaline.fr. Former fisherman François-Xavier runs this scarlet-coloured, 12-seater speedboat with 600 horsepower of outboard oomph to whisk you between the sites.

**Pass Partout** Place de la Marine; http://lepasspartout.com. This long-standing firm has small boats carrying only twelve passengers, allowing entry to narrow defiles and caves in the Calanques, as well as pink hybrid boats that seat up to 38.

**Porto Linea** Hôtel Monte Rossu, just off the square; http://portolinea.com. The smaller of this outfit's two boats is a semi-rigid that carries only twelve people.

**Via Mare** Hotel du Golfe at the foot of the tower; http://viamare-promenades.com. This outfit runs the biggest boat in the gulf, with frequent trips (at least three daily) to Scandola and the Calanques, or longer tours combining both.

interesting exhibition (free) with old photos of the Porto and Scandola area.

**Scuba diving** The clear waters of the gulf offer superlative diving. Working out of the marina next to the footbridge, Bleu Marine Plongee (https://bleumarineplongee.com) takes out beginners and more experienced divers from May to October

## ACCOMMODATION

SEE MAP PAGE 82

Competition between hotels is more cut-throat in Porto than in any other resort on the island. During slack periods towards the beginning and end of the season, some places engage in a full-on price war, pasting up cheaper tariffs than their neighbours, but if you leave until the last minute in peak season, you might find everything is booked up.

**Casa del Torrente** Route d'evisa; http://casadeltorrente.com. This campsite, on the hill above Porto, specialises in little wooden chalets that sleep four to ten people and feature small but fully equipped kitchens and outside seating on the deck. The owners have thought of everything – e-bikes, cool boxes and parasols are all available to borrow at no extra cost. There's also a woodland-fringed infinity pool. €€

**Le Colombo** At the top of the village opposite the turning for Ota; http://hotel-colombo-porto.com. An informal, sixteen-room hotel overlooking the valley. The rooms are functional but clean and airy, and there's a well-shaded garden for breakfast. €

**Les Flots Bleux** Porto Marine; http://hotel-lesflotsbleus.com. A somewhat uninspiring salmon-pink beach block where every room has an identical little balcony overlooking the bay. Functional rather than stylish, it's still reasonably priced given the location and the views are wonderful. €€

**Funtana à L'Ora Camping** Il Campo; https://funtana alora.fr. Shaded campsites along the Porto River, plus mobile homes and cabins for rent. Sites are on the small side, but facilities are top-notch, and there's a heated pool and pizzeria on-site. Campsites & mobile homes €; cabins €€

**Monterosso** Porto Marine; https://porto-corse.com. Seven simple but comfortable rooms right on the seafront. Prices shoot up over peak season, but outside of July and August, there are usually some bargains to be had. €€

**Le Romantique** Porto Marine; http://hotel-romantique-porto.com. Two-star hotel facing the marina and the Porto River. The air-conditioned rooms all have a balcony or loggia with a sea view, as well as a small fridge. €€

## EATING

SEE MAP PAGE 82

Porto's reputation for style-over-substance eateries is fast subsiding, and there are now some excellent options, although most are on the pricey side.

★ **A Stretta** Place de la marine. A quirky spot with paint-splashed tables and artfully strewn trinkets, this restaurant has earned itself a stellar reputation. The same creative flair is applied to the cuisine, which includes Thai-inspired wok dishes and fish tartares served at a leisurely pace (there's just one chef and one sitting). The owner, passionate about encouraging guests to reconnect as they dine, has banned mobile phones at the table. Cash preferred. €€

**Le Palmier** Place de la marine. Rattan furnishings and Mediterranean plants add to the beach chic vibes at Le Palmier's sweeping cliffside terrace. It's a sophisticated backdrop for tucking into a baked sea bream or a curried monkfish while sipping one of their house cocktails. €€

**Le Panorama** Route de la Marine. The panoramic views from the rooftop are the main draw to this restaurant, but the food is still a worthy sidekick. The "*burger des bergers*" is a winner, served with mayonnaise infused with herbs from the maquis, and the swordfish carpaccio is refreshingly tangy. €€

**L'Ora** Right by the footbridge along the marina. Adorned with flowers, this pretty crêperie is a great choice for a low-key lunch or a no-fuss dinner that won't break the bank. All the usual suspects are on offer, but the Corse special, laden with Corsican ham, cheese, and fig jam, is a treat. €

**El Toro** Porto Marine. The burger, made with Corsican veal, *tome corse* cheese and fig sauce, is the star of the menu here, but they also do a delicious fish soup (evening only). If you can, snag a seat on the terrace with a view over the marina. €€

**Villa Rina** Place de la Marine; https://instagram.com/la_villa_rina. As the sun sets over Porto, few restaurants twinkle quite as charmingly as this romantic bayfront restaurant with its broad flowery terrace and candlelit tables. The extensive menu features grills and tapas, but chef specials include the creamy truffle gnocchi or the "Napoleon" smash burger. €€

## SHOPPING
SEE MAP PAGE 82

**Travail de la Nacre** Porto marina; https://atelier-melisse.com. The exquisite jewellery in this seafront shop is all hand-crafted by a family team of artisans at the on-site atelier and uses prized Mediterranean red coral, harvested from the island's west coast, and mother-of-pearl, hailing from the east shore. The more eye-watering prices indicate the grade and rarity of the coral; don't be afraid to ask for explanations.

# Around Porto

Inland from Porto, a drive along the delightfully twisty D84 is an attraction in itself. You'll drive past looming rock faces, gaze down into cavernous, wooded gorges and curl through dense pine forests with sunlight strobing the road and stops every few hundred metres to allow wild boar or a flurry of goat kids to scurry across. The hillside towns of Ota and **Évisa** both make great pitstops, with short walks heading out into the **Gorges de Spelunca** and **Forêt d'Aïtone**, where the **mare à mare** and **mare à monti** long-distance footpaths interconnect.

## Évisa

**ÉVISA**'s bright orange roofs emerge against a lush background of chestnut forests about 10km from Ota, on the eastern edge of the gorge, and the village makes the best base for hiking in the area. Situated 830m above sea level, it caters well for hikers and makes a pleasant stop for a taste of mountain life – the air is invariably crisp and clear, and the food particularly good.

### ACCOMMODATION & EATING
ÉVISA

**A Tràmula** Capo Soprano. Traditional local cuisine – quality charcuterie, veal's tongue in *vin de myrte*, chestnut crêpes and other delights – with ingredients sourced in or from the farms in the immediate area. Ask for a table on the tiny balcony overlooking the valley. €€

**Camping Acciola** 3km out of Évisa along the D70; http://acciola.com. A basic site, in the depths of nowhere, with a café-bar and a great panorama over the mountains. Facilities are clean with hot showers, plus large spacious sites and a dump station on site. €

**Scopa Rossa** On the D84 at the east edge of the village; http://hotelscoparossa.com. In a lovely location elevated above the village, this unfussy hotel has simple, if unexciting, rooms and a restaurant serving Corsican specialities. Half-board is available. €

**U Caracutu** Capo Soprano. If you've worked up an appetite hiking, the perfectly cooked pizzas at this local favourite will do the trick. The Sardinian chef uses a traditional wood oven and prepares some tasty pasta dishes, too. €

## The Gorges de Spelunca

Spanning the 2km between the villages of **Ota** and **Évisa**, a few kilometres inland from Porto, the **Gorges de Spelunca** are a formidable sight, with bare orange granite walls 1km deep in places, plunging into the foaming green torrent created by the confluence of the rivers Porto, Tavulella, Onca, Campi and Aïtone. The sunlight, ricocheting across the rock walls, creates a sinister effect that's heightened by the dark, jagged needles of the encircling peaks. The most dramatic part of the gorge can be seen from the road, which hugs the edge for much of its length, but there are also several walks, most notably the mule track between the villages of Ota and Évisa, which takes about three hours.

## Forêt d'Aïtone

Forming a ravine running from the sea to the watershed of the island, the spectacular gorge de Spelunca gives access to the equally grandiose **Forêt d'Aïtone**, site of Corsica's most ancient Laricio pine trees and a deservedly popular hiking area. Throughout the forest, the river and its tributaries are punctuated by strings of *piscines naturelles* – a refreshing alternative to the beaches hereabouts. One of the most enjoyable walks is the Chemin des Châtaigniers (about two hours return) from Évisa, which weaves beneath a canopy of chestnut trees and reaches the Aïtone waterfalls, where you can cool off with a swim.

**3**

# The Calanques

The UNESCO-protected site of the **Calanques de Piana**, 5km southwest of Porto, takes its name from *calanca*, the Corsican word for creek or inlet, but the outstanding characteristics here are the vivid orange and pink rock masses and pinnacles which crumble into the green-blue sea. Liable to unusual patterns of erosion, these tormented rock formations and porphyry needles, some of which soar 300m above the waves, have long been associated with different animals and figures, of which the most famous is the Tête de Chien (Dog's Head) at the north end of the stretch of cliffs. Other figures and creatures conjured up include a Moor's head, a monocled bishop, a bear and a tortoise.

Unlike nearby Scandola, the cliffs of the Calanques can be accessed on foot and by road, but it's still well worth exploring by boat from Porto (see page 83) – the views are mesmerising from the sea. Driving along the corniche road that weaves through the granite archways on its way to Piana affords a completely different perspective of the wind-tousled landscapes. Best of all, hike around them: there are several short set routes that can also be combined into an easy half-day ramble (see page 86). Eight kilometres along the road from Porto, the *Roches Bleues* café is a convenient landmark for walkers.

**GETTING AROUND**                                    **THE CALANQUES**

**By car** In July and August, the crowds and traffic jams tend to be most oppressive along the Corniche Road, so plan an early start and avoid weekends and leave extra time for your journey, not least for the frequent photo stops that you'll be taking. The coastal road is also at risk of erosion and rockfalls, so take care when driving and keep a lookout for animals on the road.

## Piana

Picturesque **PIANA** occupies a prime location overlooking the Calanques but for some reason does not suffer the deluge of tourists that Porto endures. Retaining a sleepy feel, the village comprises a steeply sloping warren of streets with pink houses arranged around an eighteenth-century church and square, from the edge of which the panoramic views over the Golfe de Porto are sublime.

## Plage de Ficajola

From Piana, a rough track cuts down the hillside to the picturesque fisherman's cove of Ficajola, nuzzled between knobbly red sea cliffs. It's a 4km, about 1-hour walk downhill from the village, or else you can drive down to the car park and scramble down the final 800m of rocky steps to the beach. It's a photogenic spot with a crescent of sand lapped by gentle waves and framed by artfully strewn boulders and old wooden fishing cabins. In summer, it's a popular spot for swimming and picnicking, but out of season, you might even get it to yourself. Be warned: the drive here is a series of impossibly narrow switchbacks, not to be attempted in a large vehicle.

### ACCOMMODATION AND EATING                                      PIANA

Piana's diminutive size belies its excellent selection of restaurants, and it's well worth planning a longer pitstop to make the most of it.

**Les Jardins de Piana** Place de la Fontaine. What this humble little restaurant lacks in fancy surroundings, it makes up for with cheerful service and a cosy ambience, helped by the fact that it's always chockful of locals. Your hosts, Julie and Dumé, will happily talk you through everything on the menu, including where the ingredients are sourced (mostly farms in the region). Dishes are a mix of French and Italian: think linguine with crab or stuffed *escargots*. €€

**Le Josephine** Rue de la Torra; http://lejosephinepiana. fr/. The best-positioned restaurant in town is perched on the cliff edge overlooking the *calanques*. Splash out on the *magret de canard* with chimichurri sauce, or try the octopus with sweet potato purée. €€

**Residence de la Tour** Place de la Coletta; https://

---

### HIKES IN THE CALANQUES

The rock formations visible from the road are not a patch on what you can see from the waymarked **trails** winding through the Calanques, which vary from easy ambles to strenuous stepped ascents. An excellent leaflet highlighting the pick of the routes is available free from tourist offices. Whichever one you choose, leave early in the morning or late in the afternoon to avoid the heat in summer, and take plenty of water.

• **Walk one** The most popular walk is to the Château Fort (1hr), which begins at a sharp hairpin in the D81, 700m north of the *Café Les Roches Bleues* (look for the car park and signboard at the roadside). Passing the famous Tête de Chien, it snakes along a ridge lined by dramatic porphyry forms to a huge square chunk of granite resembling a ruined castle. Just before reaching it, there's an open platform from where the views of the gulf and Paglia Orba, Corsica's third-highest mountain, are superb – one of the best sunset spots on the island – but bring a torch to help you find the path back when it gets dark.

• **Walk two** For a more challenging extension to Walk one, begin instead at the *Café Les Roches Bleues*. On the opposite side of the road, two paths strike up the hill: follow the one on your left (nearest the stream, as you face away from the café), which zigzags steeply up the rocks, over a pass and down the other side to rejoin the D81 in around 1hr 15min. About 150m west of the spot where you meet the road is the trailhead for the Château Fort walk, with more superb views.

• **Walk three** A small oratory niche in the cliff by the roadside, 500m south of *Café Les Roches Bleues*, contains a Madonna statue, Santa Maria, from where the wonderful *sentier muletier* (1hr) climbs into the rocks above. Before the road was blasted through the Calanques in 1850, this old, paved path, an extraordinary feat of workmanship supported in places by dry-stone banks and walls, formed the main artery between the villages of Piana and Ota. After a very steep start, the route contours through the rocks and pine woods above the restored mill at Pont de Gavallaghiu, emerging after one hour back on the D81, roughly 1.5km south of the starting point. Return by the same path.

residencedelatour.fr. Tucked away at the bottom of the village, this traditional family home has been renovated into two bright modern studio apartments. Both have stunning views of the gulf, fully equipped kitchens, and dining tables. The optional breakfast brought to your room is a nice touch. €€

★ **Les Roches Rouges** Rte de Porto; http://lesroches rouges.com. This elegant old *grand hôtel* rising from the eucalyptus canopy on the outskirts has been restored with most of its original fittings and furniture intact, and possesses loads of *fin-de-siècle* style. The rooms are huge and light, with large, shuttered windows, but make sure you get one facing the water and be warned – there's no lift! €€

# Cargèse and around

Sitting high above a deep-blue bay on a cliff scattered with olive trees, **CARGÈSE** (Carghjese), 20km southwest of Porto, exudes a lazy charm that attracts hundreds of well-heeled summer residents to its pretty white houses and hotels. The full-time locals, half of whom are descendants of Greek refugees who fled the Turkish occupation of the Peloponnese in the seventeenth century, seem to accept with nonchalance this inundation – and the proximity of a large Club Med complex. If you're travelling between Porto and Ajaccio, Cargèse is a worthwhile place to break the journey, but the best times to visit are May and late September, when it's all but empty.

## The Roman Catholic and Greek churches

Two churches stand on separate hummocks at the heart of the village, a reminder of the old antagonism between the two cultures (resentful Corsican patriots ransacked the Greeks' original settlement in 1715 because of the newcomers' refusal to take up arms against their Genoese benefactors). The **Roman Catholic church**, built for the minority Corsican families in 1828, is one of the latest examples of Baroque in Corsica, with a trompe l'oeil ceiling. The **Greek church**, however, is the more interesting of the two: a large granite Neo-Gothic edifice built in 1852 to replace a building that had become too small for its congregation. Inside, the outstanding feature is an unusual iconostasis, a gift from a monastery in Rome, decorated with uncannily modern-looking portraits. Behind it hang icons brought over from Greece with the original settlers – the graceful Virgin and Child, to the right-hand side of the altar, is thought to date as far back as the twelfth century.

## Port de Plaisance

To reach the waterfront of Cargèse, with its small marina, it's about a 20-minute walk downhill from the top of the village. Here, you'll find a handful of seafront restaurants and a string of tour companies offering boat cruises and snorkelling excursions along the Golfe de Sagone to the south or north to Capo Rosso. Boat rentals, parasailing and jet skiing are also available.

### ARRIVAL AND INFORMATION

### CARGÈSE AND AROUND

**By bus** Buses to and from Ajaccio and Porto (http://autocars-ceccaldi-ajaccio.fr) pass through Cargèse en route, stopping outside the tiny main square in the centre of the village. The service runs three times daily in July and August and twice a day (Mon-Sat) from September to June.

**Tourist office** The village's tourist office stands on rue Sampiero and has maps of the town as well as walks in the area (http://ouestcorsica.com).

**Boat trips** Croisieres Grand Bleu (https://www.croisieres grandbleu.com/) run daily boat trips to the Calqanques and Scandola out of Cargèse from May to October.

### ACCOMMODATION

**Camping Mandriale** Route de Lozzi; http://lemandriale. com. 3km north of Cargèse, this local farm is part of the "Bienvenue à la ferme" network. Pitch a tent under the olive trees or park your campervan or caravan on the hard-standing. The hosts are exceedingly friendly, and you can also join them to eat at the farm (by reservation) and pet the llamas, donkeys and lambs. €

★ **Les Lentisques** Plage de Pero; http://leslentisques. com. Head down the lane dropping downhill from the junction at the top of the village to reach this congenial, family-run three-star. Nestled in the dunes behind the area's nicest beach, it has a large, breezy breakfast hall and simple rooms (fully en suite and sea-facing), though some could do with an update, and there's also a fair-sized pool. €€€

**Punta e Mare** Up the lane past the Spar supermarket; https://www.locations-cargese.com. Secluded, unpretentious hotel tucked away on the quiet outskirts of the village. There's ample parking, and the rooms, though on the small side, are bright, well-kept and have little loggias. Apartments are also available. €€

## EATING

A fair number of restaurants are scattered about the village, as well as the standard crop of basic pizzerias, but the most tempting place to eat is down in the harbour.

**Le Cabanon de Charlotte** Chem. du Port. Corkboard ceilings, flower-adorned menus, and a plant-lined terrace strewn with curiosities add a quirky touch to this shabby chic restaurant. Right on the marina, it's little surprise to find an abundance of seafood dishes, but they often come with a twist, like red mullet tacos or smoked tuna served with immortelle-infused quinoa. €€

**Crêperie Lortu** down an alleyway off Chemin du port. The seats on this verdant, shady terrace fill up fast at this popular crêperie come lunchtime. There's an extensive menu of crêpes and galettes – try the "Corse", filled with melted *muntagnolu* cheese and parma ham. €

**U Rasaghiu** In the marina; http://restaurant-urasaghiu. fr. Consists of two adjacent outlets: the first does *spécialités corses* and seafood dishes (including lobster in garlic sauce), at reasonable prices; the second offers huge pizzas to eat in or takeaway. They also lay on live polyphony music two or three evenings each week in season; it gets very popular (and lively). €€

## Beaches around Cargèse

Cargèse is well situated for exploring the coast, where you'll find several sandy beaches, but you'll need your own wheels to get around. The best beach in the area, **plage de Pero**, sits 2km north of the village – head up to the junction with the Piana Road and take the left fork down to the sea. Just to the north, **plage de Chiuni** has a long stretch of sand that is rarely overcrowded, even in peak season. Alternatively, head south of Cargèse along the north shore of the Golfe de Sagone, where the beaches of Menasina, Capizollu, and Stagnoli all have calm, crystal-clear waters ideal for swimming.

### Genoese Towers

The rocky coast between Piana and Cargèse isn't just known for its beaches; it's also home to the ruins of four Genoese towers, all of which make popular coastal hikes. From north to south: the dramatically situated **Tour de Turghju** (3.5-hour return) is perched at 330m atop the high cliffs of Capo Rosso and affords views over the Golfe de Porto, the Calanques and the distant peaks of Scandola. The less-visited ruins of the **Tour d'Orchinu** (a 1.5-hour return walk) lie about a half-hour drive south, but a more impressive hike follows the narrow peninsula north of the plage de Pero to reach the remarkably well-preserved **Tour d'Omigna** (2.5-hour return). Finally, the crumbling remains of the **Tour de Cargèse** lie just north of the village (1-hour return). All of the hikes cover uneven terrain with no shade, so come prepared.

# Sagone

The principal seaside resort along the Golfe de Sagone is the eponymous village of **Sagone**. It's an attractive village with a small port, a long sandy beach, and a derelict tower standing on the hillside. The village harbours roots dating back to Roman times, but the ruins of the Cathédrale Sant'Appianu, believed to date from the 5th century, are sadly closed to the public.

**EATING**

★**Glacier Pierre Geronimi** Résidence De La Plage; https://glacespierregeronimi.com. Local ice cream master Pierre Geronimi's flagship ice cream parlour (he now has franchises in Paris and Monaco) is a detour-worthy addition to any road trip. With sit-down service, decadent *canistrelli*-topped sundaes and artisan flavours inspired by his homeland – the chestnut and *nucellina* (Corsican Nutella) are winners – your inner child will be living out their wildest dessert fantasies. €

3

# The Ajaccio Region

STATUE OF NAPOLEON BONAPARTE

# The Ajaccio Region

The maquis-scented homeland of Napoleon Bonaparte and the 18th-century stronghold of the French, the Ajaccio region is rooted in history, and it's a striking proposition, from the demure capital city to the majestic silhouette of its offshore islands. Ajaccio itself clings to the north shore of its namesake gulf, where its palm-studded promenade and once-mighty citadel are a faded postcard in comparison to the golden beaches, coral-laced shores, and verdant hinterlands that lie beyond the city limits. Corsica's mountainous heartlands are within easy reach but don't dash off into the hills just yet, as the capital region has plenty to offer beyond its urbanized frontline.

Home to Corsica's largest airport and ferry port, many travellers arrive in the island capital of Ajaccio, but few linger long enough to appreciate its slightly dog-eared charm. Among the many highlights is the teal-shuttered **Maison Bonaparte**, where the city's most famous son spent his early years, and the lively **Marché d'Ajaccio**, where the stalls brim with the aromatic flavours of the French Emperor's beloved maquis.

Mere minutes from the city centre, the mist-enshrouded peaks of the **Îles Sanguinaires** frame one of Corsica's most dramatically situated Genoese towers, the emblematic **Tour de la Parata**. Sandy beaches speckle the gulf on both sides of Ajaccio, but none more enticing than **Porticcio**, the city's sun-kissed sidekick that lies just a ferry hop away. The beaches give way to craggy capes and rocky coves the further you head out along the gulf, affording some invigorating seafront walks and culminating in the sensational views from the **Capo di Muro**.

There are plenty of other surprises within day-trip distance of the city, whether cooling off at the tree-fringed **Lac de Tolla** in summer, visiting Europe's largest tortoise and **turtle sanctuary** or hitting the ski slopes.

## GETTING THERE AND AROUND THE AJACCIO REGION

Although many tours leave from the capital, it's challenging to get around in the Ajaccio region without a car.

**By train** Trains run to Ajaccio from Bastia year-round, several times daily in high season or twice a day in winter; you can also connect to Calvi by changing trains in Ponte Leccia. Timetables are updated regularly and available at tourist offices and online (https://cf-corse.corsica).

# Ajaccio and around

Despite being the island's administrative capital and one of its main transport hubs, **AJACCIO** barely grazes the list of Corsica's most beautiful towns. There's the air of a timeworn Côte d'Azur town with its boat-filled harbour, palm-studded promenade and bustling open-air food market, but the faded shopfronts and graffiti-splashed side streets feel somewhat neglected in comparison to the island's other tourist hubs. The birthplace of Napoleon still has a few jewels to its crown, namely the aforementioned **Maison Napoléon**, the island's leading art museum, and a wealth of cafés, restaurants, and shops. Just outside the city limits, the **Îles Sanguinaires** are a magnificent sight, especially at sunset.

The core of the **old town** – a cluster of ancient sprawling streets spreading north and south of **place Foch**, which opens out to the seafront by the port and the

# Highlights

**❶ Maison Bonaparte** Peek inside the eighteenth-century townhouse where Napoleon Bonaparte was born and French history was made. See page 95

**❷ Marché d'Ajaccio** Sample smoky charcuterie, delicious creamy cheeses, or anise-infused *canistrelli* at the island's largest daily food market. See page 97

**❸ Îles Sanguinaires** Sail out to the cluster of rocky isles off the western cape of Ajaccio at sunset or admire the views from the coastal tower. See page 100

**❹ A Cupulatta** This leafy hillside hideaway snags the title of Europe's largest tortoise and turtle sanctuary, home to 170 species. See page 101

**❺ Lac de Tolla** Swathes of emerald-green woodlands tumble down to the shores of the dam, where you can fish, kayak or stand-up paddleboard. See page 101

**❻ Porticcio** Hop aboard a ferry and you can be lounging on Porticcio's sandy shores within 20 minutes. See page 102

**❼ Capo di Muro** Couple a walk along the wooded peninsula to this coastal tower with a well-deserved lunch at the ocean-view restaurant. See page 103

**HIGHLIGHTS ARE MARKED ON THE MAP ON PAGE 94**

marina – holds the most interest. Nearby, to the west, **place de Gaulle** forms the modern centre and is the source of the main thoroughfare, the **cours Napoléon**, which extends parallel to the sea almost 2km to the northeast. West of place de Gaulle stretches the modern part of town fronted by the **beach**, overlooked at its eastern end by the citadelle.

## Brief history

Although it's an attractive idea that Ajax, hero of the Trojan War, once stopped here, the name of Ajaccio actually derives from the Roman *Adjaccium* (place of rest), a winter stop-off point for shepherds descending from the mountains to stock up on goods and sell their produce. This first settlement was destroyed by the Saracens in the tenth century, and modern Ajaccio grew up around the citadelle founded in 1492. **Napoleon** gave the town international fame, but though the self-designated *Cité Impériale* is littered with statues and street names related to the Bonaparte family, you'll find that the Napoleonic cult has a less dedicated following here than you might imagine: the emperor is still considered by many Ajacciens as a self-serving Frenchman rather than as a Corsican.

Since the early 1980s, Ajaccio has gained an unwelcome reputation for nationalist violence. The most infamous terrorist atrocity of recent decades was the murder, in February 1998, of the French government's most senior official on the island, Claude Érignac, who was gunned down as he left the opera. However, separatist violence rarely (if ever) affects tourists here, and for visitors, Ajaccio remains memorable for the things that have long made it attractive – its battered old town, relaxing cafés and the encompassing view of its glorious bay.

**HIGHLIGHTS**

1 Maison Bonaparte
2 Marché d'Ajaccio
3 Îles Sanguinaires
4 A Cupulatta
5 Lac de Tolla
6 Porticcio
7 Capo di Muro

**THE AJACCIO REGION**

## Place Foch

Once the site of the town's medieval gate, **place Foch** lies at the heart of old Ajaccio.
A delightfully shady square sloping down to the sea, it gets its local name – place des
Palmiers – from the row of palms bordering the central strip. Dominating the top
end, a fountain of four marble lions provides a mount for the inevitable statue of
Napoleon. A humbler effigy occupies a niche high on the nearest wall – a figurine of
Ajaccio's patron saint, **La Madonnuccia**, dating from 1656, a year in which Ajaccio's
local council, fearful of infection from plague-struck Genoa, placed the town under the
guardianship of the Madonna in a ceremony conducted on this spot.

### Salon Napoléonien

Hôtel de Ville, Av Antoine Serafini • Charge • http://ajaccio.corsica

At the northern end of place Foch stands the **hôtel de ville** of 1826. Its first floor is
given over to the **Salon Napoléonien**, which contains a replica of the ex-emperor's death
mask, along with a solemn array of Bonaparte family portraits and busts. A smaller
medal room has a fragment from Napoleon's coffin and part of his dressing case, plus a
model of the ship that brought his body back from St Helena.

## South of place Foch

The south side of place Foch, standing on the former dividing line between the port
and the bourgeoisie's territory, gives access to **rue Bonaparte**, the main route through
the latter quarter. Built on the promontory rising to the citadelle, the secluded streets
in this part of town – with their dusty buildings and hole-in-the-wall restaurants lit by
flashes of sea or sky at the end of the alleys – retain more of a sense of the old Ajaccio
than anywhere else.

**4**

### Maison Bonaparte

Rue Saint-Charles • Charge • http://musee-maisonbonaparte.fr

Napoleon was born in what's now the colossal **Maison Bonaparte**, on rue Saint-
Charles, off the west side of rue Bonaparte. The house passed to Napoleon's father in
the 1760s, where he lived with his wife and family until his death. But in May 1793,
the Bonapartes were driven from the house by Paoli's partisans, who stripped the place
down to the floorboards. Requisitioned by the English in 1794, Maison Bonaparte
became an arsenal and a lodging house for English officers until Napoleon's mother,
Letizia, funded its restoration. Owned by the state since 1923, the house now bears few
traces of the Bonaparte family's existence. One of the few original pieces of furniture
left in the house is the wooden sedan chair in the hallway – the pregnant Letizia was
carried back from church in it when her contractions started. The upper floors house
an endless display of portraits, miniatures, weapons, letters and documents.

### La Grotte Napoléon

Rue Saint-Charles • Charge • https://napoleon1769.corsica

Fans of Napoleon can also enjoy a fun retelling of the French Emperor's history at
the **Grotte Napoléon**, just a few doors down from the Maison Bonaparte. Set in an
authentic cave decked out with period-style furnishings, the hour-long audio-visual
experience (available in multiple languages, including English) is accompanied by a
traditional *Spuntinu*, a tasting of typical Corsican delicacies (vegetarian option also
available).

### The cathedral

Rue Saint-Charles • Free

Napoleon was baptized in 1771 in the **cathedral** on rue Forcioli-Conti. Modelled on St
Peter's in Rome, it was built in 1587–93 on a much smaller scale than intended, owing

↑ & Napoleon Bonaparte Airport     ↑ Parc Naturel Régional de Corse

**EATING**

| | |
|---|---|
| Le 20123 | 8 |
| A Nepita | 2 |
| L'Ardoise | 3 |
| Le Bilboq "Chez Jean-Jean" | 6 |
| Esprit Sushi | 1 |
| Le Poseidon | 7 |
| Le Temps des Oliviers | 4 |
| Maison Galeani | 5 |

**ACCOMMODATION**

| | |
|---|---|
| Camping Les Mimosas | 1 |
| Fesch | 5 |
| Kallisté | 3 |
| Le Napoléon | 4 |
| Du Palais | 2 |
| Pozzo di Borgo | 6 |
| San Carlu | 7 |

**SHOPPING**

| | |
|---|---|
| La Cave du Cardinal | 2 |
| La Maison de Mina | 1 |
| La Maison du Corail | 3 |
| Nanarella | 4 |

**DRINKING & NIGHTLIFE**

| | |
|---|---|
| 10 rue des Halles | 1 |
| Camden Pub | 3 |
| Micro Brasserie Impériale | 2 |
| Shamrock | 4 |

N

Port de Plaisance Charles d'Ornano

Jetée du Margonajo

Port de Commerce

Marseille & Nice →

Toulon →

Gare d'Ajaccio

PLACE DE LA GARE

RUE DU DR DEL PELLEGRINO

AVENUE COLONEL COLONNA

RUE SAINT-ANTOINE

BOULEVARD CHARLES BONAPARTE

COURS NAPOLÉON

AVENUE BÉVÉRINI VICO

BOULEVARD JÉRÔME ET BARTHÉLEMY MAGLIOLI D'ORNANO

RUE HYACINTHE CAMPIGLIA

RUE MICHEL BOZZI

CHEMIN DE LA PIETRINA

Palais de Justice

BOULEVARD MADAME MÈRE

RUE SAN LAZARO

RUE COMTE BACCIOCHI

AVENUE NAPOLÉON III

RUE CARDINAL FESCH

BOULEVARD SAMPIERO

Gare Routière (bus station)

Hospital

RUE DES 3 MARIE

Chapelle Impériale

Musée des Beaux Arts

Gare Maritime (ferry terminal)

RUE LORENZO VERO

AVENUE IMPÉRATRICE EUGÉNIE

RUE SERGEANT CASALONGA

RUE GÉNÉRAL CAMPI

RUE MARÉCHAL

RUE GEN LEVIE

D'ORNANO

RUE GÉNÉRAL FIORELLA

Le Préfecture

BOULEVARD DU ROI JÉRÔME

Marché

RUE E. CONTI

PLACE CÉSAR CAMPINCHI

Palais des Congrès

QUAI L'HERMINIER

Hôtel de Ville

PLACE FOCH

AVENUE A. SERAFINI

Marina Tino Rossi

Jardins du Casone

AVENUE DE PARIS

PLACE DE GAULLE

COURS GRANDVAL

AVENUE EUGÈNE MACCHINI

RUE EMMANUEL ARÈNE

RUE DE LA PORTA

RUE DES GLACIS

QUAI NAPOLÉON

Maison Bonaparte

RUE ROI DE ROME

RUE ST-CHARLES

RUE ZEVACO MAIRE

Cathédrale

RUE NOTRE DAME

RUE FORCIOLI-CONTI

Musée du Capitellu

Église St-Érasme

Casino

BOULEVARD PASCAL ROSSINI

BOULEVARD LANTIVY

Plage St-François

Citadelle

Jetée de la Citadelle

**AJACCIO**

0     100
metres

to lack of funds – an apology for its diminutive size is inscribed in a plaque inside, on the wall to the left as you enter. Inside, to the right of the door, stands the font where he was dipped at the age of 23 months. Before you go, take a look in the chapel to the left of the altar, which houses a gloomy Delacroix painting of the Virgin.

### The citadelle
Free • Guided tours available in French; book online • https://ajaccio-tourisme.com/en/la-citadelle

Previously occupied by the French military and closed to the public, Ajaccio's **citadelle** has now been reclaimed by the city and is currently undergoing restorations. Open to the public throughout, you can explore the old ramparts and bastion in various states of repair. More interestingly, a number of artists and artisans have taken up residence in the buildings around the main square, plus there's a recently opened terrace restaurant. Built by the Genoese in 1492 and expanded by the French in the 16th century, the citadelle has a fascinating history, passing hands between the French and Genoese through the centuries. It was here that WWII French resistance hero Fred Scamaroni took his own life, leaving a message in blood declaring, "Long live France, long live de Gaulle".

# North of place Foch

The dark, narrow streets backing onto the port to the north of place Foch are Ajaccio's traditional trading ground. Each weekday and Saturday morning (and on Sundays during the summer), the square directly behind the *hôtel de ville* hosts the popular **Marché d'Ajaccio** (Place du Marché; Tues-Sun mornings) where you can browse and buy top-quality fresh produce from around the island, including myrtle liqueur, wild-boar sauces, ewe's cheese from the Niolo valley and a spread of fresh vegetables, fruit and flowers.

### Palais Fesch: Musée des Beaux Arts
50–52 rue Cardinal Fesch • Charge • http://musee-fesch.com

The principal road leading north off the place Foch is rue **Cardinal-Fesch**, a delightful meandering street lined with boutiques, cafés and restaurants. Halfway along, set back from the road behind iron gates, stands Ajaccio's – indeed Corsica's – finest art gallery, the resplendent **Palais Fesch: Musée des Beaux-Arts**. Cardinal Joseph Fesch was Napoleon's step-uncle and bishop of Lyon, and he used his lucrative position to invest in large numbers of paintings, many of them looted by the French armies in Holland, Italy and Germany. His bequest to the town includes seventeenth-century French and Spanish masters, but it's the Italian paintings that are the chief attraction: Titian, Bellini, Veronese, Botticelli and Michelangelo are all represented in state-of-the-art air-conditioned galleries.

### Chapelle Impériale
50–52 rue du Cardinal-Fesch • Charge

The **Chapelle Impériale** stands across the courtyard from the Musée des Beaux-Arts. With its gloomy monochrome interior, the chapel itself is unremarkable, and its interest lies in the crypt, where various members of the Bonaparte family are buried. It was the cardinal's dying wish that all the Bonaparte family be brought together under one roof, so the chapel was built in 1857, and the bodies – all except Napoleon's – subsequently ferried in.

**ARRIVAL AND DEPARTURE**                                   **AJACCIO AND AROUND**

**BY PLANE**
Served by domestic and international flights, Ajaccio's

Napoléon Bonaparte (formerly Campo dell'Oro) Airport (https://ajaccio-aeroport.cci.corsica) is 8km south of town

4

around the bay. *Navettes* (hourly to coincide with first/last flights) provide an inexpensive link with the centre, stopping at the train station. It's cheapest to purchase tickets in advance from the ticket machines.

### BY BOAT
Ferries dock at the Gare Maritime on quai L'Herminier. Facilities are limited to a toilet and waiting area; there's no left luggage here at present.
**Ferry offices** Corsica Ferries, counter inside the Gare Maritime (http://corsicaferries.com); La Méridionale, on the quayside a 5min walk north of the terminal building along bd Sampiero (http://lameridionale.fr).
Destinations Marseille (up to 4 weekly; 12hr overnight); Nice (up to 6 weekly; 5hr 25min); Toulon (up to 3 daily; 5hr 55min).

### BY BUS
**Long-distance buses** (https://www.corsicabus.org/bus Ajaccio/) leave from the lay-by outside the Gare Maritime. The tourist office provides timetables.
Destinations Bonifacio (1–2 daily; 3hr 15min); Porto-Vecchio (1–2 daily; 3hr 10min); Propriano (1–2 daily; 1hr 35min); Sartène (1–2 daily; 1hr 45min).

### BY TRAIN
The train station lies almost a kilometre north along bd Sampiero, a continuation of the quai l'Herminier. Timetables change seasonally (https://cf-corse.corsica).
Destinations Bastia (4 daily; 3hr 30min); Calvi (2 daily; 4hr); Corte (4 daily; 1hr 30min); L'Île Rousse (2 daily; 3hr 35min).

## GETTING AROUND AND INFORMATION

**By bike** Corsica Electric Bike (https://corsicaelectricbike.com) and Appebike (https://appebike.com) offer half- and full-day bike rentals.
**By boat** Muvimare shuttle boats (https://promenades-en-mer.org) run from Ajaccio to Porticcio up to nine times daily (a 20-minute journey), leaving from Port Tino Rossi. Corsica Croisières (https://corsicacroisieres.fr) provide taxi boats to and from coastal hotels.
**By bus** The most useful of the Municipal bus routes (https://mobilite.muvitarra.fr) crisscrossing the city is line

#5, which runs a few times hourly from place de Gaulle to Parata for the Îles Sanguinaires.
**Car rental** Rent-a-Car, 52 cours Napoléon (https://rent-car-corsica.com/) and the airport; and Enterprise at the airport (https://www.enterprise.fr).
**Tourist office** 3 boulevard du Roi-Jérôme (http://ajaccio-tourisme.com). They hand out free maps, post public transport timetables and sell the Ajaccio CityPass, which includes entrance to top attractions and various discounts on tours and activities.

## ACCOMMODATION                                SEE MAP PAGE 96

Ajaccio is a safe bet for finding inexpensive accommodation, but it's essential to book ahead, especially in summer, when beds are virtually impossible to come by at short notice.
**Camping Les Mimosas** 3km northwest of town; http://camping-lesmimosas.com. A shady and well-organized site with clean toilet blocks, friendly management and fair rates. Along with tent and caravan sites, there are cottages and mobile homes available for rent. €
**Fesch** 7 rue du Cardinal-Fesch; http://hotel-fesch.com. Surprisingly smart three-star hotel in a superb, central location. More expensive rooms benefit from private terraces, plus there's a spa, an excellent restaurant and a rooftop terrace with views over the city. €€
**Kallisté** 51 cours Napoléon; http://hotel-kalliste-ajaccio.com. Efficient hotel in an eighteenth-century tenement with plenty of parking space. Soundproofed rooms for up to four people, all with cable TVs and bathrooms. The staff speak English. €
**Le Napoléon** 4 rue Lorenzo-Vero; https://www.hotel-napoleon-ajaccio.fr. Dependable upper-mid-scale hotel slap-bang in the centre of town, on a side road off cours

Napoléon, in a revamped Second Empire building. Comfortable, very welcoming and good value for the location, though peak season tariffs are high. €€
**Du Palais** 5 av Bévérini-Vico; http://hoteldupalais.corsica. Well-run mid-scale place, a 10-minute walk north of the centre, within easy reach of the train station. The rooms are on the small side, but they're impeccably clean. Ask for one at the rear of the building if you want peace and quiet. €
**Pozzo di Borgo** 17 rue Bonaparte; http://palazzu-domu.fr. Ajaccio's only boutique hotel, housed in a former mansion of the Pozzo di Borgo clan. Using natural materials such as teak and slate, it manages to fuse Imperial elegance with contemporary designer chic. The effect of all the dark wood and stone is a touch sombre, and some of the rooms are on the gloomy side, but this is as cool as accommodation in the Imperial City gets. €€€€
**San Carlu** 8 bd Danielle-Casanova; http://hotelsancarlu.com. Sited opposite the citadelle and close to the beach, this three-star hotel is the poshest option on the waterfront, with sunny, well-furnished rooms, all fully a/c, and a special suite for disabled guests in the basement – but no parking. €€

## EATING                                        SEE MAP PAGE 96

At mealtimes, the alleyways and little squares of Ajaccio's    old town become one large, interconnecting restaurant terrace lit by rows of candles. Bars and cafés jostle for pavement space along cours Napoléon, while old-fashioned cafés and *salons de thé* offer a more sedate scene on place de Gaulle.

★ **Le 20123** 2 rue du Roi-de-Rome; http://20123.fr. Decked out like a small hill village, complete with a fountain and parked Vespa, the decor here's a lot more frivolous than the food: serious Corsican gastronomy features on a single *menu*. Top-notch cooking and organic AOC wine. €€€

**A Nepita** 4 rue San Lazaro; https://anepita.fr. Named after the most pungent of the maquis herbs, this effortlessly elegant terrace restaurant is the brainchild of British chef Simon Andrews and inspired by his adopted homeland. Grilled octopus, roasted veal and lobster risotto are flecked with local flavours. Open Wed-Sat. €€€

**L'Ardoise** 11 Bd du Roi Jérôme; https://lardoiseajaccio. fr. This contemporary restaurant is a good induction into Corsican cuisine, including *bocconcini de veau à la tomme* (rolls of ham, veal and cheese) and *terrine de sanglier* (wild boar terrine). There's a good selection of Corsican wines and aperitifs, too. €€

★ **Le Bilboq "Chez Jean-Jean"** 2 rue des Glacis, just off place Foch. The eponymous patron (a former fisherman and boxer) of this legendary seafood joint is Ajaccio's undisputed "lobster king" – and there's only one thing on the menu: local *langouste*, served grilled with spaghetti. Dine alfresco on a narrow alley terrace, or inside, regaled by the music of

Ajaccien opera singer Tino Rossi. Dessert, should you have room, is a creamy chestnut tart. €€€€

**Esprit Sushi** 69 Cr Napoléon; https://espritsushiajaccio. fr. Bright, friendly restaurant that whips up colourful poke bowls, expertly crafted sushi and deliciously fresh *shirashi*. Prices are reasonable too. €

**Le Poseidon** Vieux Port Tino Rossi. This seafood restaurant onboard a boat could be really gimmicky but manages to pull it off with aplomb, creating the perfect place to sip chilled rosé and watch the (other) boats bob in the harbour. The short carte is resolutely anchored in the sea, with dishes such as *soupe de poisson* to start and grilled red mullet for mains. €€

**Le Temps des Oliviers** 1 rue des Halles. Run by a pair of young sisters, this upbeat backstreet bistro occupies a secluded spot on a traffic-free alley behind the tourist office. It serves quality Italian dishes: the pizzas (cooked on a state-of-the-art Morello oven) are sublime, and so are the risotto and *grillades*. Get there early for a table outside on the terrace. €

**Maison Galeani** 3 Rue Cardinal Fesch; https://instagram. com/boulangerie.galeani/. The decadent pastries, freshly baked breads, and fanciful desserts on display here are as eye-catching as the bakery's candy pink, flower-bedecked façade. Try the *beignets au lait brebis* or the *fondant chataîgne*. €€

4

## DRINKING AND NIGHTLIFE
SEE MAP PAGE 96

Ajaccio's nightlife is concentrated around a handful of bars and the seafront casino; if you fancy a view of the bay, try one of the flashy cocktail bars that line the seafront on bd Lantivy.

**10 rue des Halles** 10 Rue des Halles; https://facebook. com/10ruedeshalles. In an atmospheric stone-walled cavern, this bar hosts live music several nights a week.

**Camden Pub** 1 Bd Lantivy; https://camdenpub.fr. A lively after-work pub that draws crowds to watch sports matches (a great atmosphere if France is playing) or watch a band;

there's live music every weekend from September to May.

**Micro Brasserie Impériale** 5 Rue Zevaco Maire. The small selection of craft beers, including a blonde and an IPA, are brewed on-site at this popular microbrewery. Pair them with a planche of cheese and charcuterie for the full effect.

**Shamrock** 9 Rue Notre Dame. Grungey Irish pub serving a wide selection of international beers, cheap cocktails and shooters, as well as a small selection of Corsican wines. If you get hungry, pizzas and hot dogs are served until 2am.

## SHOPPING
SEE MAP PAGE 96

Most of Ajaccio's shops are packed along the pedestrianized rue Cardinal Fesch and cours Napoléon, one block over.

**La Cave du Cardinal** 18 Cr Napoléon; http://lacave ducardinal.corsica. In an authentic stone-arched cave, this shop is brimming with wines from all corners of Corsica. Staff will be happy to guide you.

**La Maison de Mina** 64 Cr Napoléon; https://maison demina.fr. Quality artisanal produce from the finest local winemakers, brewers, cheesemakers and farmers. They also sell charcuterie, oils, jams, and terrines.

**La Maison du Corail** 1 Rue Cardinal Fesch; https:// lamaisonducorail.com. Corsica's most prestigious coral jeweller sells some exquisite – and expensive – pieces forged from the prized red coral that is harvested from the depths of the ocean around Ajaccio.

**Nanarella** 26 rue Bonaparte; https://nanarella.com. Corsican artist and jewellery designer Antoinette Nunzi now has boutiques all around the island, including one at Ajaccio airport. Her unique designs are inspired by Corsican places, plants and iconography.

## DIRECTORY

**Hospital** Centre Hospitalier, Route du Stilleto 04 95 29 90 90; for an ambulance, call 15.

**Police** Rue Général Florella 04 95 11 17 99.

## La Route des Sanguinaires

West of Ajaccio, the **route des Sanguinaires** is the city's very own "Sunset Boulevard", running for about 10 kilometres from the city all the way to the Pointe de la Parata and the **Îles Sanguinaires**. The road hugs the coast, affording glittering views across the Golfe d'Ajaccio and home to some of the city's best beaches.

**Plage Trottel** is the closest, with a soft shingle beach and a patrolled swimming area, while the rock-fringed **plage de Barbicaja** is ideal for swimming and snorkelling. Neighbouring **plage d'Ariadne** has jet-ski and kayak rentals, while the **plage de la Terre Sacrée** is overlooked by a poignant monument to the Corsican soldiers of WWI.

Note that this road becomes clogged with traffic through the summer months, so if your goal is to reach the peninsula, it's often better to follow the inland D11B through the hills. Better yet, rent a bike and cycle the seaside promenade or hike the Chemin des Crêtes (see page 100).

### Les Îles Sanguinaires

Ajaccio's much-photographed **Îles Sanguinaires**, a rocky quartet of isles standing guard over the mouth of the Golfe d'Ajaccio, are found at the very tip of the Parata peninsula. The largest of the islets, Mezzo Mare (or Grande Sanguinaire), is topped by a lighthouse where Alphonse Daudet spent ten days in December 1862. Tufts of gorse, a square watchtower (la Tour de Castellucciu) and crashing surf give the place a dramatic air, and it's most atmospheric at sunset.

Without the luxury of your own vessel, the only way to get a close look at them is on a boat tour; alternatively, enjoy the iconic view of the islands from **Punta della Parata**, the narrow, rocky headland facing them from the mainland. It's about a 20-minute walk from the car park, and a further short scramble takes you to the **Tour de la Parata**, a 12m-tall watchtower built of dark grey granite in 1608. One of the last of its kind erected by the Genoese to guard the coast against Barbary pirates, it sports the rusting remains of Corsica's first aerial telegraph, installed in the latter half of the eighteenth century.

**GETTING AROUND AND INFORMATION**            **LA ROUTE DES SANGUINAIRES**

**By car** Most of the beaches have paid parking, but spaces   are limited, so get here early, especially in summer. There's a

### CHEMIN DES CRÊTES

The most gratifying way to reach the **Tour de la Parata** is by following the Chemin des Crêtes footpath from Ajaccio. The path follows the old route of the customs officers; an easy, gently sloping route that follows the cliff-tops, winding through the scented maquis and affording panoramic views over the beaches of the Route des Sanguinaires.

You can join the Chemin de Crêtes at various points, but the official starting point is just north of the place d'Austerlitz with its grand monument to Napoleon, about a kilometre west of the place Foch. Shortly after leaving Ajaccio, the footpath forks off into an upper, more steeply climbing path and a lower, flatter path – they both come out at the same spot, from where it slowly zig-zags down to join the coastal road.

On arrival at the Tour de la Parata, you can explore three routes: the main coastal footpath (20-minute return) that leads to the viewpoint over the Îles des Sanguinaires, a steep scramble up to the tower itself (12-minute return), and a full loop around the peninsula (about 30 minutes). Enthusiastic hikers can also connect with the Chemin de la Corniche, which follows the coast north to reach the wild beach of Capo Di Feno, a popular surf spot.

In total, allow for about three hours, including the final leg to reach the Tour de la Parata and the end of the peninsula; to reach Capo Di Feno beach, count another two hours. It's rocky underfoot, so decent footwear is required, and you'll need plenty of water as, despite the refreshing ocean breeze, there's almost no shade. Bring your swimsuit to cool off at the beach post-hike, then catch the bus back.

large paid car park at the start of the Punta della Parata trail.
**By bus** Municipal buses (line #5) run roughly twice hourly to Punta della Parata from place de Gaulle, stopping at beaches including Trottel, Barbicaja, and Marinella en route.
**By bike** It's about a 12km, 40-minute bike ride from Ajaccio, with dedicated bike lanes most of the way.

**Boat tours** Nave Va (http://naveva.com) operate popular half-day cruises from Ajaccio's Marina Tino Rossi to the Îles Sanguinaires, including a 1-hour visit to the Île Mezumare. They also operate sunset *Magie des Sens* island cruises, including Corsican wine and food tastings.

## ACCOMMODATION

**Camping Le Barbicaja** 4.5km west of Ajaccio along the rte des Sanguinaires. Close to the beach and a bus ride from the city, this simple campsite has plenty of shady pitches, but it gets crowded in high season. €

★ **Marengo** 2 rue Marengo; https://hotel-marengo.com. With easy beach and city access, this 2-star hotel is arguably one of Ajaccio's best bargains. Elegantly decorated rooms are a masterclass in interior design on a budget, as is the

pretty garden courtyard, where breakfast is served. €
**Les Mouettes** 9 Cr Lucien Bonaparte; https://www.hotellesmouettes.fr/. Housed in a palm-fringed 19th-century villa right on the seafront, this luxurious 4-star hotel is worth the splurge. Enjoy ocean views from the terrace swimming pool, relax at the spa and hammam, or help yourself to one of the self-service bikes. €€€€

## EATING

**Brasserie I Sanguinari** 56 rte des Sanguinaires; https://www.facebook.com/BISanguinari. The views out to the Îles are the highlight of this terrace restaurant, and it's a well-deserved rest stop for hikers and cyclists with a range of meat, fish and pasta dishes. €€
**Grain 2 Café** 10 boulevard Albert 1er; http://www.facebook.com/LE-GRAIN-2-CAFE-159232104618689/. This cool beachside café specializes in "bistronomie", and there's a small but ever-changing menu of great-value and

stylishly presented dishes. Think poké bowls, burgers, and salads, served with strong coffee or cocktails, depending on your mood. €
**KOS restaurant** 6km west of Ajaccio along the rte des Sanguinaires; https://kosbeachclub.com. With its chic wicker furniture and leafy chill-out zones right on the sand, this private beach club is a cut above the rest. Order one of the sharing platters to accompany their signature cocktails. Open May-Sept. €€

# The Gravona and Prunelli Valleys

Northeast of Ajaccio, the road climbs steeply uphill into the mountain valleys of Gravona and Prunelli. To the north, along the T20 and the railway, the **Vallée de la Gravona** is home to the small villages of Vero, Ucciani, Tavera and Carbuccia – each of which holds its own charms. To the south, the **Vallée du Prunelli** is known for its forested landscapes, laced with scenic footpaths. Most visitors make a beeline for the **Lac de Tolla**, but there's also the village of **Bastelica**, famously the birthplace of Sampiero Corso and renowned for its traditional charcuterie.

## A Cupulatta

Along the T20 near Carbuccia • Charge • https://acupulatta.com

If you have even the slightest curiosity about tortoises and turtles, then this 2.5-hectare park entirely devoted to the slow-moving reptiles should pique your interest. This is Europe's largest tortoise and turtle sanctuary, and more than 3,000, representing 170 species, live in its natural setting. Staff are passionate about the breeding and research programmes, and you'll leave armed with a trillion fascinating facts and possibly a tortoise-themed souvenir.

## Lac de Tolla

A gleaming turquoise pool set amid the rolling tree-clad gorge of the Prunelli river, it's little surprise that the **Lac de Tolla** pulls in a crowd when the sun is shining. You can rent kayaks, pedalos, SUPs and electric paddleboards from the Nautical Centre

4

(https://centre-nautique-de-tolla.fr) to explore the manmade dam and several footpaths set out from here into the Prunelli gorge (maps available online or from the tourist office; https://www.celavuprunelli.corsica/fr/decouverte/tolla/). Alternatively, tackle the **Via Ferrata** course at the south end of the lake (https://revesdecimes.fr) or ride the **Petit Train du Maquis** (https://m.colcricheto.com/Le-Petit-Train-du-Maquis_a13.html).

## Val d'Ese

At 1,620m, the **Val d'Ese ski resort** (https://valdese.fr) crowns the Prunelli Valley with views down to the Golfe d'Ajaccio below. It's a small station, with 20 hectares of ski slopes peaking at 1,825m and six red, blue and green pistes, but skiers also have access to more than 100 hectares of off-piste terrain. The tiny ski school (https://esf-corse.fr) offers ski and snowboard lessons through ski season (Dec-April). Hikers also frequent the resort through the summer season, where a popular footpath runs leads up to the *pozzi* (alpine wetlands) above Bastelica.

### GETTING AROUND AND INFORMATION — GRAVONA AND PRUNELLI VALLEYS

**By car** You'll need a car to reach most destinations in the Gravona and Prunelli valleys. The T20 runs all the way from Ajaccio to Corte, passing through the heart of the Gravona valley, while the smaller and windier D3 and D27 carve through the Prulleni valley.

**By train** There's also a slow and infrequent train service from Ajaccio to Carbuccia, Ucciani, Tavera, and Bocognano villages in the Gravona valley.

**Tourist office** The Office du Tourisme du Celavu Prunelli (U Palazzu Quartier; https://celavuprunelli.corsica/en/) in Bocognano is a great resource for hiking maps and local attractions.

### ACCOMMODATION AND EATING

★ **Auberges de Prunelli** Pisciatello Bridge, Bastelicaccia; http://auberge-du-prunelli.fr. This traditional country inn has been serving up the region's finest veal, lamb, and goat since 1957. Recipient of the prestigious "Gusti di Corsica" label for its commitment to local produce, eating here is an experience to be savoured. €€€

**Bergeries Du Prunelli** Lieu dit Perosso, Cauro; http://bergerieduprunelli.com This authentic old bergerie has been transformed into a luxurious chambre d'hôte, full of traditional charm. There's a huge breakfast spread of local goodies, lunch available on request, or you can spend your time flitting between the indoor/outdoor pools, hammam and jacuzzi. €€€€

# Porticcio and around

From Ajaccio, the vista of whitewashed villas and sandy beaches lining the opposite side of the gulf may tempt you out of town when you first arrive. On closer inspection, however, **Porticcio** turns out to be a faceless string of leisure settlements for Ajaccio's smart set, complete with tennis courts, malls and flotillas of jet-skis. Don't be put off exploring, as the south shore of the **Golfe d'Ajaccio** boasts some 30km of beaches, among them the **plage d'Isolella** with its rose-hued sands and rocky promontory. Just north of the beach, the coastal walk to the **Tour de Capitello** is perennially popular, but the region's most rewarding hike is to **Capo di Muro** at the southwesternmost tip.

### GETTING AROUND AND INFORMATION — PORTICCIO AND AROUND

**By boat** Muvimare shuttle boats (https://promenades-en-mer.org) connect Ajaccio to Porticcio up to nine times daily (a 20-minute journey), arriving at the pier outside the tourist office.

**By bus** In summer, the *navette des plages* shuttle bus runs between the beaches on the south shore; timetables are posted at the tourist office, and they stop right outside.

**Tourist office** (Parking des Marines; https://taravo-ornano-tourisme.corsica) has all the need-to-know details about the south shore beaches and footpaths.

### ACCOMMODATION AND EATING

Porticcio's portfolio of hotels and eateries is geared towards the well-heeled; budget travellers may be better off staying in Ajaccio and hopping over on a day trip.

**A Bona Stella** Plage de la Viva. Good old-fashioned Corsican homecooking is elevated to an art form at this popular restaurant right on the main drag. The *sauté de veau aux olives* is a classic dish, but the lamb with sauce *à la myrte* is also delicious. €€

**Camping U Prunelli** Grosseto-Prugna, off the T40; http://camping-prunelli.com. Set back from the beach, this tranquil 4-star campsite has more than 200 pitches, multiple swimming pools, a pizzeria grill, and a tennis court. There are also chalets for rent by the week only. Camping €

**L'Alta Rocca** plage de Capitello; https://alta-rocca-porticcio.com. Swish beachfront restaurant where you can curl up on cushioned benches and dip your toes in the sand while you're waiting for your tapas to arrive. The best time to come is a toss-up between brunch on the beach or dancing the night away as you work your way through the cocktail list. €€

**Hôtel Suite Home** Lieu Dit Scaglione, http://suitehome-porticcio.com. This swanky 4-star hotel is one of the best of Porticcio's central options, within a short walk of the port. There are 60 spacious suites available, each with a fully equipped kitchenette and a mixture of garden or sea views. Rooms are considerably cheaper in shoulder season. €€€

## Capo di Muro

Free • No public transport; free parking on site

Among Corsica's many coastal walks to Genoese towers, the **Tour de Capo di muro** stands out for its unique location on the bush-clad frontier between the Golfe d'Ajaccio and the Golfe de Valinco. The walk along the promontory takes about 45 minutes each way, with some steep and uneven sections, although the dense maquis provides some welcome – if prickly – shade along the way. You can't go inside the tower, but the view, spanning both gulfs, is reward enough.

**EATING**                                                        **CAPO DI MURO**        **4**

★ **Le Capo di Muro** Monte Biancu; https://lecapodimuro.com. Few strategically located restaurants live up to the hype, but the only eatery on the cape serves up more than just the glittering views from its terrace. Succulent *gambas*, *langoustine* and octopus are cooked to perfection (although the prices might put you off), but there are also more wallet-friendly options like burgers and generous salads. €€

# The South

KAYAKING IN THE WATERS OF BONIFACIO

# 5 The South

From the dazzling alabaster cliffs that ripple up from the ocean around Bonifacio to the emerald-green gorges of the central Alta Rocca mountains, the South packs in a plethora of panoramic views. Forested headlands sweep out along the coast, capped by the distant ruins of Genoese towers; tiny granite islands pepper the shoreline; and glitzy yachts bob hull-to-hull in the busy harbours. While mountain hikes and prehistoric treasures draw travellers inland, some of the best beaches in Corsica can also be found along the southern shore. They are just as majestic as you might expect, whether plunging into a crystalline lagoon fringed with umbrella pines or bathing in a cocoon of pink rocks and ivory sand.

Dense thickets of maquis smooth the transition from coast to mountains as you leave the Golfe d'Ajaccio and round onto the oceanfront road of the **Golfe de Valinco**, where the most worthwhile detour is a visit to the prehistoric menhirs of **Filitosa**, notable for their charmingly chiselled faces.

Further south, the beaches of **Propriano** draw crowds in summer, as do the coastal footpaths of **Campomuro**, where you can wander along rock-strewn shores and sandy beaches, as well as climb Corsica's tallest **Genoese tower**. Nearby **Sartène**, with its sombre granite buildings and warren of alleys creeping up the hillside, is dubbed the most "Corsican" of all towns, and it's easily explored on a day trip.

The headline acts sit along the island's southeastern heel, starting with the majestic white cliffs and spectacular natural harbour of **Bonifacio**, where boat cruises and scuba diving excursions leave for the **Îles Lavezzi**, part of the Bouches de Bonifacio Nature Reserve. From Bonifacio, a string of gorgeous beaches, among them the much-photographed **Plage de Palombaggia** with its pink-hued boulder stones and the perfectly curved **Plage de Rondinara**, stud the coast up to the south's other major resort town, **Porto Vecchio**.

If you tire of the drinking and dining options in Porto Vecchio's cobbled citadelle, escaping into the mountainous belt of the **Alta Rocca** is a favourite for day-trippers. The cloud-grazing pinnacles of the **Aiguilles de Bavella** are a short drive away, where hiking, canyoning and wild swimming are the main activities, while nearby **Conca** marks the finish line (or starting line, if you prefer) of the epic **GR20 footpath**.

North of Porto Vecchio, the upper shore of the **Golfe de Porto-Vecchio** has more fine sandy beaches, from the crescent-shaped **Plage de Cala Rossa** at the mouth of the bay to the pine-bordered **Plage de Pinarellu**, which sits at the southern end of the **Côte de Nacre**, the *Pearl Coast*.

## GETTING THERE AND AROUND                                    THE SOUTH

Bonifacio and Porto Vecchio are two of the only towns in Corsica that offer *navettes* (shuttles) to the surrounding beaches in summer (see here for timetables: https:// corsicabus.org/busPVecchio). There are more tours in this region than most but to fully explore the South, you'll need to hire a car.

# Golfe de Valinco

Driving south from Ajaccio, the T40 highway scales the **Col de Celaccia**, then winds down to the stunning **Golfe de Valinco**. A vast blue inlet bounded by rolling, scrub-covered hills, the gulf presents the first dramatic scenery along the coastal highway. It also marks the start of – if you believe the media – the militant and Mafia-ridden south

'MENHIR' AT THE PREHISTORIC SITE OF FILITOSA

# Highlights

**1 Filitosa** One of Corsica's oldest and most significant prehistoric sites, famous for its 6,000-year-old statue-menhirs. See page 110

**2 Campomuro** Powder-soft sands, miles of coastal footpaths and a restored Genoese tower that you climb for a view across the Golfe de Valinco. See page 112

**3 Bonifacio** The emblematic white-chalk cliffs and natural harbour of Bonifacio are sensational from all angles. See page 115

**4 Îles Lavezzi** A slice of paradise off the coast of Bonifacio with orange-hued rocks, marbled blue waters, and champagne-coloured sands. See page 121

**5 Porto Vecchio** The hilltop citadel has bags of character and myriad shops, restaurants and nightlife options to choose from. See page 121

**6 Plage de Palombaggia** This sandy, half-moon bay is one of Corsica's most beloved beaches, embellished with pink porphyry rocks and umbrella pines. See page 124

**7 Plage de Pinarellu** Escape the crowds for this forest-fringed beach with its off-shore island and traditional *paillotes*. See page 124

**8 Aiguilles de Bavella** Mother Nature's skyscrapers afford a thrilling backdrop for outdoor adventures, whether hiking, canyoning or wild swimming. See page 125

**HIGHLIGHTS ARE MARKED ON THE MAP ON PAGE 108**

5

Corsica, more closely associated with vendetta, banditry and separatism than any other part of the island. Many of the mountain villages glimpsed from the roads hereabouts are riven with age-old divisions, exacerbated in recent years by the spread of organised crime and nationalist violence. But the island's seamier side is rarely discernible to the hundreds of thousands of visitors who pass through each summer, most of whom stay around the small port of **Propriano**, at the eastern end of the gulf. In addition to offering most of the area's tourist amenities, this busy resort town lies within easy

Golfe
d'Ajaccio

Ajaccio

Ajaccio

Col de St-
Eustache

Petreto-
Bicchisano

Aullène

Col de
la Tana

Tour de
Capo di Muro

D155

D757

Tavaro

T40

Col de
Celaccia

Col de Siu

Capo di
Muro

Tour de
Capannelle

Filitosa

Sollacaro

Plage de
Cupabia

Porto-Pollo

Abbartello

Olmeto

Fozzano

Capo Nero

Plage
de Taravo

D157

Capicciolo

Tour de la Calanca

Golfe de Valinco

Propriano

Arbellara

Viggianello

Ste-Lucie-
de-Tallano

Plage de Capo Lauroso

Rizzanese

ALTA
ROCCA

Campomoro

Portigliolo

Sartène

Capo di
Senetosa

Bocca
Albitrina

Pont de Curgia

Ortolo

L'Uomo di
Cagna
(1217 m)

Alignement de
Palaggiu

D48

Tizzano

Cauria
Megaliths

San Gavino

Golfe de
Roccapina

T40

Pianotolli-
Caldarello

Baie de
Figari

Îlots des Moines

## HIGHLIGHTS

1. Filitosa
2. Campomuro
3. Bonifacio
4. Îles Lavezzi
5. Porto Vecchio
6. Plage de Palombaggia
7. Plage de Pinarellu
8. Aiguilles

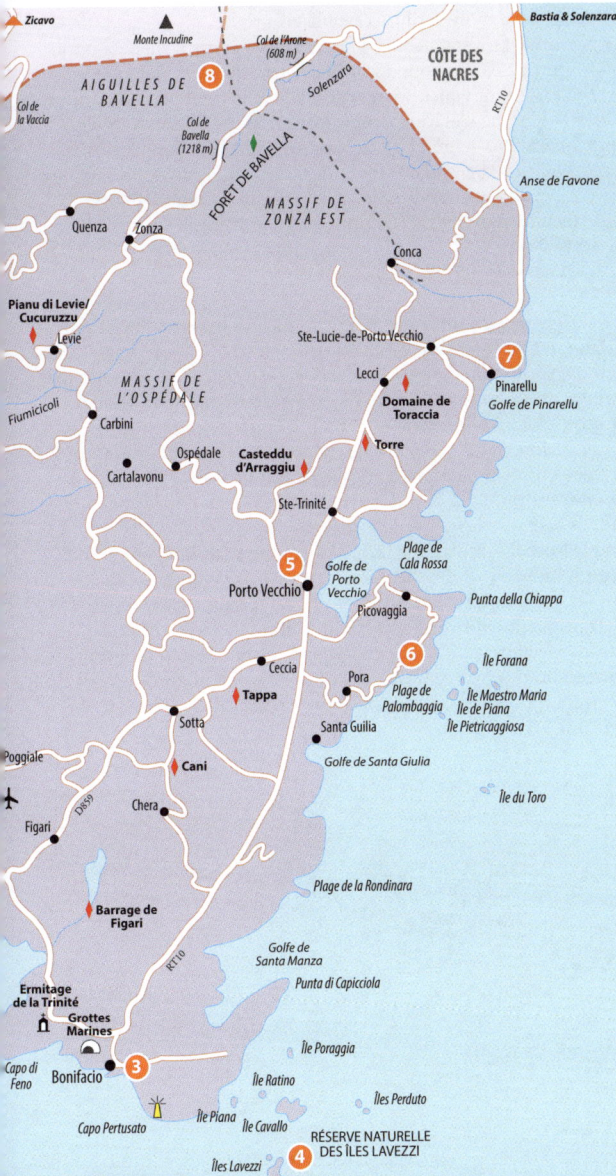

reach of the menhirs at **Filitosa**, one of the western Mediterranean's most important prehistoric sites, as well as some memorable coastal hikes.

## GETTING AROUND

The Golfe de Valinco region is reasonably well served by public transport, with buses running two to three times per day between Ajaccio and Bonifacio via Propriano and

## GOLFE DE VALINCO

Sartène. However, you will need your own transport to explore the beaches and villages, and outside July and August, there are no services along this route on Sundays.

**THE SOUTH**

N

*Zicavo*

*Bastia & Solenzara*

**CÔTE DES NACRES**

Monte Incudine

Col de l'Arone (608 m)

*AIGUILLES DE BAVELLA* ⑧

Col de la Vaccia

Col de Bavella (1218 m)

FORÊT DE BAVELLA

*Solenzara*

RT10

Anse de Favone

Quenza  Zonza

*MASSIF DE ZONZA EST*

Conca

**Pianu di Levie/ Cucuruzzu**

Levie

*MASSIF DE L'OSPÉDALE*

Ste-Lucie-de-Porto-Vecchio

Lecci

Pinarellu ⑦

*Golfe de Pinarellu*

**Domaine de Toraccia**

Fiumicicoli

Carbini

Ospédale

**Casteddu d'Arraggiu**

**Torre**

Cartalavonu

Ste-Trinité

Plage de Cala Rossa

⑤ Porto Vecchio

*Golfe de Porto Vecchio*

Picovaggia

*Punta della Chiappa*

Ceccia

Pora

⑥

*Île Forana*

**Tappa**

Plage de Palombaggia

*Île Maestro Maria*
*Île de Piana*
*Île Pietricaggiosa*

Sotta

Santa Giulia

*Golfe de Santa Giulia*

Poggiale

**Cani**

*Île du Toro*

D859

Chera

Figari

Plage de la Rondinara

**Barrage de Figari**

*Golfe de Santa Manza*

RT10

*Punta di Capicciola*

**Ermitage de la Trinité**

**Grottes Marines**

*Île Poraggia*

Capo di Feno

③ Bonifacio

*Île Ratino*

Capo Pertusato

*Île Piana*  *Île Cavallo*

*Îles Perduto*

**RÉSERVE NATURELLE DES ÎLES LAVEZZI**

④

*Îles Lavezzi*

0 ——— 5
kilometres

**5**

# Filitosa

April–Oct, out of season by arrangement only • Charge; cash only • http://filitosa.fr • Audio tours included; guided tours available in English by prior reservation • No public transport; parking on site

Set deep in the countryside of the fertile Vallée du Taravo, the extraordinary **Site Préhistorique de Filitosa**, 17km north of Propriano, comprises an array of statue-menhirs and prehistoric structures encapsulating some eight thousand years of history. Plan at least an hour to 90 minutes to visit the site, which includes audio commentary in English and a fair amount of walking over steep and uneven ground – stick to the main site at the top of the hill for a more easily accessible visit.

Filitosa was settled by Neolithic farming people who lived here in rock shelters until the arrival of navigators from the east in about 3500 BC. These invaders were the creators of the menhirs, the earliest of which were possibly phallic symbols worshipped by an ancient fertility cult. When the seafaring people known as the Torréens (after the towers they built on Corsica) conquered Filitosa around 1300 BC, they destroyed most of the menhirs, incorporating the broken stones into the area of dry-stone walling surrounding the site's two *torri*, or towers, examples of which can be found all over the south of Corsica. The site remained undiscovered until a farmer stumbled across the ruins on his land in the late 1940s.

## The Filitosas

**Filitosa V** looms up on the right shortly after the main entrance to the site. The largest statue-menhir on the island, it's an imposing spectacle, with clearly defined facial features and a sword and dagger outlined on the body. Beyond a sharp left turn lies the *oppidum* or central monument, its entrance marked by the **eastern platform**, thought to have been a lookout post. The cave-like structure sculpted out of the rock is the only evidence of Neolithic occupation and is generally agreed to have been a burial mound. Straight ahead, the Torréen **central monument** comprises a scattered group of menhirs on a circular walled mound, surmounted by a dome and entered by a corridor of stone slabs and lintels. Nobody is sure of its exact function.

Nearby **Filitosa XIII** and **Filitosa IX**, implacable lumps of granite with long noses and round chins, are the most impressive of the menhirs. Filitosa XIII is typical of the figures made just before the Torréen invasion, with its vertical dagger carved in relief – **Filitosa VII** also has a clearly sculpted sword and shield. **Filitosa VI**, from the same period, is remarkable for its facial detail. On the eastern side of the central monument stand some vestigial Torréen houses, where fragments of ceramics dating from 5500 BC were discovered; they represent the most ancient finds on the site, and some of them are displayed in the museum.

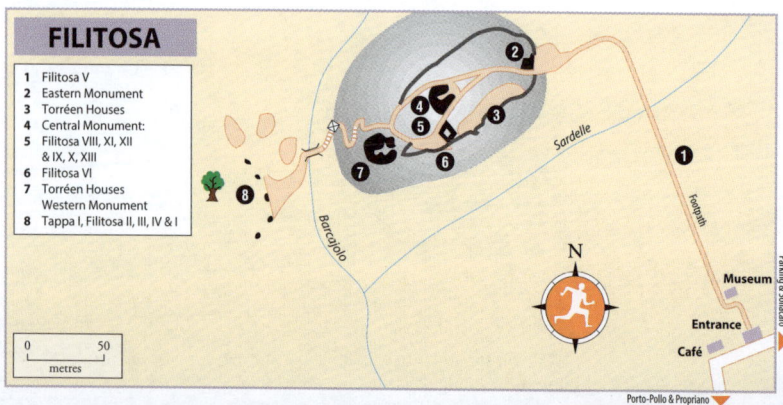

**FILITOSA**

1 Filitosa V
2 Eastern Monument
3 Torréen Houses
4 Central Monument:
5 Filitosa VIII, XI, XII
   & IX, X, XIII
6 Filitosa VI
7 Torréen Houses
   Western Monument
8 Tappa I, Filitosa II, III, IV & I

Sardelle
Barcajolo
Footpath
Parking & Sollacaro
Museum
Entrance
Café
N
0    50
metres

Porto-Pollo & Propriano

### The western monument

5

The **western monument**, a two-roomed structure built underneath another walled mound, is thought to have been some form of Torréen religious building. A flight of steps leads to the foot of this mound, where a footbridge opens onto a meadow that's dominated by five statue-menhirs arranged in a semicircle beneath a thousand-year-old olive tree. A bank separates them from the quarry from which the megalithic sculptors hewed the stone for the menhirs – a granite block is marked ready for cutting.

### The olive tree

From the western monument, rough stone steps lead quite steeply downhill and across the Barcajolo stream to the foot of the valley where a thousand-year-old olive tree stands. In the shade of the tree, a series of five menhirs (**Filitosa III, Filitosa IV, Filitosa I, Tappa I** and **Filitosa II**) stand gathered together. Originally found face down, the statues were later erected here to facilitate viewing.

### The museum

The **museum** is small but packed with fascinating artefacts, along with comprehensive information panels (in French and English) that detail the island's history, the excavation of Filitosa, and the site itself. The major item here is the formidable **Scalsa Murta**, a huge menhir dating from around 1400 BC and discovered at Olmeto. Like other statue-menhirs of this period, this one has two indents in the back of its head, which are thought to indicate that these figures would have been adorned with headdresses. Other notable exhibits are **Filitosa XII**, which has a hand and a foot carved into the stone, and **Trappa II**, a strikingly archaic face.

## Propriano and around

Tucked into the narrowest part of the Golfe de Valinco, the small port of **PROPRIANO**, 57km southeast of Ajaccio, centres on a fine natural harbour that was exploited by the ancient Greeks, Carthaginians and Romans, but became a prime target for Saracen pirate raids in the sixteenth century, when it was largely destroyed. Redeveloped in the 1900s, it now boasts a thriving marina and handles ferries to Marseille and Sardinia.

### The beaches

During the summer, tourists come here in droves for the area's **beaches** and aside from day trips to the surrounding sights, there's little to do in Propriano except hit the beach or take a boat cruise (https://propriano-promenadeenmer.fr). The nearest of these are the sandy **plage de Mancinu**, right in town, and the **plage du Lido**, 1km west, just beyond the Port de Commerce, both of which can get crowded in summer. Prettier options lie in the coves strung along the northern shore of the gulf around **Olmeto plage**, or to the south, where the rocky pools around **plage de Capu Laurosu** are a favourite for snorkelling.

#### ARRIVAL AND DEPARTURE | PROPRIANO AND AROUND

**By boat** Ferries from the mainland and Sardinia dock in the Port de Commerce, a 10-minute walk from rue du Général-de-Gaulle, the town's main street. La Méridionale operate all services from here, represented in Propriano by Voyages Sorba (http://sorba-voyages.com).

**By bus** Buses (https://bit.ly/3NLn2J7) go from the Gare Routière on rue des Pêcheurs.
Destinations Ajaccio (2–3 daily; 1hr 45min); Porto-Vecchio (2–3 daily; 1hr 45min); Sartène (2–3 daily; 20min); Bonifacio.

#### INFORMATION AND ACTIVITIES

**Tourist office** 21 Av Napoléon III (http://lacorsedesorigines.com) provide maps, transport timetables, and plenty of advice on regional attractions.

**Water sports** Jet 7 (plage de Mancinu; http://jet7propriano.com/) rents boats, jet-skis, and underwater scooters, as well as offering flyboarding tours.

**5**

## ACCOMMODATION

**Beach Hôtel** 38 av Napoléon; http://beachhotel-propriano.com. Spacious and comfortable en-suite rooms, all with small balconies, in a leafy four-storey block overlooking the Port de Commerce. The location, within strolling distance of the plage du Lido, is a big plus. €€

**Camping TIKITI** Rue d'Ajaccio; https://campingtikiti.com. The closest campsite to town has shady, powered campsites, a recently renovated amenities block, and chalet and mobile home rentals. There's also a large swimming pool with a waterfall and an on-site pizzeria. €

**Le Lido** 42 av Napoléon; http://le-lido.com. This low-rise hotel on the outskirts of Propriano, which dates from the 1930s, is head and shoulders above the competition – not least in its unsurpassed beachside location. The eleven rooms are ranged around a cool courtyard – seven have terraces jutting on the sand behind – and there's also a very sophisticated gourmet restaurant. €€€

★ **Domaine de Logliastru** Along the Golfe de Valinco; https://www.domaine-de-logliastru.com. If your idea of fun is sleeping in a luxurious treehouse or renting a converted shepherd's hut in the middle of nowhere, Domaine de Logliastru has you covered. Most exciting is the opportunity to rent out the Tour de Micalona, a fully refurbished 16th-century Genoese tower, with a rooftop terrace, private rock pool, and dazzling ocean views. There's nowhere like it on the island. Weekly bookings only in high season. €€€€

## EATING AND DRINKING

Propriano has more than its fair share of duff restaurants – most of them with a prime view of the marina – but a few quality establishments are starting to spring up.

★ **Chez Charlot** Viggianello, 4.4km east up the D19. Down-to-earth village cuisine – Corsican soup, veal bruschettas, stuffed courgettes, roast pork, tripe, rabbit stew and pan-fried snapper – offered on a superb-value *menu*. You can eat indoors or out on the fabulous narrow terrace next to the church, which surveys the entire gulf. Reservations are essential in high season. €€

**Le Peché Mignon Bischof** 24 av Napoléon. This cosy tearoom is the go-to spot for morning croissants or afternoon *goûter*. There's a wide selection of teas, accompanied by tempting homemade treats with some gluten-free options available too. €€

★ **Tempi Fa** 7 rue Napoléon; http://tempi-fa.com. Done out in rustic Corsican style, with exposed stone walls and sides of ham dangling from the roof, *Tempi Fa* functions as a local *epicerie* by day and a lively tapas bar in the evenings, where you can order plates of top-notch charcuterie, local cheese, Alta Rocca olives and Rizzanese wines, while perched on stools around old barrels on the terrace or inside a cosy dining hall with antique tiled floors and wooden ceilings. €€

**Terra Cotta** 31 av Napoléon; +33495742380. One of the swankiest restaurants in town, with tables in a cool, Moroccan-style bistro, or out on the breezy seafront terrace. The cooking is uncompromisingly sophisticated, using only the freshest local seafood, and the service smiling. €€€

**U Tavonu** 1 rue Camille Pietri; https://instagram.com/utavonu. Decked out like an authentic old wine *cave* with a veritable smorgasbord of Corsican charcuterie swinging from the rafters, this is the spot to try and buy local specialities. Better yet, take a seat and order a *plateau découverte* laden with cheeses, charcuterie and aubergine caviar. €€

# Tour de Campomoro

Charge • https://campomuru-senetosa.corsica • No public transport; paid parking in the village

Perched on the southwest shore of the Golfe de Valinco, the **Tour de Campomuro** was once one of the south's best-kept secrets – today, it's such a tourist magnet in the summer months that you'll need to arrive before 10am to grab a parking spot. The restored Tour de Campomuro, now home to a small but interesting museum (English translations available from the ticket office), is the focal point of a popular walk that sets out from the fishing village of Campomuro (about 30 minutes one-way). From the tower, additional footpaths of varying lengths run south along the coast. From here to the **Phare de Sentosa**, where you can spend the night, it's a 5-hour hike.

## ACCOMMODATION

★ **Refuge de Phare de Sentosa** Morta Spana, reachable only on foot; https://www.campumoru-senetosa.corsica/boutique/. Among the most memorable of Corsica's *refuges*, hikers can stay at the old Sentosa Lighthouse, with a magnificent oceanfront setting. Basic rooms and dorms are available or you can pitch a tent; tents and bedding are available to hire. €

# Sartène (Sartè) and around

5

Prosper Mérimée famously dubbed **SARTÈNE** *"la plus corse des villes corses"* ("the most Corsican of Corsican towns"), but the nineteenth-century German chronicler Gregorovius put a less complimentary spin on it when he described it as a "town peopled by demons". Sartène hasn't shaken off its hostile image, despite being a smart, better-groomed place than many small Corsican towns. The main square, place Porta, doesn't offer many diversions once you've explored the enclosed *vieille ville*, and the only time of year Sartène teems with tourists is at Easter for **U Catenacciu**, a Good Friday procession that packs the main square with onlookers.

Close to Sartène are some of the island's best-known **prehistoric sites** (see page 114), most notably, the megaliths of **Cauria** and the **Alignement de Palaggiu**, monuments from which are displayed in the town's excellent museum.

## Place Porta and Santa Anna

**Place Porta** – its official name, place de la Libération, has never caught on – forms Sartène's nucleus. Once the arena for bloody vendettas, it's now a well-kept square opening onto a wide terrace. Flanking the north side is the **church of Ste-Marie**, built in the 1760s but completely restored to a smooth granitic appearance. Inside the church, the most notable feature is the weighty wooden cross and chair carried through the town by hooded penitents during the Easter **Catenacciu** procession.

A flight of steps to the left of the **hôtel de ville**, formerly the governor's palace, leads past the post office to a ruined **lookout tower** (*échauguette*), which is all that remains of the town's twelfth-century ramparts. This apart, the best of the *vieille ville* is to be found behind the *hôtel de ville* in the **Santa Anna** district, a labyrinth of constricted passageways and ancient fortress-like houses. Featuring few windows and often linked to their neighbours by balconies, these houses are entered by first-floor doors which would have been approached by ladders – dilapidated staircases have replaced these necessary measures against unwelcome intruders.

## Musée Départemental de Préhistoire Corse et d'Archéologie

Bd Jacques-Nicolai • Charge • https://isula.corsica/patrimoine/Musee-d-archeologie-de-la-Corse

A noteworthy attraction in Sartène is the swish **Musée Départemental de Préhistoire Corse et d'Archéologie**. Exhibits comprise mostly Neolithic and Torréen pottery fragments, in addition to some bracelets and glass beads from the Iron Age, and painted ceramics from the thirteenth to sixteenth centuries.

### ARRIVAL AND INFORMATION

SARTÈNE AND AROUND

**By bus** Arriving in Sartène by bus, you'll be dropped either at the top of av Gabriel-Péri or at the end of cours Général-de-Gaulle.
Destinations: Ajaccio (1–3 daily; 1hr 45min); Propriano (1–3 daily; 10min).
**Tourist office** Cours Soeur-Amélie (http://lacorsedesorigines.com).

### ACCOMMODATION

**Camping Olva** Rte de la Castagna, 6km north of Sartène; https://camping-olva.com. Shady three-star site, with lots of hiking trails into the forest on its doorstep. There's a lovely pool, sports field, tennis court and even a gym, plus a variety of lodges, bungalows and mobile homes. Camping €, bungalow €€

★ **Domaine de Murtoli** Vallée de l'Ortolu; https://murtoli.com. If you've got money to splurge, this 5-star

paradise is a veritable village of stone-built heritage houses converted into luxury villas and set amid fragrant maquis, vineyards, and farmlands. Wooden beams, natural brick and sumptuous furnishings make each suite stand out, plus there's a 20-metre-long stone pool, a Michelin-starred restaurant (see below), and a custom-designed golf course amid the maquis. €€€€

**Hôtel Les Roches** Av. Jean Jaurès; https://les-roches-

**5**

## MEGALITHIC SITES IN SOUTH CORSICA

Sparsely populated today, the rolling hills of the southwestern corner of Corsica are rich in **prehistoric sites**. The megaliths of **Cauria**, standing in ghostly isolation 10km southwest of Sartène, comprise the **Dolmen de Fontanaccia**, the best-preserved monument of its kind on Corsica, and the nearby alignments of **Stantari** and **Renaggiu**, which also have an impressive congregation of statue-menhirs.

As you snake your way through the maquis, the **Dolmen de Fontanaccia** eventually comes into view on the horizon, crowning the crest of a low hill amid a sea of vegetation. A blue sign at the parking space indicates the 15-minute track to the dolmen. Known to the locals as the **Stazzona del Diavolu** (Devil's Forge), a name that does justice to its enigmatic power, the Dolmen de Fontanaccia is in fact a burial chamber from around 2000 BC. This period was marked by a change in burial customs – whereas bodies had previously been buried in stone coffins in the ground, they were now placed above, in a mound of earth enclosed in a stone chamber. What you see today is a great stone table, comprising six huge granite blocks nearly 2m high, topped by a stone slab that remained after the earth eroded away.

The twenty "standing men" of the **Alignement de Stantari**, 200m to the east of the dolmen, date from the same period. All are featureless except two, which have roughly sculpted eyes and noses, with diagonal swords on their fronts and sockets in their heads where horns would probably have been attached. Across a couple of fields to the south is the **Alignement de Renaggiu**, a gathering of forty menhirs standing in rows amid a small shadowy copse, set against the enormous granite outcrop of Punta di Cauria. Some of the menhirs have fallen, but all face north to south, a fact that seems to rule out any connection with a sun-related cult.

Northwest of Cauria, **Palaggiu** is another rewardingly remote site and holds the largest concentration of menhirs in Corsica. Stretching in straight lines across the countryside like a battleground of soldiers are 258 menhirs, among them three statue-menhirs with carved weapons and facial features – they are amid the first line you come to. Dating from around 1800 BC, the statues give few clues as to their function, but it's a reasonable supposition that proximity to the sea was important – the famous Corsican archaeologist Roger Grosjean's theory (and the most popular) is that the statues were some sort of magical deterrent to invaders.

Further afield, the prehistoric sites of **Cucuruzzu and Capula** sit on a forested plateau in the Alta Rocca, just north of Levie. The **Castello di Cucuruzzu** is the most notable site, a Bronze Age hill fort perched on a rocky spur and surrounded by a series of stone huts and terraces. Northeast of the site stand the remains of a tower, believed to have been used for storing crops, while a further 20-minute walk will bring you to the medieval fortress of **Capula**. Plan about an hour to visit the whole site.

Numerous prehistoric monuments also dot the coast between Porto-Vecchio and Solenzara, but the most impressive, **Casteddu d'Araggiu**, lies 12km north along the D759. From the site's car park (signposted off the main road), it's a twenty-minute stiff uphill climb through maquis and scrubby woodland to the ruins. Built in 2000 BC, the *casteddu* consists of a complex of chambers built into a massive circular wall of pink granite from the top of which the views over the coastal belt are superb.

### GETTING THERE & INFORMATION

All sites are managed by the Collectivité de Corse (https://isula.corsica) and are free to visit, except for Cucuruzzu and Capula, which has a small charge (audio guides are also available). You'll need your own transport to reach the sites and roads are unpaved and sometimes inaccessible due to periods of heavy rain. The region's tourist offices can provide details of the sites and advise of local guides, but there are currently no guided tours.

sartene.com. Open April to November, this 3-star hotel sits at the top of the village, looking out over the emerald hills of the Rizzanese Valley below. Opt for a superior room with a balcony; the views are worth the extra fee. Bonus points are awarded for the free parking with electric charge points and excellent on-site restaurant. €

**San Damianu** Montée Saint Damien; http://sandamianu. fr. This four-star hotel, now a Best Western, occupies a plum spot with spectacular views over the town and valley. Rooms are airy, bright and minimalist, and it offers all the comforts and amenities you'd expect for a hotel in this class, including a lovely pool and teak sun terrace. €€

## EATING

In addition to the restaurants listed below, cafés cluster around place Porta, and are great places for crowd-watching.
**Le Jardin de l'Échauguette** Place de la vardiola. Delightful garden restaurant on a shade-dappled terrace, tucked away on the edge of the medieval ramparts (get here early for a table with the best valley views). The food's refined *gastro corse* at friendly prices: grouper *croustillant* with almonds in red wine sauce; chicken liver with fresh mint; *Sartenaise* veal stew on a bed of creamy polenta. €€
**La Storia** Rue Jean Codaccioni; http://lastoria-sartene.fr. Traditional *sartenaise* cuisine served in a rustic stone-walled tavern where dinner is often accompanied by delicately

strummed live guitar or polyphonic chants. Pasta is the star here, whether *cannelloni* stuffed with *brocciu* and fresh mint or the Coriscan lasagne layered with stewed wild boar. €€
★ **La Table de la Ferme** Domaine de Murtoli; https:// murtoli.com. In the Vallée de l'Ortolo, south of Sartène, this Michelin-starred experience is part of the 5-star Domaine de Murtoli (see above). Mere mortals, albeit ones bearing credit cards, are also invited to sample the estate-bred veal, east coast lobster, and other creations. If you can, take a table in the courtyard, where ancient olive trees burst through the terrace canopy, providing a dramatic centrepiece for your culinary voyage. €€€€

# Bonifacio

BONIFACIO enjoys a superbly isolated location at Corsica's southernmost point, a narrow peninsula of dazzling white limestone creating a town site unlike any other. The much-photographed **haute ville**, a maze of narrow streets flanked by tall Genoese tenements, rises seamlessly out of sheer cliffs that have been hollowed and striated by the wind and waves, while on the landward side, the deep cleft between the peninsula and the mainland forms an impregnable natural harbour. A haven for boats for centuries, this inlet is nowadays a chic marina that attracts yachts from around the Med. Its geography has long enabled Bonifacio to maintain a certain temperamental detachment from the rest of Corsica, and the town today remains distinctly more Italian than French in atmosphere. It retains Renaissance features found only here, and its inhabitants have their own dialect based on Ligurian, a legacy of the days when this was practically an independent Genoese colony.

Such a place has its inevitable drawbacks: exorbitant prices, overwhelming crowds in July and August and a commercial cynicism that's atypical of Corsica as a whole. However, the old town, which sits on a narrow clifftop, forms one of the most arresting spectacles in the Mediterranean and warrants at least a day-trip. If you plan to come in peak season, try to get here early in the day before the bus parties arrive at around 10am.

## Haute Ville

Most of Bonifacio's sights lie within the **Haute Ville**, the old citadel built high on the cliffs. At the end of the café-lined **quai Comparetti**, just before the **ferry port**, a long-cobbled walkway – **Montée Rastello** – leads uphill to the citadel and the entrance to the **Bastion de l'Etendard**. The climb is rewarded by a magnificent view of the white limestone cliffs tapering to Capu Persutau, and the huge lump of fallen rock face called the Grain de Sable. The tiny **Chapelle St-Roch**, at the head of the steps, was built on the spot where the last plague victim died in 1528; another, narrower stone staircase twists down to the tiny beach of **Sutta Rocca**. From the marina, you can also take the staircase up from the end of the harbour on Quai Banda del Ferro, which comes out by the tourist office on Via Fred Scamaroni.

**5**

# Bastion de l'Étendard

Charge

Montée St-Roch takes you up the final approach to the citadelle walls, entered via the great **Porte de Gênes**, once the only gateway to the *haute ville*. It opens on to the place des Armes, where you can visit the **Bastion de l'Étendard**, sole remnant of the fortifications destroyed during a siege in 1554. While exploring the narrow streets, look out for flamboyant marble escutcheons above the doorways and double-arched windows separated by curiously stunted columns. Many of the older houses did not originally have doors; the inhabitants used to climb up a ladder which they would pull up behind them to prevent a surprise attack.

# Ste-Marie-Majeure

Cutting across rue du Palais de Garde brings you to the church of **Ste-Marie-Majeure**, originally Romanesque but restored in the eighteenth century, though the richly sculpted belfry dates from the fourteenth century. The facade is hidden by a loggia where the Genoese municipal officers used to dispense justice in the days of the republic. The church's treasure, a fragment of the True Cross, was saved from a shipwreck in the Straits of Bonifacio; for centuries after, the citizens would take the relic to the edge of the cliff and pray for calm seas whenever storms raged. It is kept

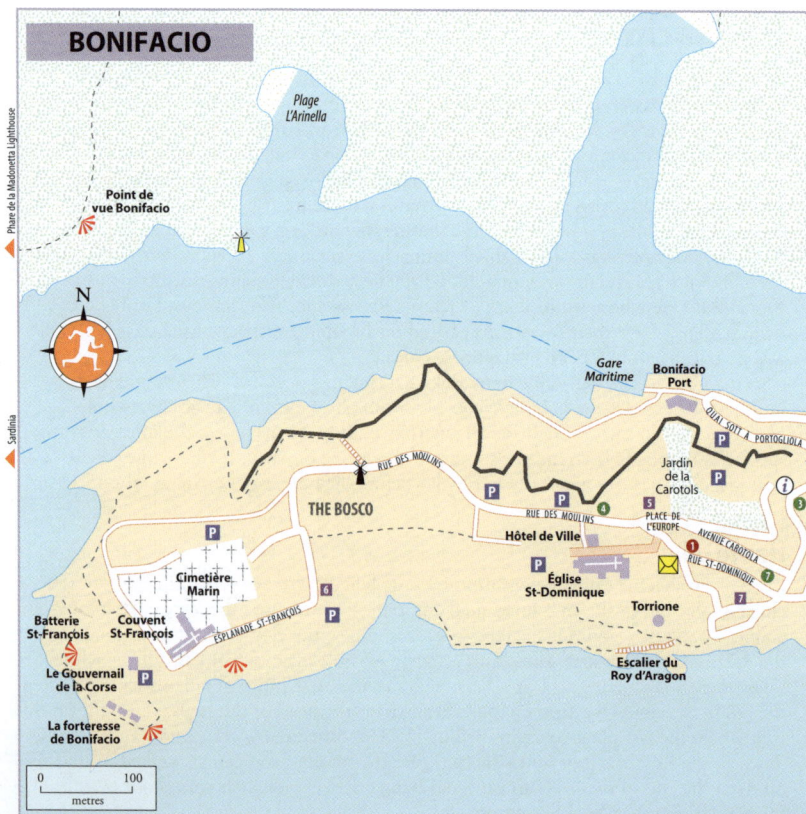

BONIFACIO

Plage L'Arinella

Phare de la Madonetta Lighthouse

Point de vue Bonifacio

N

Sardinia

Gare Maritime

Bonifacio Port

QUAI SOTT A PORTOGLIOLA

Jardin de la Carotols

RUE DES MOULINS

THE BOSCO

RUE DES MOULINS

PLACE DE L'EUROPE

AVENUE CAROTOLA

Hôtel de Ville

RUE ST-DOMINIQUE

Cimetière Marin

Église St-Dominique

Batterie St-François

Couvent St-François

ESPLANADE ST-FRANÇOIS

Torrione

Le Gouvernail de la Corse

Escalier du Roy d'Aragon

La forteresse de Bonifacio

0        100
metres

**5**

under lock and key in the sacristy, along with an ivory cask containing relics of St Boniface.

## Torrione and the Escalier du Roi d'Aragon

**Escalier du Roi d'Aragon** charge

Rue Doria leads towards the Bosco; at the end of this road, a left down rue des Pachas will bring you to the **Torrione**, a 35-metre-high lookout post built in 1195 on the site of Count Bonifacio's castle. Descending the cliff from here, the 187 steps of **Escalier du Roi d'Aragon** cut right through the cliff face and descend all the way to the seafront. Following the carved path around the cliff with the sea lapping at your heels is one of the most thrilling views in the city. The stairs are said to have been built in one night by the Aragonese in an attempt to gain the town in 1420, but in fact they had already been in existence for some time and were used by the people to fetch water from a well. The only downside is you have to walk back up; a feat that ensures even the fittest will break a sweat.

## The Bosco

To the west of the Torrione lies the **Bosco**, a quarter named after the wood that used to cover the far end of the peninsula in the tenth century. In those days, a community

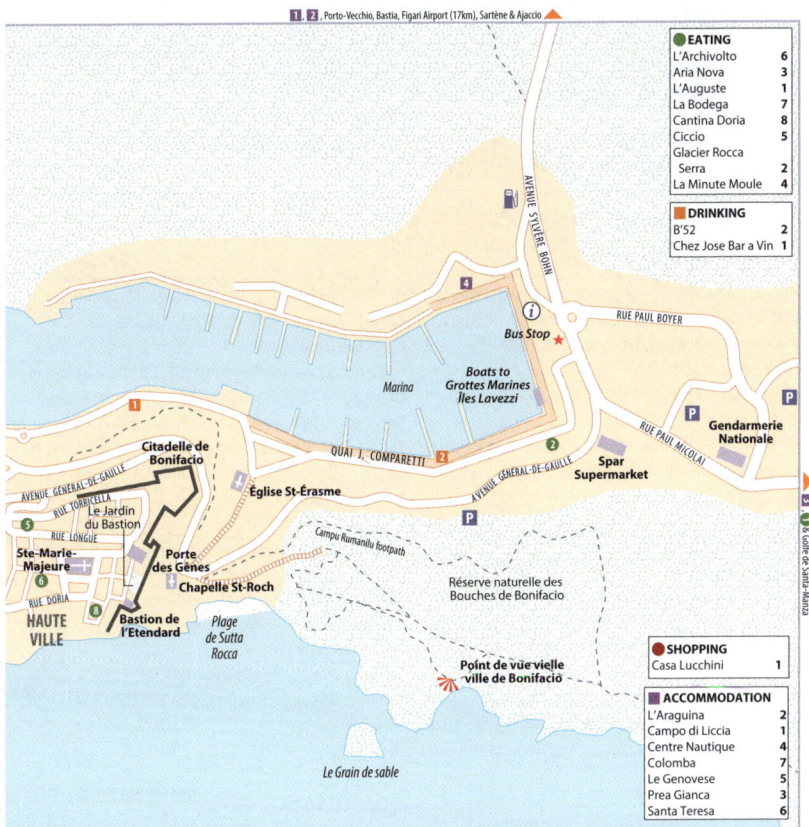

| ● EATING | |
| --- | --- |
| L'Archivolto | 6 |
| Aria Nova | 3 |
| L'Auguste | 1 |
| La Bodega | 7 |
| Cantina Doria | 8 |
| Ciccio | 5 |
| Glacier Rocca Serra | 2 |
| La Minute Moule | 4 |

| ■ DRINKING | |
| --- | --- |
| B'52 | 2 |
| Chez Jose Bar a Vin | 1 |

| ● SHOPPING | |
| --- | --- |
| Casa Lucchini | 1 |

| ■ ACCOMMODATION | |
| --- | --- |
| L'Araguina | 2 |
| Campo di Liccia | 1 |
| Centre Nautique | 4 |
| Colomba | 7 |
| Le Genovese | 5 |
| Prea Gianca | 3 |
| Santa Teresa | 6 |

5

of hermits dwelt here, but nowadays, the vast limestone plateau is accessed by a series of footpaths that follow the recently restored ramparts and afford some great views along the coast. The entrance to the Bosco is marked by the **Église St-Dominique**, a rare example of Corsican Gothic architecture – it was built in 1270, most probably by the Templars, and later handed over to the Dominicans.

Beyond the church, rue des Moulins leads on to the ruins of three **windmills** dating from 1283, two of them decrepit, the third restored. Behind them stands a memorial to the 750 people who died when a troopship named *Sémillante* ran aground here in 1855 on its way to the Crimea: one of the many disasters wreaked by the notoriously windy straits.

The tip of the Bosco plateau is occupied by the **Cimetière Marin**, its white crosses standing out sharply against the deep blue of the sea. Open until sundown, the cemetery is a fascinating place to explore, with its flamboyant mausoleums displaying a jumble of architectural ornamentations. Next to the cemetery stands the **Couvent St-François**, allegedly founded after St Francis sought shelter in a nearby cave – the story goes that the convent was the town's apology to the holy man, over whom a local maid had nearly poured a bucket of slops. Immediately to the south, the **Esplanade St-François** commands fine views across the bay to Sardinia.

## Le Gouvernail de la Corse & Batterie St François

**Le Gouvernail** charge • **Batterie St Francois** free

South of the cemetery, across the car park, an ongoing restoration project has seen two new sites open up to the public. The **Batterie St François**, a defensive area that dates back to the 12th century, has now been restored to its former glory, allowing you to descend the steps that tunnel through the ramparts and gaze out across towards Sardinia, as well as explore part of the old batteries. A short walk away, the **Gouvernail de la Corse** is an old military surveillance site built in 1880 to guard the strait of Bonifacio. A hang-dug tunnel, with 168 steps, leads down to a hidden bunker and lookout point at the far end of the peninsula – nicknamed "the rudder" – just 10m above sea level. It's a magnificent, and unexpected, view.

### ARRIVAL AND DEPARTURE BONIFACIO

**By car** There are 13 car parks (charge; https://www. bonifacio-mairie.fr/ma-commune/parkings), located around the marina and throughout the Haute Ville; watch out for spaces marked "réservées aux abonnés" as these are residents only. In summer, the Parking des Valli, 3km north of town, offers a day rate and free shuttles to town.

**By bus** Buses drop passengers in the marina, next to the tourist information point. For services to Ajaccio, you'll need to change buses at Scopeto.

Destinations Ajaccio (2–3 daily; 3hr 30min) via Sartène (1hr 20min); Porto-Vecchio (2–4 daily; 30–40min)

**By plane** Figari airport, 17km north of Bonifacio (https:// figari-aeroport.cci.corsica), handles flights from mainland France and a few charters from the UK. A seasonal *navette* runs two to four times daily from the airport to Porto-Vecchio, from where you can pick up a connecting bus to Bonifacio. The only other option (aside from car hire) is to take a taxi into town.

### GETTING AROUND AND INFORMATION

You can get around Bonifacio on foot, as long as you don't mind clocking up some miles. If you want to avoid the steep uphill paths and many flights of steps, the best bet is to hop on the Petit Train (April–October; every 30 minutes; charge), which leaves from the marina.

**By bike or scooter** Tam-tam (rue Paul Nicolai; https:// tam-tam.fr) rents bikes and e-bikes by the day; Scoot-rent (3 Quai Banda del Ferro; https://bonifacioscootrent.com)

rents 50cc and 125cc scooters.

**Tourist office** The tourist office in the *haute ville*, 2 rue Fred Scamaroni (http://bonifacio.fr), has audioguides for hire in English and French (charge).

**Car hire** Avis, at Figari airport (http://avis.fr); Europcar, Port de Plaisance (http://europcar.fr); Hertz, at Figari airport (http://hertz.fr).

### ACCOMMODATION SEE MAP PAGE 116

Bonifacio's hotels and campsites demand some of the highest tariffs on the island and finding a place to stay can be a chore, as hotels book up quickly in high season. For a room near the centre, reserve well in advance, and brace yourself for noise at night if you nab a room on the quayside – Bonifacio becomes a proper party town in August. Better still, save yourself the trouble, and the money, by finding a room elsewhere and visiting on a day trip.

**L'Araguina** Av Sylvère-Bohn; http://campingaraguina.fr. The closest campsite to town, but unwelcoming, cramped in season, and with inadequate washing and toilet facilities. Avoid unless desperate – though it's undoubtedly the most convenient option if you're backpacking. €

**Campo di Liccia** 3km north towards Porto-Vecchio; http://campingdiliccia.com. Well shaded and large, so you're guaranteed a place. There's a pleasant pool (plus a kids' pool), a playground and an outdoor gym. €

**Centre Nautique** On the marina; http://centre-nautique.com. Very chic (with prices to match) but relaxed hotel on the waterfront, fitted out with mellow wood and nautical charts. No rooms here – just suites and apartments, all stylishly furnished and most benefitting from sea views. €€€€

**Colomba** Rue Simon-Varsi; https://hotel-bonifacio.fr. The only hotel worthy of note in the thick of the old quarter occupies a smartly renovated medieval tenement on one of the *haute ville's* prettiest streets. It offers twelve classically furnished, en-suite rooms, some with shuttered windows

opening to magnificent sea views. Parking available. €€€

★ **Le Genovese** 1 Pl. de l'Europe; https://hotel-genovese.com. Built within part of the old Geonese ramparts, this four-star stunner occupies prime turf at the heart of the Haute Ville. The bustle of the city feels far away when relaxing on the rooftop pool terrace, while the 14 rooms have an understated elegance about them and effective soundproofing. There's also a sauna, hammam, and indoor pool. €€€€

★ **Prea Gianca** 3km from Bonifacio, along the rte de Santa Manza; https://preagianca.fr. Earning the Eco Label in 2023, this three-star hotel sweeps out like an Italian villa around a central swimming pool; its 25 rooms fanned out beneath the surrounding olive trees. Recently renovated, each one is unique, named after Bonifacio's beaches and bays and embellished with an artful splash of colour. There's an excellent restaurant, too. Prices soar in summer, but it's much more affordable off-season. €€€€

**Santa Teresa** Quartier St-François; http://hotel-santateresa.com. Large and modern three-star on the clifftop overlooking the Cimetière Marin, noteworthy for its stupendous views across the straits to Sardinia. Rooms are elegant with some playful pops of colour, but not all are sea-facing, so make sure to choose the "*terrasse vue mer*" when you book. €€€

## EATING

SEE MAP PAGE 116

Eating possibilities in Bonifacio might seem unlimited, but it's best to avoid the chintzy restaurants around the marina, few of which merit their exorbitant prices.

**L'Archivolto** Rue de l'Archivolto. With its candlelit, antique- and junk-filled interior, this would be the most commendable place to eat in the *haute ville* were the cooking a little less patchy and the prices fairer. But it still gets packed out – reservations are recommended – and the couple that own it are charming. €€€

★ **Aria Nova** 4 Rue Fred Scamaroni; https://restaurant-aria-nova.com. Sourcing the finest ingredients from regional farmers, this fashionably rustic restaurant adds a gastronomic twist to timeless Corsican recipes. Try the menu corse, where you'll be treated to *migliaccioli* (Corsican pancakes), a reenvisioned *civet de sanglier*, and *figadone* all in one sitting. €€€

★ **L'Auguste** rte de Santa Manza; https://preagianca.fr. Prea Gianca's excellent hotel restaurant, also open to non-guests, creates gastronomic magic up in the hills while everyone else is dining in the Old Town. Meat dishes like the *filet mignon de porc à la chataîgne* and *tagliata de veau* are worthy of attention, but there are also some surprising vegetarian dishes. Don't miss out on the heavenly mousses – it's impossible to choose between the chestnut and the clementine, so you'll just have to order both. €€

**La Bodega** 1 Av. de la Carotola; https://m.facebook.com/LaBodegaBonifacio. Time-honoured establishment that

serves honest, no-frills Corsican cuisine like lamb chops garnished with fragrant maquis herbs and local speciality, *aubergines a la Bonifacienne*. Don't miss the *moelleux au chataîgne* for dessert. €€

**Cantina Doria** 27 rue Doria. Down-to-earth Corsican specialities at down-to-earth prices. Their popular three-course *menu* – which includes the house speciality, aubergines *à la bonifacienne* – offers unbeatable value for the *haute ville*, though you'll soon bump up your bill if you succumb to the temptations of the excellent wine selection. €€

**Ciccio** 6 Rue Saint-Jean Baptiste; https://cicciobonifacio.com. Tucked down an alleyway in the Old Town, this stone-walled cavern of a restaurant makes everything in-house – they even have their own bakery, a few doors down. The honey-glazed *porc Nustrale* melts in your mouth, and the tiramisu with *canistrelli* and *Nucciola* is a hat-trick for dessert lovers. €€€

**Glacier Rocca Serra** 17 Quai Jérôme Comparetti; https://instagram.com/glacierroccaserra. The best *glacier* in the city also has two other smaller branches in the haute-ville, ensuring you're never more than a stroll away from an ice cream. Look out for local flavours like *farine de chataîgne*, *figue de Bonifacio* or *clementine de Corse*. €€

**La Minute Moule** Rue des moulins; https://fr-fr.facebook.com/laminutemoulebonifacio. Look beyond the fast-food-esque décor and the tacky plastic chairs because this

5

## BOAT TOURS FROM BONIFACIO

From the moment you arrive in Bonifacio, you'll be pestered by touts from the many boat companies running excursions out of the harbour. There are more than a dozen of these, but they all offer more or less the same routes at the same prices. Lasting up to an hour, the shorter trips take you out along the cliffs to the *grottes marines* (sea caves) and *calanques* (inlets) below the old town.

Longer excursions (2 hours up to a full day) head out to the **Îles Lavezzi**, part of the archipelago to the east of the straits of Bonifacio. Many companies offer a shuttle (*navette*) service, allowing you to spend as much time as you like on the islands before returning. Boats go out past the Grain de Sable and Phare du Pertusato and then moor at the main island of **Lavezzi**, beside the **cimetière Achiarino**. Buried in two walled cemeteries are the victims of the *Sémillante* shipwreck of 1855, in which 773 crew members and soldiers bound for the Crimean War were drowned after their vessel was blown onto the rocks.

Classified as a nature and marine park since 1982, the *Réserve naturelle des Bouches de Bonifacio* is home to several rare species of **wildflowers**, and offer fabulous **snorkelling**, **scuba diving** and some exquisite shell-sand **beaches**. A network of footpaths runs between them, well-waymarked, as you're not permitted to wander off into the fragile vegetation.

### BOAT TRIPS AND EXCURSIONS

**Bonifacio Excursions** (https://bonifacio-excursions.com) and **SPMB** (https://spmbonifacio.com) both offer a variety of boat tours; **Pintarella Vision** (https://instagram.com/piantarellavision) offer 50-minute tours of the marine park in a semi-submarine; and **Briseis Croisieres** (https://briseis-croisieres.com/fr/yacht) organise full-day private yacht cruises. **Bonifacio Plongee** (https://bonifacioplongee.corsica) organise scuba dives for beginners and certified divers around the Îles Lavezzi, while **Bonif'Kayak** (https://bonifacio-kayak.com) offer guided kayaking tours, as well as kayak and SUP rentals.

---

humble little seafood shack is one of the best finds in the city. There's just one thing on the menu – *moules* – served with your choice of sauce. Fresh as they come, and you can enjoy them on the panoramic terrace. €̄

## DRINKING AND NIGHTLIFE                    SEE MAP PAGE 116

**B'52** Quai Comparetti. Hippest of the waterfront lounge bars, hosting DJs on weekends and throughout peak season. There's a pleasant outdoor deck.

**Chez Jose Bar a Vin** 31 quai Banda del Ferro. Bonifacians frequent this convivial wine bar as much as tourists, and the bartenders will be happy to talk you through the wine list. There's a substantial list available by the glass, including some sparkling wines and local digestifs.

## SHOPPING                                    SEE MAP PAGE 116

★**Casa Lucchini** 28 rue Saint Cominique; https://instagram.com/casalucchini_epicerie. This treasure-trove of a shop is brimming with *figatellu*, *coppa*, *lonzu*, and *panzetta*, all 100 percent Corsican charcuterie, raised and cultivated from owner Jean-Baptiste Lucchini's own farm, where the free-roaming nustrale pigs feed on chestnuts and acorns. The charcuterie, unsurprisingly, is top-notch, and the passionate staff will happily give you a tasting.

## DIRECTORY

**Banks** Bonifacio only has two central ATMs: at Société Générale, 38 rue St-Érasme, and La Banque Postale, rue St-Dominique, and they frequently run out of bills, so go early in the day if you need cash.

**Hospital de Bonifacio** Lieu dit Valle; emergency unit 24/7
**Police Muncipale** Rue Paul Nicolaï; for emergencies, call 15.

# Around Bonifacio

At the head of the Montée Rastello, the cobbled stone pathway known as the **Sentier Campu Rumanilu** climbs up to the clifftops east of the city, affording spectacular views.

The main trail up to the viewpoints and back will take you about an hour, but you can also continue for another hour or so, along the maquis-clad Pertusatu trail.

## Îles Lavezzi

Perhaps the most impressive views of Bonifacio are from the sea, and each day a flotilla of excursion **boats** (see page 120) ferry visitors out to the best vantage points, most notably the **Îles Lavezzi**, the scattering of small islets where the troop ship *Sémillante* was shipwrecked in 1855, now designated as a nature reserve. The whole experience of bobbing around to an amplified running commentary is about as touristy as Bonifacio gets, but it's well worth enduring just to round the mouth of the harbour and see the *vieille ville*, perched atop the famous chalk cliffs. The Lavezzi islets themselves are surrounded by wonderfully clear sea water, offering Corsica's best snorkelling. Clouds of fish swirl around in front of you, giving the impression that you're in the Indian Ocean rather than the Mediterranean. On your way back, you skirt the famous **Île Cavallo**, or "millionaire's island", where the likes of Princess Caroline of Monaco and other French and Italian glitterati have luxury hideaways.

## The beaches

The **beaches** within walking distance of Bonifacio are generally smaller and less appealing than most in southern Corsica. For a dazzling splash of turquoise, you'll have to follow the narrow, twisting lane east of town in the direction of Pertusatu lighthouse, turning left when you see signs for **Piantarella**, Corsica's kitesurfing hotspot. A twenty-minute walk south around the shore from there takes you past the remains of a superbly situated Roman villa to a pair of divine little coves, **Grand Sperone** and **Petit Sperone** – both shallow and perfect for kids.

Another superb beach in the area is **Rondinara**, a perfect shell-shaped cove of turquoise water enclosed by dunes and a pair of twin headlands. Located 10km north (east of N198), it's sufficiently off the beaten track to remain relatively peaceful (outside school holidays). Facilities are minimal, limited to a smart wooden beach restaurant, a paying car park and a 4-star resort (see below). Shade is at a premium, so come armed with a parasol.

**ACCOMMODATION**                                **AROUND BONIFACIO**

**Camping Rondinara** Rondinara beach; https://camping-rondinara.com. This brand-new 4-star campsite is the only one at Rondinara, with sites scattered between clumps of maquis. There's a bar and pizzeria, a mini-supermarket and a swimming pool, but ecolodge tents and mobile homes to rent. Ecolodge tents & Caravans €; mobile homes €€

**Terrasses de Rondinara** Rondinara beach; https://lesterrassesderondinara.com. Lavish 4-star villas with space for up to six people, nestled in the maquis with a direct access road to the beach. There's also a restaurant and cocktail bar overlooking the ginormous ocean-view infinity pool. €€€€

# Porto-Vecchio and around

Set on a hillock overlooking a beautiful deep blue bay, **PORTO-VECCHIO**, 25km north of Bonifacio, was rated by James Boswell as one of "the most distinguished harbours in Europe". It was founded in 1539 as a second Genoese stronghold on the east coast, Bastia being well established in the north. The site was perfect: close to the unexploited and fertile plain, it benefited from secure high land and a sheltered harbour, although the mosquito population spread malaria and wiped out the first Ligurian settlers within months. Things began to take off mainly thanks to the cork industry, which still thrived well into the twentieth century. Today most revenue comes from tourists, the vast majority of them well-heeled Italians who flock here for

Bastia

Hyper U
supermarket

Golfe de Porto Vecchio

# PORTO VECCHIO

| EATING | |
|---|---|
| A Cantina di l'Orriu | 2 |
| L'Allegria | 3 |
| L'Ardoise | 6 |
| Chez Pino | 1 |
| Nymphea | 5 |
| Sushi Bar | 4 |

AVENUE GEORGES POMPIDOU

RUE HENRI FRENAY

AVENUE GEORGES POMPIDOU

Ospedale & Zonza

RUE GIUDICE DI CINARCA

CHEMIN DE COVASINA

RUE DI STAZZALE

AVENUE MARÉCHAL LECLERC

RUE PASTEUR

RUE JOHN ANTOINE NAU

AVENUE GEORGES POMPIDOU

Buses to Bonifacio

RUE TOUSSAINT CULIOLI

RUE BORGO

Mairie

La Citadina
bus stop

RUE DES OLIVIERS

AVENUE MARÉCHAL LECLERC

PLACE
DE LA
RÉPUBLIQUE

R. DR. C. P. ROCCA SERRA

Citadelle de
Porto-Vecchio

HAUTE
VILLE

R. A. MICHELIN

R. BONAPARTE

Église St-Jean Baptiste

R. QUENZA

CONS. R. PORTE GÉNOISE

Porte Génoise

QUAI PASCAL PAOLI

RUE JEAN NICOLI

R. GÉNÉRAL DE GAULLE

RUE BAPTISTE MARCELLESI

RUE COMMANDANT L'HERMINIER

Airport
bus stop

Marina

QUAI PASCAL PAOLI

RUE JEAN JAURÈS

RUE SAINT VINCENT

RUE DE QUNTANA-VECCHIA

RUE DRAGUT

STRETTA DI U PURGATORIU

RUE COMMANDANT L'HERMINIER

VOIE ROMAINE

RUE MARSHAL ALESSANDRINI

RUE DENIS DE OCCA SERRA

CHEMIN DE MARINA VILLAGE

QUAI DE SYRACUSE

Ferries to Marseille and Livorno

N

RUE DE LA BCR

| ACCOMMODATION | |
|---|---|
| Camping Arutoli | 1 |
| Camping La Matonara | 2 |
| Hôtel Casadelmar | 5 |
| Holzer | 4 |
| Mistral | 3 |
| San Giovanni | 6 |

| DRINKING & NIGHTLIFE | |
|---|---|
| Bar a Bière Corse | 3 |
| Le Pointe de Vue | 1 |
| La Taverne du Roi | 4 |
| Le Vinyle | 2 |

0                    100
metres

Palombaggia, Santa Giulia, Figari Airport & Bonifacio

the fine outlying **beaches**. To the northwest, the little town of **Zonza** makes a good base for exploring the dramatic forest that surrounds one of Corsica's most awesome road trips, the **route de Bavella**.

Around the centre of town, there's not much to see apart from the well-preserved **fortress** and the small grid of **ancient streets** backing onto the main place de la République, packed with independent boutiques, bars and restaurants. East of the square you can't miss the **Porte Génoise**, which frames a delightful expanse of sea and saltpans and through which you'll find the quickest route down to the modern marina, which is lined with cafés and restaurants.

## ARRIVAL AND INFORMATION PORTO-VECCHIO AND AROUND

**By plane** Figari airport (https://figari-aeroport.cci.corsica), 28km southwest, is served mostly by domestic departures to the French mainland. A seasonal *navette* runs two to four times daily from the marina (https://cc-sudcorse.fr/navettes-aeroport-figari-sud-corse/).

**By bus** Porto-Vecchio doesn't have a bus station; instead, the various companies who come here stop and depart by the marina. The tourist office has information on departure times and stops.

Destinations Ajaccio (2–4 daily; 3hr 30min); Bastia (2 daily; 2hr 45min–3hr); Bonifacio (1–4 daily; 30–40min); Propriano (2–4 daily; 1hr 40min); Sartène (2–4 daily; 1hr 35min).

**Tourist office** Porto-Vecchio's large tourist office (http://ot-portovecchio.com) is at the Espace Jean-Paul de Rocca Serra on Rue Fred Scamaroni.

## ACCOMMODATION SEE MAP PAGE 122

As most visitors staying in this region during the summer come for fly-drive villa holidays, hotel accommodation is thin on the ground, especially at the bottom end.

**Camping Arutoli** 1 route de l'ospédale; http://arutoli.com. Tall pines and cork oaks provide welcome shade at this three-star campsite. There are 110 pitches for tents, campervans and caravans, plus a range of accommodation, the cheapest of which are the tiny wooden "pods". Tents & pods €

**Camping La Matonara** Rue Giudice de Cinarca; http://camping-matonara.fr. North of the city and within easy reach of the Hyper U supermarket, this is the most easily accessible site in the area. Pitches are shaded by cork trees, but bring plenty of mozzie repellent. €

**Hôtel Casadelmar** Route de Palombaggia; https://casadelmar.fr. East of Porto-Vecchio, in a spectacular spot looking out over the Gulf, this five-star hotel is a stunning

accomplishment of modern architecture. Clean lines and beach-inspired minimalism take precedence throughout the rooms, and the oceanfront pool is mesmerising. €€€€

**Holzer** 12 rue Jean-Jaurès; http://hotel-holzer.com. Labyrinthine place with rather cramped, unexciting rooms, but immaculately clean and very central. They also have triple and quad rooms. €€

**Mistral** Rue Jean-Nicoli; http://lemistral.eu. Comfortable mid-range three-star, slightly removed from the noisy centre of town. There's a lovely flower-filled, shady terrace outside, and rooms are sleek, if a little old-fashioned, with air-conditioning and wood floors. €€

**San Giovanni** 2km south on route d'Arca; http://hotel-san-giovanni.com. Thirty comfortable, bright and airy rooms set in landscaped gardens, with a heated pool, jacuzzi, sauna, tennis court, ping pong table and children's games area. It's well-run, peaceful and great value. €€€

## EATING SEE MAP PAGE 122

You won't go hungry in Porto Vecchio: there's a wealth of excellent restaurants catering for all tastes and cuisines, many of which are deservedly popular (reservations are highly recommended).

★ **A Cantina di l'Orriu** 5 cours Napoléon; https://lorriu.fr. In a leafy garden setting, the city's most popular epicerie – selling the highest quality regional produce – opens its door for a menu inspired by said produce. The flavours of the terroir shine through whether you're tucking into a juicy *jarret de bœuf de montagne* or a *filet mignon de cochon noir*, all expertly paired with a regional red. €€

**L'Allegria** Rue Dr Camille de Rocca Serra. Perennially popular spot just off the main drag. Simple dishes executed well are the name of the game here. The seafood is

particularly good – try the fried calamari or the piquant *ragout de calamars au chorizo*. The homemade brioche perdue au speculoos is a velvety dream. €€

**L'Ardoise** Rue Maréchal Juin; https://ardoise.restaurant. five-minute drive out of town, this casual eatery cooks up some of the best *pot au feu* and *roll bavette à l'Italienne* in the South. Cap it off with a tangy *tartlette clémentines et crumble*. €

★ **Chez Pino** 7 Rue Pasteur. You know you're onto a good thing when you keep getting turned away because it's full. Lesson learned: book a table at this hugely popular Italian restaurant. Luckily, it's worth the wait – the pizzas are baked to doughy perfection, staff are good-humoured, and the aromas wafting over from the open kitchen will have

5

you salivating in anticipation. €
**Nymphea** Mnt de la Prte Génoise. This chic little eatery is one of few vegan places in Corsica, and its diminutive menu packs a nutrient punch. Tuck into a peanut and ginger poke bowl or a creamy vegan lasagne; they also serve a selection of homemade desserts and sweet treats. Lunchtimes only. €

★ **Sushi Bar** 18 Rue du Général de Gaulle; http://sushibar.fr. This atmospheric sushi emporium put a lot more effort into their cuisine than they did coming up with their name. You'll find all the usual suspects on the menu, and the sushi is as fresh as it gets. They have some unusual but delicious, cocktails too. €€€

### DRINKING & NIGHTLIFE

SEE MAP PAGE 122

**Bar a Bière Corse** 14 Rue U Borgo. This hole-in-the-wall beer bar always seems to have a crowd outside, but they're generally a friendly bunch, and the owner loves nothing more than introducing a newcomer to the world of Corsican beer. There are only a couple of *Pietra* beers on tap; the rest are bottled, but they have plenty of beers that are hard to find elsewhere, as well as mixing up some beer-based cocktails.
**Le Pointe de Vue** Av. du Maréchal Leclerc. Located within the Best Western Hôtel Alcyon, this swanky cocktail bar has a glittering view over the gulf and some fabulous – and inventive – cocktails.

**La Taverne du Roi** 43 Rue U Borgo. Built right into the wall of the old medieval city gate is an atmosphere nightclub and intimate live music venue. There's a cover charge, and expect to be turned away if you don't meet the smart-casual dress code.
**Le Vinyle** 10 Rue U Borgo. This slick, black-painted bar decorated with old vinyl records is one of the coolest places to drink in town, and they sometimes host live bands, too. There's a lengthy wine list, but they also make a mean cocktail and some delicious tapas, all named after music icons.

# Golfe de Porto-Vecchio

Much of the coast of the **Golfe de Porto-Vecchio** and its environs is characterised by ugly development and hectares of swampland, yet some of the clearest, bluest sea and whitest beaches on Corsica are also here. The most frequented of these, Palombaggia and Santa Giulia, can be reached by **bus** from the town in summer, timetables for which are posted in the tourist office; at other times, you'll need your own transport.

## The beaches

A golden semicircle of sand edged by short, twisted umbrella pines and red rocks, the **plage de Palombaggia** is south Corsica's trademark beach and indisputably one of the most beautiful bays in Europe. Come here outside the school holidays and you'll find it hard to resist the striking colours and clear water. But in summer the crowds can be simply overwhelming. One possible compromise is to press on south to two other smaller, less famous beaches just beyond Palombaggia – **Cala di la Folaca** and the **plage d'Acciaju** – where the sand is just as white and the water equally translucent. Narrow access lanes and *pistes* drop down to them from the main road at regular intervals, but the best way to enjoy this exquisite string of coves is by walking along them.

A few kilometres further south along the same road takes you over the Bocca di l'Oru to the plage de **Santa Giulia**, a spectacular white-sand beach and turquoise bay. The presence of several sprawling holiday villages and facilities for windsurfing and other watersports ensures large crowds from early in the season, but the colours alone warrant a detour. Shallow and crystal-clear, the water is especially good for little ones.

North of Porto-Vecchio, the first beach worth a visit is **San Ciprianu**, a half-moon bay of white sand, reached by turning right off the D468 at the VITO petrol station and following the road down to the sea. If you instead carry on for another 8km, you'll come to the even more picturesque beach at **Pinarellu**, an uncrowded, long sweep of soft white sand with a Genoese watchtower and, like the less inspiring

5

beaches immediately north of here, benefiting from the spectacular backdrop of the Massif de l'Ospédale.

## The route de Bavella

Starting from just north of the resort of **Solenzara** on the east coast, and winding 40km through the mountains to the picture-postcard-pretty mountain village of **ZONZA**, the D268 – known locally as the **route de Bavella** – is among the most dramatic roads in Corsica. To get there from Porto Vecchio, follow the squiggly D368 up through the mountains to Zonza, stopping along the way at the idyllic **Ospédale Dam**. The surrounding **forêt de l'Ospédale** is home to a treetop adventure park and several via ferratas (https://xtremsud.com), while just to the north, a trail runs to the **Piscia di Gallu** waterfall.

From Zonza, the road penetrates a dense expanse of old pine and chestnut trees as it rises steadily to the **Col de Bavella** (1218m), where a towering statue of **Notre-Dame-des-Neiges** marks the windswept pass itself. An amazing panorama of peaks and forests spreads out from the col: to the northwest, the serrated granite ridge of the Cirque de Gio Agostino is dwarfed by the pink pinnacles of the **Aiguilles de Bavella**; behind soars Monte Incudine.

### Bavella

Just below the Col de Bavella, the seasonal hamlet of **BAVELLA** comprises a handful of congenial cafés, corrugated-iron-roofed chalets and hikers' hostels from where you can follow a series of waymarked **trails** to nearby viewpoints. Deservedly the most popular of these is the two-hour walk to the **Trou de la Bombe**, a circular opening that pierces the Paliri crest of peaks. From the car park behind the *Auberge du Col* follow the red-and-white waymarks of GR20 for 800m, then head right when you see orange splashes. The Bavella area is also among the most popular places on the island for canyoning (https://corsica-forest.com).

**ACCOMMODATION AND EATING**        **GOLFE DE PORTO-VECCHIO**

★ **Cocoon Village** Along the D638 opposite the Ospedale dam; http://glampingcorsica.com/. Pack light as you'll be climbing ladders and shuffling across swing bridges to reach these extraordinary glamping "cocoons". Set high in the clifftops of the Vizzavona forest, there are five geodesic domes – all unique – either suspended from the trees or perched on dizzying treetop terraces. Not only will you fall asleep beneath the stars and wake up to the forest canopy, but you can sleep easy knowing that this back-to-nature hotel with its solar showers and compost toilet is also eco-certified. €€€€

★ **L'Eternisula** Along the D420 in Zonza; https://leternisula.com/. Hearty and healthy sustenance for adventurers served in a bright and airy dining room or beneath the fairy lights in the courtyard. Classic dishes each get a local twist – think crispy courgette fritters fragranced with Corsican mint, nutty bowls of homemade humous with a swirl of local olive oil, or *croque-monsieurs* oozing with *fromage corse*. Closed on Mondays. €

# Eastern Corsica

IDYLLIC SCENES NEAR ALÉRIA

# Eastern Corsica

If you've cut your teeth on the mighty peaks and canyons of the central massifs or the white-chalk bluffs and bustling beach resorts of the south, then Eastern Corsica might appear, at first glance, to have little to offer. The eastern plain has little in the way of star attractions and distinguishing landmarks, but between its lacklustre towns, agricultural foothills, and sleepy fishing villages, you'll find some idyllic spots far from the crowds. This is the place to embrace slow travel, lingering along near-deserted beaches, sampling fresh-from-the-lagoon oysters and exploring the ruins of the island's once-mighty Roman capital.

Travelling up from the south, **Solenzara** is the first major town of the *Corse Orientale* and home to one of the best beaches on the eastern shore, the **Plage de Scaffa Rossa**. It's a quiet base for beach-hopping along the **Côte des Nacres**, named for the priceless mother-of-pearl that was once harvested along its shores, or excursions into the mountains, with the jagged skyline of the Aiguilles de Bavella and the shaded woodlands of the **Forêt de Tova** both within easy reach.

More beautiful beaches await along the **Costa Serena** between **Ghisonaccia** and **Aléria,** bejewelled with oyster-filled saltwater lagoons. The **site archéologique d'Aléria** is the east coast's headline act, where the treasures include Roman ruins, a Genoese fortress and artefacts excavated from fourth-century BC Etruscan tombs. In-between beaches and ancient finds, you can also stroll through the beachside **Forêt de Pinia**, enjoy oyster tasting at the **Étang de Diana** or discover the miracle plant that brought luxury brand L'Occitane en Provence to Corsica at the immersive **Musée d'Immortelle**.

**Moriani-plage** is the flagship beach resort of the sun-soaked **Costa Verde**, but the simple pleasures of inland **Casinga** and **Castagnicca** will soon entice you into the mountains. Beneath the veil of chestnut and hazelnut forests, the sloping hills are home to picturesque stone villages and ambling footpaths, where you can swim beneath waterfalls, admire sequestered Baroque churches, and visit the childhood home of Corsican revolutionary hero **Pascal Paoli**.

## GETTING THERE AND AROUND

The infrequent buses from Bastia to Porto Vecchio (https://rapides-bleus.com) stop at Ghisonaccia and Aléria en route, but aside from this, public transport is pretty much non-existent in eastern Corsica and renting a car is essential.

**By car** The RT10 highway, one of the straightest, smoothest roads in all of Corsica, runs the entire of the east coast, making navigating a cinch. All of the main towns lie along the highway; from there, you can head west into the mountains or east to the beaches and lagoons.

**By plane** Bastia's Poretta airport (http://bastia.aeroport.fr) is 25km north of Moriani-Plage, while Figari airport (https://figari-aeroport.cci.corsica) is 60km from Solenzara. Neither offer shuttles to towns along the east coast, so you would need to take a taxi or rent a car.

# Solenzara and around

Straddling the RT10, about 40km north of Porto Vecchio, **Solenzara** is the obvious choice for exploring the southern reaches of the *Corse Orientale*. The village itself has little to offer aside from a smattering of shops and cafés and a small marina, but set at the mouth of the Solenzara River, it's a strategic base for exploring the much-photographed **Aiguilles de Bavella**, and it's far quieter than nearby Porto Vecchio, especially in summer.

From Solenzara, follow the **Route de Bavella** (see page 125) along the scenic D268 into the mountains, where you can hike, go canyoning or enjoy **wild swimming** at one of the

SCULPTURE AT THE MUSÉE D'ARCHÉOLOGIE D'ALERIA

# Highlights

**❶ Plage de Scaffa Rossa** Flanked by rocky coves, Solenzara's most handsome beach has fine shingle sands and crystalline waters. See page 131

**❷ Musée d'Immortelle** Local legends and global beauty brands like L'Occitaine en Provence swear by this wrinkle-zapping, acne-soothing yellow flower. See page 133

**❸ Forêt de Pinia** Maritime pines stretch from the sea up to the Étang d'Urbino lagoon, hiding some rare and endangered bird species in their folds. See page 134

**❹ Site archéologique d'Aléria** On a hilltop just south of the modern town, the well-preserved ruins of Alalia tell the story of Corsica's ancient Roman capital. See page 135

**❺ Étang de Diana** Breathe in the ocean air and sample some fresh-from-the-sea oysters at this idyllic coastal lagoon. See page 136

**❻ Chestnuts** The humble chestnut gets a makeover in the tree-studded foothills of Castagniccia, where they are dried, roasted, and milled into flour according to age-old traditions. See page 138

**❼ Musée Pascal Paoli** The hero of Corsican independence and one-time head of the Corsica Republic is the subject of this small museum in the heart of Castagniccia. See page 140

**HIGHLIGHTS ARE MARKED ON THE MAP ON PAGE 130**

# EASTERN CORSICA

0 — 5 kilometres

N

**CASINCA**

→ Bastia    Casamozza
Vescovato    Venzolasca
Campile
San Tomaso
di Pastoreccia    Loreto di Casina
Valle di Rostino
Santa Maria
di Riscamone
Morosaglia    Col di Prato
La Porta    ⑥
**CASTAGNICCIA**    Pruno-Casette
Monte San
Petrone
(1767 m)    Piazzole
Campana    Valle
Piedicroce    d'Orezza    San
Stazzona    Giovanni
di Moriani
Carcheto    Felce    San-Nicolao
Santa
Reparata
di Moriani    Cervione
Col d'Arcarotta    Prunete
Alesani

⑦

Corte

Corte

Calvi

**COSTA VERDE**

Moriani-Plage

**BOZIO**

Phare d'Alistro    🗼

Bravone

Antisanti

**Tour de Diane** 🏰    ⑤
Étang
de Diane
Aléria/Cateraggio
Site archéologique d'Aléria    ④    Plage de
Padulone

Ghisoni
Défilé de L'Inzecca

**TYRRHENIAN
SEA**

**FIUMORBO**    Étang
d'Urbino

Prunelli di Fiumorbo    ③    **FORÊT DE PINIA** 🌲
GR20    Ghisonaccia
Punta di a
Cappella
(2042 m)    Pietrapola    ②    **Musée d'Immortelle**
San Gavino    Plage de Vignale
di Fiumorbo    Serra di Fiumorbo

Ventiseri
Mare a Mare Centre    Étang
de Palo

Chisà Via Ferrata    ✈ **Airforce Base**
d'U Calanconu
Solaro    Travo    Marine de Solaro

**COSTA SERENA**

**FORÊT DE
TOVA**    ①    Plage de Scaffa Rossa
Solenzara

---

## HIGHLIGHTS

① Plage de Scaffa Rossa
② Musée d'Immortelle
③ Forêt de Pinia
④ Site archéologique d'Aléria
⑤ Étang de Diane
⑥ Chestnuts
⑦ Musée Pascal Paoli

numerous natural pools along the Solenzara Village (ask for a map from the tourist office). Just to the north, the **Forêt de Tova** and the mountain village of **Chisa** are equally popular spots for outdoor activities, and far less frequented than the canyons of Bavella.

## Plage de Scaffa Rossa

Over the river on the north side of town, Solenzara's biggest draw is the gloriously sandy **Scaffa Rossa** beach, a long crescent of sun-bleached sands that tapers out into a series of rocky coves at the north end. In summer, you can rent sunbeds and parasols from La Voile Rouge (https://la-voile-rouge.edan.io) and kayaks and SUPs from (https://corse-canyoning-parc.com/). There's free parking available and a large campsite by the beachside.

**6**

### ARRIVAL AND DEPARTURE      SOLENZARA AND AROUND

**By boat** Solenzara's small marina welcomes private vessels (https://portdesolenzara.com).

**By bus** Long-distance buses (https://rapides-bleus.com) between Bastia and Porto-Vecchio stop along the RT10 right in the centre of town. Times vary throughout the year and services are limited in low season.

**Destinations** Aléria (1–2 daily; 40 mins); Bastia (1-2 daily; 2hr 10); Porto-Vecchio (1–2 daily; 50min).

### INFORMATION AND GETTING AROUND

**Tourist office** Place des Ancienne Ecoles (https://www.alta-rocca-tourisme.com) hands out free maps of the region and has plenty of info about hiking trails and activities.

**Car rental** Hertz Along the RT10, right by the tourist office

(https://hertz.fr).

**By boat** Marine Voile Location (Solenzara marina; https://corse-location-voilier.fr) offers boat cruises and motorboat rentals.

### ACCOMMODATION

Solenzara has slim pickings when it comes to hotels, but there are some great campsites along the river.

**Les 3 Terrasses** 49 Via di u Commandanti Poli; http://les3terrasses.com. Bright, wood-floored rooms with comfy beds, right in the centre of town – ask for a room with a sea view. There's a busy restaurant downstairs, but it can get loud on weekend evenings, so be warned. €€

**Camping Cote des Nacres** Solaro; off the RT10; http://campingdesnacres.fr. There's both beachside and riverside camping here, and you can pitch your tent right on the sand if you want. The campsite has a shop, restaurant and games areas, and they run a shuttle to the Aguilles de Bavella in

season. The only downside is the distinct lack of shade. €

**Case Vanille** 9 A Muvra d'Oru; http://casevanille.com. Set on the hillside above town with a large pool and flowery gardens, this gite has space for four or six people. Rooms are all individually decorated and you'll be welcomed with open arms by your hosts. Weekly bookings only. €€€

**Sole di Sari** 1000 Strada Di Bavella; https://soledisari.com. The best of the tourist residences that Solenzara is known for, with a lush canopy of trees overlooking the four-pool complex and activities organised for kids in summer. Lodges and mobile homes €€; ecolodge tents €

### EATING

**L'Acinu** Along the RT10 in the centre of town. Drawing a big crowd on Friday and Saturday evenings, this tapas bar has a reliable cocktail list and a decent selection of wines from around the island. Pair your drink with a planche of charcuterie or a variety of tapas to share – the *beignets aux fleurs de courgettes* are the perfect finger food. €

★ **Le Bar Jean "LBJ"** Along the RT10 in the centre of town; https://lebarjean.fr. A rare find in a small town, this modern haunt has an innovative cocktail list, a mouth-watering tapas list, and a menu replete with tasteful puns

and fun, tongue-in-cheek references. Snag a spot on the olive tree-studded terrace and order yourself a veal tajine or a sea bream ceviche, all sourced from local producers. €€

**O Resto**      Maison Medori, Via di U Commandanti Poli. Fish, fresh from the local harbour, is the order of the day here. The *plats du jours* depend on the daily catch, but you can count on a generous bowl of *moules nustrale* or a seared red tuna steak. If you're not in the mood for seafood, the pasta – homemade on-site – is a close contender. €€

## Chisa and the Forêt de Tova

About a half-hour drive northwest of Solenzara, the tiny village of **Chisa** occupies an idyllic leafy enclave in the foothills of Monte Incudine. A number of footpaths set out from here, and there are several *gîtes d'etapes* catering to hikers passing through on the **mare è monte** long-distance trail. Another highlight for adventurers is the **via ferrata** (https://alpacorse.com) that scales the rocky crag just outside of town. South of the village, the Mare e Monte continues through the dense woodlands of the **Forêt de Tova**, where old shepherd's huts dot the mountainsides.

### ACCOMMODATION                    CHISA AND THE FORÊT DE TOVA

**La pause.Chisa** South of Chisa, along the Travu River; +33628251925. A vision in oak and rattan, this delightful converted *bergerie* sits firmly on the chic side of rustic. Taking "the middle of nowhere" to new levels, the view from the deck is a thick carpet of forest in all directions, and you can enjoy it from your outdoor jacuzzi, rolltop bath or rocking chair. There's also a pool. **€€€**

# Costa Serena

Long tracts of white sand contour the east coast around **Ghisonaccia** and **Aléria**, bestowing the **Costa Serena** with its name. Far from the shoulder-to-shoulder crush of the southern beaches, the east coast beaches retain much of their wild side. A sweeping toupée of maritime pines hems in much of the shore, cocooning half a dozen saltwater lagoons, where coastal walks, birdwatching and oyster tasting are the preferred activities.

Aside from its serene coastline, the eastern plain has little to boast of in the way of top attractions, but the **Site archéologique d'Aléria** is worth a visit for its excellent museum, and there are some great hikes traversing the hills of the **Fiumorbo** region to the west of Ghisonaccia.

## Ghisonaccia and around

Best known as the gateway to the Forêt de Pinia (see page 134) and its beach, the **plage de Tignale**, just east of town, there's little reason to hang around in the small town of **Ghisonaccia**. The diminutive **Église Saint Michel**, a 5-minute walk from the main drag, is worth a visit for its surprising neo-Byzantine frescos, the work of Greek artist Nikos N. Giannakakis, while the town's other claim to fame – two "remarkable trees" – lie 5km out of town along the Fiomurbo River. One, a marvellously overgrown pistachio tree, is said to be more than a thousand years old; the other, a 500m walk away, is a cork oak nicknamed the "bird tree" for its knobbled trunk in the shape of a raptor.

### ARRIVAL AND DEPARTURE                    GHISONACCIA AND AROUND

**By bus** Long-distance buses (https://rapides-bleus.com) between Bastia and Porto-Vecchio stop at Bar Chi Fa – THALASSA voyages along the RT10 just north of the village. Times vary throughout the year and services are limited in low season.

Destinations Aléria (1–2 daily; 25 mins); Bastia (1-2 daily; 2hr 25); Porto-Vecchio (1–2 daily; 1hr 5min).

### INFORMATION AND GETTING AROUND

**Tourist office** Rte de Ghisoni (http://corseorientale.com/) gives out free regional maps and has detailed information on hiking routes.
**Car rental** Europcar 40 Rte de Ghisoni; https://europcar.fr
**Active tours** Corsica River (https://corsicariver.fr) have canyoning, mountain biking and snorkelling excursions that depart from Ghisonaccia.

**Horse riding** Cavullu & Co (https://cavalluandco.wixsite.com/cavalluandco) offer rides in the forest or on the beach for all levels.
**Skydiving** Corse Parachutisme Tandem (https://corse-parachutisme-tandem.fr) offers tandem flights from mid-June to mid-Oct over the beaches of the East Coast.

### ACCOMMODATION AND EATING

Ghisonaccia has limited options in the village, but you'll find more options along the beach just east of town.

## IMMORTELLE: CORSICA'S SECRET CURE-ALL

Amid the fragrant herbs and shrubs that bloom throughout Corsica's wild maquis, there's one plant that you'll hear locals raving about – *helichrysum*, more commonly known as *immortelle*. If the name conjures up images of the mystic or the divine, that's probably no mistake, because this Mediterranean plant is known for its "miracle" (and later, science-based) anti-ageing properties and is infused in everything from essential oils and luxury face creams to craft beer. Emblematic of Corsica, it's been revered since ancient times, mentioned in Homer's *Odyssey* and woven into flower crowns during old summer solstice rituals.

Immortelle grows in short, dense bushes, a little over knee height, with distinctive clusters of golden yellow flowers that bloom from May to August and thrive in the arid, rocky terrain of the Corsican maquis under the hot Mediterranean sun. Rub the flowers between your fingers, and they release a pungent, curry-esque smell. There are more than 500 known species of immortelle, all of which have varying properties, but just one that is endemic to Corsica, *a Murzella*; others also grow in the hills of Sicily, Portugal and Tunisia.

The secret of immortelle is said to lie in its everlasting flowers: the sunny yellow blooms never wilt, even when picked. Of greater interest to dermatologists is the plant's high concentration of *italidiones,* known for their anti-inflammatory qualities, which – according to the research laboratories of **L'Occitaine en Provence**, who use the flower in several of their cosmetic products – also have an anti-ageing effect on the skin. The oil is also said to help with a raft of ailments from sunburn, acne and rosacea to hematomas and conjunctivitis.

For a fascinating insight into all things immortelle, **Helios di Corsica** operates the immersive full-sensory **Musée de L'Immortelle** (Route de la Mer, Ghisonaccia; free; https://heliosdicorsica.com), where you can touch and smell the flowers, as well as learn all about the complex distillation process that transforms them into essential oils – a whopping 500kg are needed to produce just 1.2 litres of the precious elixir. The museum also takes a look at the future of sustainable agriculture, detailing the steps taken by L'Occitaine en Provence to set up their 100 percent organic and sustainable immortelle plantations in Corsica.

### HOW TO TRY IMMORTELLE

The Helios di Corsica shop has a huge variety of products on sale, including natural soaps, face creams and essential oils. Other well-known local brands include **Casanera** (https://casanera.com), who produce a range of immortelle-infused oils and cosmetics, and **Mardy's Garden** (https://immortelle.pro), who operate a farm near Calvi.

**Paolina** (https://paolina.fr/) and **Ribella** (see page 58), two of Corsica's most beloved beers, also famously produce beers made with the aromas of immortelle. Look out for immortelle in a variety of local recipes and products, too, from jams and sauces to meat dishes where the flowers are used to flavour the stew.

---

**Arinella Bianca** 769 Strada di Bruschettu; https://arinellabianca.com. If you want your camping experience served with a spoonful of five-star luxury, then this sprawling mega-complex, complete with an aquatic park, a choice of restaurants and a spa, is for you. Mobile homes and chalets range in quality – and price – but there are some good deals in shoulder season. Tent spots are also available, but they book up fast. €€€€

**A Casa di Maria Cicilia** 60 rte Ghisoni; http://www.casamariacicilia.com. Housed in a former post office built in the 1930s, this hotel has a variety of room options, some of which sleep six. The rooms are nothing to write home about, but they are clean, functional and comfortable. €

**Ghiso Beach** Plage de Vignale; https://ghisobeach.com. Pull up a wicker armchair at this swish bar-restaurant right on the beach, and let yourself be tempted by the lengthy cocktail list. Food wise, the equally extensive menu covers all the bases, from the healthy (salads and poke bowls) to the hearty (300g rump steaks), with plenty of burgers, tapas and sandwiches inbetween. €€

**Lodge les Muriers** Lot les Mûriers, 2.5km south of Ghisonaccia; www.facebook.com/lodgelesmuriers. At this eco-friendly *chambre d'hôte*, you can choose between a cute wooden "tortoise cabin" (so-called because of its green, curved roof) or a safari tent in the grounds of your host's house. Breakfast, dinner and a jacuzzi are included, and you have access to a pleasant outdoor shower and compost toilet. €€

## Forêt de Pinia and Étang d'Urbino

East of Ghisonaccia town, the **Forêt de Pinia** is criss-crossed by a network of shaded footpaths that weave through the tall maritime pines and stretch for almost 5km to the southern banks of the **Étang d'Urbino**. It's the largest coastal forest on the island, with a thick fringe of maritime pines that border the wild and undeveloped **plage de Pinia**, an expanse of soft white sands and gentle waves. There are dedicated walking, horse riding and cycling trails through the forest, and you'll be able to find a quiet patch of sand along the beach, even in the depths of summer.

The forest opens out onto a vast saltwater lagoon, the **Étang d'Urbino**, a feeding and nesting ground for several rare and endangered birds. Great cormorant, great egret and great-crested grebe are frequent visitors, along with pink flamingoes.

**GETTING THERE**        **FORÊT DE PINIA AND ÉTANG D'URBINO**

**By car** There are four free car parks dotted throughout the Forêt de Pinia; the bumpy roads are accessible without a 4WD if you drive carefully, although may occasionally be impassable after rainfall. You can also reach the Étang d'Urbino by a small access lane along the northwest shore, where you'll find a free car park by the lakeside.

**EATING**

**Restaurant d'Urbino** https://www.fb.com/profile.php?id=100063582432854. On the northwest shore, this lakeside fishing hut is the place to enjoy delicious fresh oysters or *moules-frites* with views across the lagoon. Open from May to September, lunchtimes only. €€€

## Fiumorbo region

West of Ghisonaccia, the **Fiumorbo** and Abatesco rivers snake their way up into the mountains flanked by rolling woodlands that extend along the coast to Aléria. The dozen rural villages perched on the hillsides each have their own charm, as do the interlinking footpaths that run between them, many passing natural pools and old Genoese bridges, and some joining up with the Mare è Monte Livantinu and Mare à Mare long-distance trails. Enthusiastic hikers can even walk far enough to join part of the GR20, which passes west of the village of **San Gavino di Fiumorbo**. Pick up a map from the tourist office (see page 132) detailing the various footpaths before setting out or enquire about hiring a local guide (A Sarrada Randonées offer guided excursions year-round in French; https://asarrada.com).

Highlights include the panoramic views from **Prunelli di Fiumorbo**, the 10th-century ruins of the Château de Covasina in **Ventiseri**, and the aforementioned San Gavino di Fiumorbo, known for its seventeenth-century Baroque church. There's also **Pietrapola**, famous for its thermal waters since Roman times, and the picturesque **Serra di Fiumorbo**, around which you can explore the ruins of two Romanesque chapels.

# Aléria and around

Built on the estuary at the mouth of the River Tavignano, **ALÉRIA** was first settled in 564 BC by a colony of Greek Phocaeans as a trading port for copper and lead, as well as wheat, olives and grapes. After an interlude of Carthaginian rule, the Romans arrived in 259 BC, built a naval base and re-established its importance in the Mediterranean. Aléria remained the east coast's principal port right up until the eighteenth century. Today, little is left of the historic town except for its hilltop Roman ruins and nearby Genoese fort, which are among the most visited attractions of Eastern Corsica. The modern town, known as **Cateraggio**, lies just northeast of the archaeological site. It's little more than a strip of modern buildings straddling the main road, and the nearby **Étang de Diana** is a far better use of your time once you've explored the ruins.

# Site archéologique d'Aléria

Charge • https://bit.ly/48q1hlk • Free parking available

Set aside at least a couple of hours to explore the **site archéologique d'Aléria**, which stands high on the hilltop surrounded by chequered fields and green vineyards. From the car park, follow the road up the hill and around to the right until you reach the hamlet of **Le Fort**, a cluster of old buildings that date between the eleventh and thirteenth centuries, some using a base of stones from the Roman city. Tickets can be purchased in the yellow-painted **Maison Rossi** and include admission to the museum and the archaeological site.

**6**

## Le Fort

The hamlet is part-way through an extensive renovation project to restore the old buildings, destined to house exhibitions and study facilities to aid ongoing excavations of the archaeological site. However, progress is slow, and the various buildings seem to open and close to the public somewhat spontaneously, depending on the current restoration schedule. Panels (in English, French and Corsican) throughout introduce the restorations and the history of each building, and it's worth spending 15 minutes wandering around. If you're lucky, you'll be able to peek inside the **Église Saint Marcel**, originally built in the fifteenth century, although most of its façade dates from the seventeenth century, but most captivating is the **Musée d'archéologie d'Aleria**, opposite. There's also a temporary exposition space (additional charge), a restaurant, toilets and a snack bar.

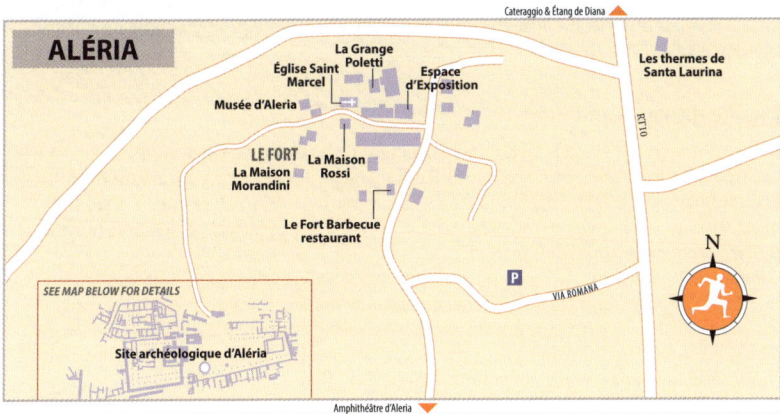

ALÉRIA

Cateraggio & Étang de Diana
La Grange Poletti
Église Saint Marcel
Espace d'Exposition
Les thermes de Santa Laurina
Musée d'Aleria
RT10
LE FORT
La Maison Rossi
La Maison Morandini
Le Fort Barbecue restaurant
P
VIA ROMANA
N
SEE MAP BELOW FOR DETAILS
Site archéologique d'Aléria

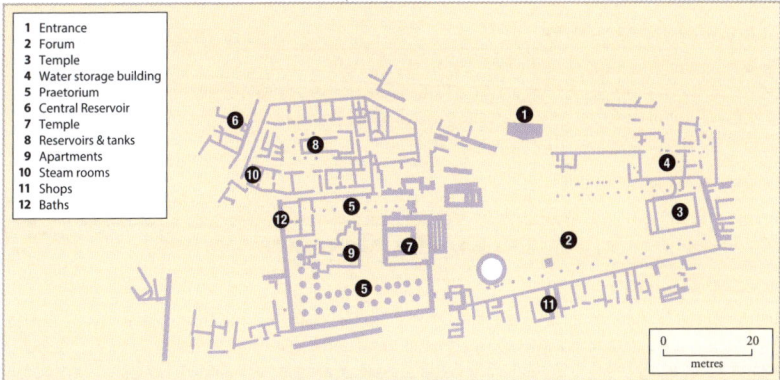

Amphithéâtre d'Aleria

1 Entrance
2 Forum
3 Temple
4 Water storage building
5 Praetorium
6 Central Reservoir
7 Temple
8 Reservoirs & tanks
9 Apartments
10 Steam rooms
11 Shops
12 Baths

0   20
metres

## Musée d'archéologie d'Aleria

Across the square from the church stands the **Fort Matra**, a small but mighty Genoese fortress dating from the fourteenth century, now home to the excellent **Musée d'archéologie d'Aleria** (formerly the Musée Jérôme Carcopino). Plan at least an hour to browse the four floors of exhibitions (currently in French only), which hold finds from the **Roman site**, including Hellenic and Punic coins, rings, belt links, elaborate oil lamps decorated with Christian symbols, Attic plates and a second-century marble bust of Jupiter Ammon. Etruscan bronzes fill another room, with jewellery and armour from the fourth to the second century BC.

Most compelling are the reconstructed Etruscan tombs and artefacts excavated from the nearby necropolis. In 2019, there was much excitement about the discovery of an Etruscan hypogeum from the fourth century BC, the most important archaeological excavation in Corsica since the 1960s.

## The site

To the left of the Fort Matra, a dusty track leads down the hill to the Roman site itself, where most of the excavation was done as recently as the 1950s. Much of the site still lies beneath ground and is undergoing continuous digging, but the balneum (bathhouse), the base of Augustus's triumphal arch, the foundations of the forum and traces of shops have already been unearthed. A colour-coded map with explanations in English is provided, making it easy to orientate yourself.

To the south, you can glimpse the ruins of the **amphithéâtre d'Aléria**, currently closed to the public, but plans are underway to create an open-air event space around the ancient ruins. Built in the fourth century AD, the theatre is thought to be one of the smallest in the Roman world.

# Étang de Diana

A short drive northeast of Aléria and Cateraggio, the **Étang de Diana** was also frequented by the ancient Greeks and Romans, who harvested its abundant oysters. Oyster farms are still the lifeblood of the saltwater lagoon, so time your arrival for lunchtime when the waterfront restaurants serve heaped platters of deliciously fresh *huîtres* (oysters) and *moules* (mussels).

Patchwork vineyards skirt the south bank, from where a footpath (about 45 minutes) loops around the coast and the lagoon, passing by the ruins of the Tour de Diana. On the north coast, a scenic footpath leads down to the white sand plage de Tallone. Across a narrow spit to the north sits one of the island's most renowned thalassotherapy spas, while the adjoining plage de Riva Bella is a popular naturist beach and resort. Nudity is not required at the spa, but you've been warned.

## ARRIVAL AND DEPARTURE                                      ALÉRIA AND AROUND

**By Bus** Long-distance buses (https://rapides-bleus.com) between Bastia and Porto-Vecchio stop along the RT10 in the centre of town by the turnoff to the Leclerc supermarket. Times vary throughout the year and services are limited in low season.

Destinations Bastia (1-2 daily; 1hr 30); Porto-Vecchio (1–2 daily; 1hr 30min).

## INFORMATION

**Tourist office** 80 Avenue St Alexandre Sauli, Caterragio (http://oriente-corsica.com) hands out free maps of the area, including the centre-ville, site antique and the Étang de Diana footpaths.

## ACCOMMODATION

**Les Orangers** 95 route du roi Theodore; http://hotel-lesorangers.com. Well-located on a quiet side street on the edge of town and right off the T50, this friendly hotel has ten comfortable but somewhat bland rooms and parking on-site. The selling point is the price, which doesn't double come July like so many others. €

**Marina d'Aléria** plage de Padulone; https://www.capfun. com/camping-france-corse-marina_aleria-FR.html. Right by the beach, this large campsite has plenty of space for tents, as well as mobile homes and chalets to rent. A great choice for families, there's an outdoor pool and aquapark. Tent € Chalets/Mobile homes €€

**Riva Bella Thalasso & Spa** Rte de Riva Bella; http:// rivabella-spa.com/fr. The East Coast's leading spa retreat is this huge thalassotherapy spa, set right on the narrow spit between the coast and the *Étang de Terrenzana*. Most visitors opt for some kind of spa treatment package with accommodation included, and it's worth keeping an eye on their offers and promotions throughout the year. There's also an oceanside restaurant and easy access to the sandy *plage de Riva Bella*. €€€

**6**

### EATING AND DRINKING

★ **Aux Coquillages de Diana** 1.2km north of Aléria: look for a sign on the right (east) side of the road pointing the way down a surfaced lane. This famous seafood restaurant, resting on stilts above the water, is the place to sample the local Nustale oysters, hauled fresh each day from the nearby Étang de Diane lagoon. It serves a great-value seafood platter featuring clams, mussels and a terrine made from dried mullet's eggs called *poutargue* – the kind of food one imagines the Romans must have feasted on when they farmed the *étang* two millennia ago. €€

**Clos Canereccia** Chem. de Rotani, 10 minutes' drive from town; https://closcanereccia.com. Established in the 1970s, this two-generation family-run winery specialises in organic wine growing, and their 24-hectare vineyards produce a variety of red, white and rosé wines. Book ahead to enjoy their winemaker's aperitif with wine and food tasting €€ or a picnic in the vineyards lunch experience. €€€

★ **Le Fort Restaurant** Le Fort, Aléria, at the entrance to the archaeological site; https://instagram.com/lefortaleria. This seasonal (May-Sept) restaurant is the highlight of any visit to the Roman site, with homecooked cuisine served on a breezy terrace beneath twinkling fairy lights. There are some great lunchtime salads and seafood-based tapas to share, but their speciality is delicious, barbecued meats, priced by the kg and served with a smile. €€

**L'imprévu** 160 Imp. Sant'Agata. A rustic *paillotte* on the southwest shore of the Étang de Diana with a view across the water. A carefully curated menu of seasonal tapas forms the basis of dining here, along with plates of charcuterie. Order a selection based on the chef's recommendation – he'll be happy to advise. €

**L'Ortu Di Rotani** Imp. de Rotani. Worth the drive out of town for, this farm-to-table restaurant is made with the freshest ingredients sourced from the food bowl that is eastern Corsica – many of the herbs and vegetables come from their own garden. Dishes are lovingly prepared and artfully presented with an emphasis on high-quality meat cuts, all paired with regional wines. €€€

# Moriani-Plage

Situated along the RT10, 40km south of Bastia, Moriani-Plage is the largest town along the **Costa Verde**, the expanse of fine sandy beaches that run along the East Coast from Aléria up to the mouth of the Fium'altu River. If you're not in the mood for sun-seeking or water sports, there's little reason to swing by here, but it's well placed for day-trips to the city and neighbouring Castagniccia as well as sitting at the trailhead of the **Mare à Mare Nord** hiking trail. With 17km of **beaches**, you're guaranteed a place to lay your beach towel even in midsummer; the most popular spots are the dunes of **Prunette** and **plage de Santa Lucia** where you can rent jet skis, peddle boats and SUPs (LS Location; http://ls-location-jetski.corsica/).

### ARRIVAL AND DEPARTURE                                          MORIANI-PLAGE

**By bus** Long-distance buses (https://rapides-bleus.com) between Bastia and Porto-Vecchio stop along the RT10 right outside the Office de Tourisme. Times vary throughout the year and services are limited in low season.
Destinations Aléria (1–2 daily; 40 mins); Bastia (1-2 daily; 50 mins); Porto-Vecchio (1–2 daily; 2hr 10min).

**By Boat** Port Taverna (https://port-taverna.fr), just 4km south of Moriani-Plage welcomes private (and rented) boats and yachts.

### INFORMATION

**Tourist office** 430 Route de Moriani Plage (https:// castagniccia-maremonti.com). Housed in a striking old stone building with wooden beams, this stylish tourist office covers the Costa Verde and the southern villages of Castagnicca, and also has a boutique of hand-crafted souvenirs and local products.

6

## A TASTE OF CASTAGNICCIA

Still celebrated as the food bowl of Corsica, Castagniccia is not only renowned for its sweet chestnuts but for the hazelnuts, olives, figs, Corsican clementines and wild mushrooms that grow in abundance. Whether browsing the farmers' markets, helping out with the chestnut harvest (Oct-Nov) or visiting the region's artisan producers, you can taste AOC/AOP-labelled delicacies such as charcuterie, chestnut flour, and chestnut honey, and experience the age-old traditions associated with them.

### VISIT THE PRODUCERS

Pick up a copy of the *Route des Sens Authentiques* (https://gustidicorsica.com) booklet from tourist offices, which will guide you to local producers and farm shops. Pig and chestnut farmer Jean-Paul Vincensini (https://corse-bio.fr/fr/) in San Lorenzu and dairy farmer Carine Croce (c.oricelli@gmail.com) organise visits on request, and chestnut flour producer Stéphane Guerrini (guerrini.stephane@gmail.com) hosts guests on his chestnut farm. You can also purchase hazelnut products from **L'Atelier de la Noisette** in San-Giuliano (http://atelierdelanoisette.com) or visit farm-to-table restaurants **La Bergerie** ( https://labergeriegiustiniani.fr) in Penta-di-Casinca or **A Cinderella** (https://instagram.com/cinderellasaveuretvindecorse) in Santa Maria Poggio.

### ATTEND A TRADITIONAL FAIR

Local fêtes celebrating local produce are held throughout the year, the most notable of which are the **Autre Foire artisanale** held in Piedicroce over Easter weekend, the **Foire de la Casinca/ Fiera Di San Branca** held in Castellare di Casinca in May, the **Fiera di a Bocca à u Pratu** in Col de Pratu at the end of July, and the **Festa di a Nuciola** (Hazelnut Festival) in Cervione in August. Somewhat bizarrely, the island's biggest chestnut fair actually isn't in Castagniccia – the village of Bocogano, between Ajaccio and Corte, hosts the popular **Foire de la Chataîgne** (chestnut festival) on the first week of December, drawing up to 20,000 visitors.

### SPECIALITIES TO TRY

Traditional Corsican products to look out for include *farine de châtaigne (*chestnut flour), which is used to make local specialities such as *pulenta* (chestnut bread), *canistrelli* (crunchy biscuits), and *migliacciu* (pizza-like savoury snacks with cheese). Also, look out for local craft beer Pietra, brewed with barley malt and chestnut flour, and Corsican "Nutella" made with Cervione hazelnuts – Nuciola, Nucellina, and Nocetta are favourite local brands.

## ACCOMMODATION

There's a glut of hotels and campsites in Moriani-Plage, but the best book up quickly for July and August.

**Camping Merendella** Corsica Vacanze; https://merendella.com. The best of the coastal campsites, this large site has 220 pitches and 88 rentals ranging from 2-bed mobile homes to 10-bed cottages. There's a pool, water slides and direct access to the beach. Tent €; mobile home €€

**La Demeure Coloniale** 60 rue Jean Tafani; http://la-demeure-coloniale.com. Five rooms with retro-style furnishings in an old 1930s colonial-style house. The beds are more comfortable than they look, which is a plus, but note that the cheapest have the toilet and shower in the same room. €

## EATING

**Abri des flots** route de la plage; http://abridesflots.com. Beneath arches of mulberry trees, this broad terrace serves tasty BBQ veal skewers, grilled fish, *moules* and wood-fired pizzas. A highlight is the artisanal ice creams, of which there are myriad flavours served in a cone or whipped into a flurry of sundaes and milkshakes. €€€

**Les Arbousiers** lieu dit l'Avidanella, Poggio-mezzana; https://www.maquis-plage-corse.com/page/restaurant. Even if you're not staying at the Maquis Plage hotel, it's worth swinging by its atmospheric terrace restaurant for a dinner date. The menu might look textbook – think *entrecôte grillée* or a *filet de dorade* – but the execution is divine. For dessert, try the baked Alaska flambéed in *chestnut eau de vie*. €€

# Casinga and Castagnicca

In ancient times, **Castagniccia** was dubbed the "*grenier de Rome*" (the attic of Rome), a reference to the fertile hills that rose up above the coastal ports, their dense canopy of trees swollen with chestnuts, olives and hazelnuts ripe for the picking. The modern name, Castagniccia, comes from the Corsican *castagnu* (chestnut) and is often used as a catch-all for the mountainous region – encompassing neighbouring Casinga – that rambles down from Ponte Leccia and Corte towards the coast.

Castagniccia doesn't have a central hub or big attractions to its name, but somehow, the Land of the Chestnut Trees still invokes misty-eyed nostalgia among locals, all of whom seem to talk of it fondly. This might be the ultimate slow tourism destination, not least because the twisty mountain lanes and wandering livestock make it impossible to get anywhere fast. Its highlights, which include woodland walks to waterfalls and pretty stone villages, and the hometown of Corsican icon Pascal Paoli, are scattered through the hills and the best way to explore is slowly, hopping from village to village and enjoying the views along the way.

**6**

## Cervione

Towards the south of the region, **Cervione** is best known for its production of hazelnuts and much-loved hazelnut *fête* (see page 138). In the village, you'll find the eighteenth-century Baroque-style *cathédrale Sant'Erasmu* and the small *Musée Ethnographique* (charge; in French only), which has an interesting collection looking at Corsican art and cultural traditions through the ages. Another worthwhile diversion is the hike (about 1hr) up to the hilltop **A Madonna di a Scupiccia chapel**, which affords magnificent views.

## San-Nicolao

A popular stopover for hikers, **San-Nicolao** sits along the final stretch of the Mare a Mare Nord, but the big trek is just one of several scenic walks around the village. Follow the Route de la Corniche (about 7km) south to Cervione via the village of Santa Maria Poggio and the Ucelluline waterfall, or take the footpath from Hell's Bridge to the **abandoned village of Fiuminale**. In San-Nicolao itself, the most memorable landmark is the seventeenth-century Baroque Église San-Nicolao (free; ask at the Mairie for opening times as they vary) with its towering bell tower and eighteenth-century frescos.

## Penta di Casinca

Further north, in the Casinga region, **Penta di Casinca** boasts the classification of "Picturesque Site of Corsica", the only village on the island to receive the honour. Its slate-roofed stone houses and eighteenth-century baroque church live up to the hype, as do the magnificent panoramic views down to the sea.

## Piedicroce

In the shadows of Monte San Petrone, the highest point of the region and a popular challenge for hikers, **Piedicroce** is one of Castagniccia's most emblematic villages. The seventeenth-century church is a focal point with its ornate interiors and old organ, while nearby points of interest include the enigmatic ruins of the 15th-century Orezza convent and the Struccia waterfall, where you can swim beneath the falls. Don't forget to swim by **Eaux d'Orezza** (https://orezza.fr) nearby, where you can fill up your water bottle with naturally sparkling spring water from the fountain and visit the official shop of the island's most famous water brand.

## Morosaglia

Perched high on the mountainside at about 800m, Morosaglia marks the northern boundary of Castagniccia. Forever synonymous with its most famous son, Corsican revolutionary and one-time General of the Corsican Republic, Pascal Paoli was born in the village and a museum dedicated to his legacy is its biggest tourist attraction. After exploring the small **Musée Pascal Paoli** (charge; French/Corsican only), you can also visit the adjacent chapel where Paoli's ashes are housed.

**6**

### GETTING AROUND AND INFORMATION                                   CASINGA AND CASTAGNICCIA

There's no public transport in the Casinga and Castagniccia regions, so the only practical way to get around is by renting a car in either Bastia or Corte.

**On foot** The Mare a Mare Nord long-distance trail passes through several Castagniccia villages, and almost every village has at least one footpath – many link multiple villages. Pick up a map from the tourist office at Moriani-Plage (see page 137).

**By bike** For the strong of quads, a vast (and very hilly) network of cycling trails covers the entire region; pick up a map from the tourist office at Moriani-Plage (see page 137).

### ACCOMMODATION

There's no main hub for exploring Casinga and Castagniccia; instead, you'll find small guesthouses and *chambres d'hôtes* dotted throughout the villages. The following are just a few of the region's more unique stays.

**Buller dans le maquis** Route d'Anghione, Cervione; https://debulleetdecorse.com. Spend a night in a glamping dome beneath the stars surrounded by towering cork oaks. This quirky eco glampsite has three domes to choose from, all with double beds, plus there's an outdoor jacuzzi to lull you off to sleep. €€

**Le Refuge** Piedicroce; http://lerefuge-orezza.com. Friendly and affordable two-star eco-hotel with ten basic rooms, some looking out over the valley. Good enough for a night's stay, and you can enjoy your evening meal at the adjoining restaurant. €

**Gîte Luna Piena** Hameau de Penti, Santa-Reparata-Di-Moriani; https://gitelunapiena.com/. Cheap, cheerful, with a hot shower and a comfy pillow to lay your head, this homely *gîte d'étape* along the Mare à mare nord footpath checks all the boxes. There are doubles and bunk beds spread across six rooms, two spotless shared bathrooms, and you can pay extra for an evening meal, breakfast or packed lunch. €

**A Piattatella** Chem. Saint-François, Monticello; https://www.apiattatella.fr. A jagged mountain skyline and vast jungle-like maquis stretch on the horizon at this five-star eco-hotel. Breathtaking views envelop the 17 small villas dotted around the domain, where you'll sleep in your own little cocoon of luxury. There's also a panoramic infinity pool. €€€€

# Central Corsica

PASCAL PAOLI STATUE, CORTE TOWN

# Central Corsica

Hulking mountain ranges and gaping canyons etch out the ragged skyline of Central Corsica, the island's alpine heartland. Wild, unchartered and formidable, the one-time stomping ground of bandits, guerrilla armies and nationalist rebels is studded with hardy mountain villages and steeped in centuries-old traditions. For hikers and outdoor enthusiasts, the central massifs unfold into a vast adventure playground with a nonstop parade of stupendous scenery. Gnarly peaks frame the horizon, many of them over 2,000m, funnelling down into verdant wooded gorges, maquis-clad valleys and glittering glacial lakes – all of it contained within the sprawling *parc naturel régional de Corse.*

**7**

All roads in Central Corsica lead to the former capital and nationalist stronghold of **Corte**, where centuries of hardships have done nothing to extinguish the town's traditional spirit. As such, it's a great place to dig into hearty **Corsican cuisine** and dive into local culture, as well as being strategically located for exploring.

**Getting outdoors is the only way** to experience this mountainous region, and the ever-expanding network of trails and forest tracks can be tackled on foot, by bike or on horseback. The ridge of granite peaks forming the spine of the island is closely followed by the legendary **GR20** footpath (see page 74), which can be picked up from various villages and is scattered with *refuge* huts, most of them offering no facilities except shelter. Several other long-distance footpaths also cut through the centre, while the most popular short trails journey to the dazzling **Lac de Nino** and the magnificent **gorges** of **La Restonica** and **Tavignano**, all within easy reach of Corte.

To the north, **Ponte Leccia** is the gateway to the high-altitude peaks of the **Asco Valley**, where you can swim in the river in summer and hit the ski slopes in winter. The jagged summit of **Monte Cinto**, Corsica's highest peak, presides over the region, but it's a drive through vertiginous cliffs of **Scala di a Santa Regina** to the south that unveils the most jaw-dropping scenery, giving way to the rural villages and wooded trails of the **Niolo valley**.

South of Corte, the **forested mountains and canyons** around **Venaco**, **Vivario** and **Vizzavona** are replete with opportunities for **canyoning**, rock climbing and hiking, and there are some great short walks such as the **Cascade des Anglais**, which sits along the GR20. At Vivario, the roads branch off, with the T20 snaking down to Ajaccio and the D69 traversing the epically windy Col de Sorba to **Ghisoni** before descending into the verdant hills of the **vallée du Taravo.**

## GETTING THERE AND AROUND

While you can reach the central region by train, without your own vehicle, you'll be reliant on taxis to reach trailheads.
**By train** Regular trains connect Corte with Bastia, Ajaccio, and Calvi several times daily in high season, reducing to twice a day in winter. Timetables are updated regularly and available at tourist offices and online (https://cf-corse. corsica).

# Ponte-Leccia and around

Set between the lofty peaks of the Asco Valley and the forested highlands of Castagniccia, the small town of **Ponte-Leccia** (U Ponte à a Leccia) marks the start of Corsica's mountainous central region. The town itself is little more than a smattering

# Highlights

**❶ Scala di a Santa Regina** This rock-hewn mountain road is a thrill-a-minute drive with hairpin bends, plunging canyon walls and gurgling waterfalls below. See page 144

**❷ GR20** If the island's most challenging footpath is too much, there are plenty of opportunities to hike shorter sections. See page 147

**❸ Lac de Nino** Backdropped by snowy peaks and lush, grassy *pozzi* (alpine wetlands), wild horses often graze the banks of this glacial lake. See page 149

**❹ Corte** The timeworn streets and mountain vistas of Pasquale Paoli's late 18th-century capital are steeped in history. See page 149

**❺ Corsican cuisine** Slow-cooked stews with wild boar and cannelloni stuffed with creamy *brocciu* cheese provide hearty sustenance for hikers. See page 152

**❻ Gorges de la Restonica** The region's flagship day hike is a rolling slideshow of wildflower-speckled valleys, rock-strewn gorges, and alpine lakes. See page 152

**❼ Canyoning** Dramatic mountain canyons and thundering waterfalls provide ample terrain for thrill-seekers of all levels. See page 155

**❽ Cascade des Anglais** Among the most rewarding of the region's short hikes, hidden away in the Vizzavona Forest. See page 156

**HIGHLIGHTS ARE MARKED ON THE MAP ON PAGE 146**

# CENTRAL CORSICA

## HIGHLIGHTS

1 Scala di a Santa Regina
2 GR20
3 Lac du Nino
4 Corte
5 Corsican cuisine
6 Gorges de la Restonica
7 Canyoning
8 Cascade des Anglais

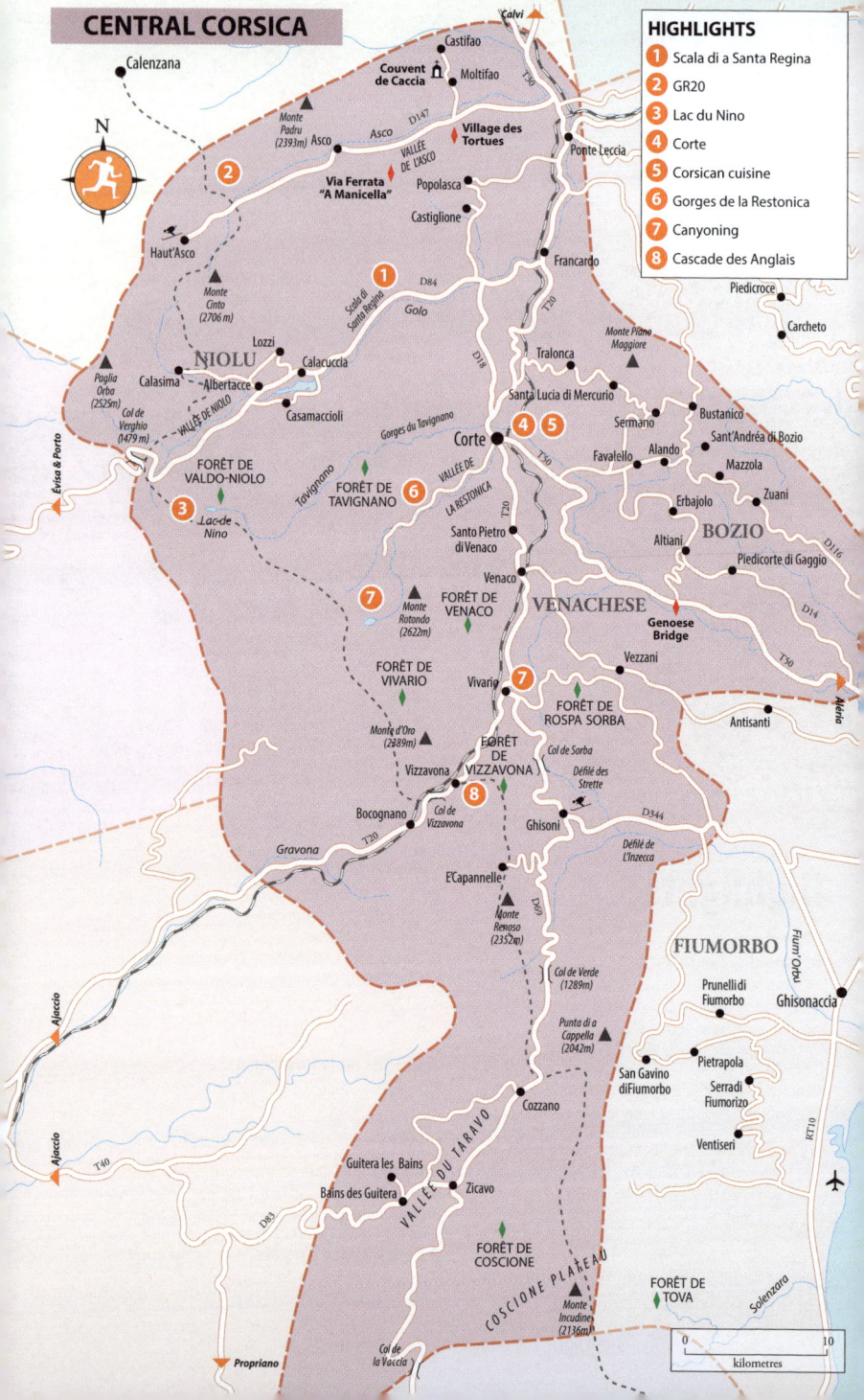

Calvi

Calenzana

Castifao

Couvent de Caccia

Moltifao

Monte Padru (2393m)

Asco

VALLÉE DE L'ASCO

Village des Tortues

Ponte Leccia

Via Ferrata "A Manicella"

Popolasca

Castiglione

Haut'Asco

Monte Cinto (2706 m)

Francardo

Piedicroce

Carcheto

Scala di a Santa Regina

Golo

NIOLU

Lozzi

Calacuccia

Tralonca

Monte Piano Maggiore

Paglia Orba (2525m)

Calasima

Albertacce

Casamaccioli

Santa Lucia di Mercurio

Bustanico

Col de Verghio (1479 m)

VALLÉE DE NIOLU

Gorges du Tavignano

Corte

Sermano

Sant'Andréa di Bozio

Mazzola

Favalello

Alando

Zuani

FORÊT DE VALDO-NIOLU

FORÊT DE TAVIGNANO

Erbajolo

Tavignano

VALLÉE DE LA RESTONICA

BOZIO

Altiani

Piedicorte di Gaggio

Lac de Nino

Santo Pietro di Venaco

Venaco

VENACHESE

Vezzani

FORÊT DE VENACO

Monte Rotondo (2622m)

Genoese Bridge

FORÊT DE VIVARIO

Vivario

FORÊT DE ROSPA SORBA

Antisanti

Monte d'Oro (2389m)

FORÊT DE VIZZAVONA

Col di Sorba

Défilé des Strette

Vizzavona

Bocognano

Col de Vizzavona

Ghisoni

Défilé de L'Inzecca

FIUMORBO

Gravona

Ghisonaccia

E'Capannelle

Prunelli di Fiumorbo

Monte Renoso (2352m)

Col de Verde (1289m)

Pietrapola

San Gavino di Fiumorbo

Serradi Fiumorizo

Punta di a Cappella (2042m)

Ventiseri

Ajaccio

Cozzano

Guitera les Bains

Bains des Guitera

Zicavo

VALLÉE DU TARAVO

FORÊT DE COSCIONE

FORÊT DE TOVA

Solenzara

Propriano

Monte Incudine (2136m)

COSCIONE PLATEAU

Col de la Vaccia

Aléria

Évisa & Porto

0          10
kilometres

of buildings straddling the Golo River and its only landmark of note is the striking Genoese bridge that you'll drive over on the way through. It's still a key transport hub, sitting at the meeting point of the T20, which runs from Bastia through Corte to Ajaccio, and the T30, which heads northwest to Île Rousse and Calvi. Just to the north, the D47 branches off west into the **Asco Valley**.

## ARRIVAL AND DEPARTURE PONTE-LECCIA AND AROUND

**By bus** The daily buses between Bastia and Calvi stop in Ponte Leccia (https://www.corsicar.com) but are best kept as a last resort.

**By train** Trains from Corte, Bastia, and Calvi all alight in Ponte Leccia, making this a more viable option for getting around. Timetables change throughout the year and are available online (https://cf-corse.corsica) or from the tourist office.

**Destinations** Ajaccio (3–5 daily; 3hr); Bastia (3–6 daily; 1hr 10min); Calvi (3 daily; 2hr); L'Île Rousse (3 daily; 1hr 45min).

**By car** Driving is by far the best way to get around; fill up here before heading out into the mountains. There's free parking at the train station.

## GETTING AROUND AND INFORMATION

**Taxis** Taxi Etienne (06 09 40 61 09) and Taxi Luciani (06 09 40 61 09) both operate 24/7 by reservation.

**Tourist office** Outside the train station (http://www. tourisme-pasqualepaoli.corsica) covers the Asco, Niolu and Bozio regions, as well as western Castagniccia.

**Adventure sports** In Terra Corsa (https://interracorsa.

com) offer seasonal activities, including canyoning, white water rafting, skiing and snowshoeing, via ferrata and ziplining in the Asco and Golo valleys.

**Guides** The Fédération des Guides Diplômés de Corse (https://frcgi.jimdofree.com) has a list of certified guides for the region, searchable by language and speciality.

## ACCOMMODATION AND EATING

★**Casaluna** Espace Maria Julia, 20218. A surprising find that feels underpriced (a rarity in Corsica) given the quality, presentation and service. Delicious and 100 per cent homemade, the tajine and poke bowls are as flavoursome as they come, and the *ravioles de langoustines et gambas* are a fraction of the price of the coastal resorts. €̄

**Ecolodge Ascosa** Rue de Calvi, 20218 Ponte Leccia; http://www.ascosa.corsica/. Don't be put off by the drab, warehouse-like exterior of this eco-lodge – inside, it's a feast of patterned tiles, colourful rugs and brightly painted

walls. There's also an open kitchen area with plenty of fridge space and tea/coffee available 24/7, plus a cool, graffiti-adorned pool area. €̄

**La paillote** 6 Rue de Calvi; https://www.facebook.com/ PizzaleCamion. North of town, along the T30, the sunny courtyard is the ideal spot to share a platter of Corsican charcuterie or *beignets* stuffed with Corsican cheese. The menu is limited but well-considered, with a mix of meat, seafood and pasta dishes, and a mouthwatering burger topped with sizzling *pancetta*. €̄€̄

# Vallée de l'Asco

The sky-grazing Monte Cinto massif, home to the island's highest summit at 2,706m, presides over the Asco valley, forming a natural barrier with the forested uplands of the Balagne. This region is home to some of Corsica's highest peaks, many of them crested with snow even in the summer, as well as fabulously rocky canyons and steep crags spliced by the meandering Asco River. The D147 climbs up through the lower and upper valleys, skirting around weather-sculpted cliffs, plunging gorges and cascading waterfalls as it climbs up to the ski station of **Haut Asco**, the culmination of the highest leg of the GR20. Along the way, you can stop to swim in refreshing pools along the river and follow numerous footpaths through the gorge.

Adventurers can enjoy a host of outdoor activities through all four seasons. White-water rafting is possible along the upper river in spring (April-May) and canyoning tours start around the same time, while in summer, the region's high altitude provides cooler air ideal for hiking and rock climbing. Near **Moltifao**, there's also an adventure park with ziplines and a via ferrata (https://interracorsa.com), along with some great mountain biking trails in the **forêt de Moltifao**. While you're there, a visit to the nearby **Village des Tortues** (charge; https://villagedestortues.wordpress.com), a small sanctuary of Hermann's tortoises, is a fun diversion for kids.

## SKIING IN CORSICA

Corsica's high peaks aren't only the realm of hikers; the island is also a little-known ski destination. It's far removed from the Alps, so temper your expectations, but there's still plenty of winter fun to be had on the slopes. Ski season is short (December to early April) and temperamental, but the most reliable snowfall is typically from mid-January to early March.

There are three ski resorts in Corsica: Haut Asco, Ghisoni and Val d'Ese. The small **Haut Asco ski resort** (https://asco.corsica) sits at 1,450m and has just two 600m slopes, along with a couple of beginner runs, but there's a ski and snowboard school (https://interracorsa.com), plus sledging and snowshoeing tracks. Further south, the **Ghisoni Capanelle ski station** (https://ghisoni.corsica) has seven slopes, including five red and black runs from a top height of 1,810m; there's also a ski school (https://esf-ghisoni.corsica). Finally, nearby **Val d'Ese ski resort** (https://valdese.fr) at 1,620m has six red, blue and green pistes and a ski school (https://esf-corse.fr).

In addition, there are options for off-piste and cross-country skiing in Corsica; it's even possible to ski part of the GR20, although it's a technical descent best left to the experienced (if you do want to attempt it, contact one of the official mountain guides; https://montagnesdecorse.com). The proximity of the mountains to the coast has also given rise to another daredevil feat that locals proudly attest to: hitting the ski the slopes in the morning then surfing the Mediterranean waves in the afternoon.

---

**ACCOMMODATION AND EATING**      **VALLÉE DE L'ASCO**

**Acropole** Lieu Dit Ranza, 20276 Asco; https://www.acropole-asco.com. Simple and comfy, if a little outdated, this is still one of the best-situated and most reasonably-priced places to stay in the Asco Valley. There's a restaurant on-site, plenty of parking, and amenable staff who are happy to help advise you on the region. €

**Camping Tizarella** Vallée d'Asco, 20218 Moltifao; http://www.camping-tizarella.com/. Surrounded by trees and close to the riverside, you can't beat the location of this campsite. Staff are somewhat unengaged, and the facilities are basic, but it's clean, well-equipped and has a nice swimming pool. €

**Le Chalet** Les Hauts D Asco, 20276 Asco; http://www.hotel-lechalet-asco.com/hotel-asco-corse. Gazing out over the jagged skyline of Monte Cinto as you eat your breakfast croissants is the high point of a stay at this popular ski hotel. There's a choice of rooms, including singles, twin, and dorm beds, a restaurant that serves lunch and hiker's evening menus, and it's open year-round to accommodate both the hiking and ski season. €€

# Niolo

Historically one of the most inaccessible regions of the island, the pastoral highlands of **Niolo** sit to the south of Monte Cinto, sewn in by a string of soaring peaks. Driving the D84, which slashes west through the mountains from the D18 turnoff, is an exhilarating ride and surely ranks among the island's most scenic drives, providing you have a head for heights.

The **Scala di Santa Regina** section – literally the "staircase" – serves up some of the most jaw-dropping views. Chock-full of dizzying switchbacks, narrow passageways and roof-grazing overhangs, it clings to the banks of the Golo River and often swings out to reveal the gaping chasm of the canyon below. Unsurprisingly, this is a favourite route for motorcyclists. Handy car-sized lay-bys are strategically positioned to allow passing traffic, but they also make it easy to dash out and snap some photos, so take the opportunity while you can.

## Calacuccia

The glittering reward at the end of the Scala di Santa Regina is the **lac de Calacuccia**, a manmade reservoir backdropped against snow-hatted peaks and encircled by three villages. On the northeast shore, the eponymous **Calacuccia** has the majority of accommodation and dining options, while **Albertacce** to the west boasts a magnificent swimming spot along the Golo River, beneath the picturesque arches of an old Genoese bridge. South of the lake, **Casamaccioli** is best known for its annual Santa di u Niolu fair, held around Sept 8th to celebrate the birth of the Virgin Mary. It's Corsica's oldest country fair and far more than just a religious celebration with artisan markets, traditional foods and traditional entertainment.

South of Calacuccia, more showstopping scenery awaits as you traverse the sinuous **Col de Verghio** mountain pass, heading down towards the west coast. You might prefer to linger longer in the **Vallée de Niolo**, where you'll find a network of hiking trails, many of which join up with the Mare à Mare Nord and the GR20, as well as activities from horse riding to rock climbing.

### GETTING AROUND AND INFORMATION                                   NIOLO

**Taxi** Taxi JMG (06 24 68 10 31) covers all distances by reservation only.

**Tourist office** 30 avenue Valduniellu, Calacucccia (http://www.tourisme-pasqualepaoli.corsica). It's not a patch on the larger regional office in Ponte Leccia (see page 144), but they will give you the lowdown on the area's footpaths.

**Outdoor activities** AS Niolu (Albertacce; https://haute-montagne-corse.com) organize hiking, rock climbing and canyoning tours in the Niolo region, as well as operating the Valduniellu treetop adventure park. Ranch U Niolu (https://ranchunioluacavallu.fr) offers horse treks through the Niolu Valley and to the Lac de Nino.

### ACCOMMODATION AND EATING

**Les Chalets de Lozzi** Muro Nuovo, 5km north of Calacuccia; https://www.les-chalets-de-lozzi.com/. In the hills above town, these four cosy wooden chalets are perched right on the hillside looking out over the mountainscapes. The chic cabins are heated and well-furnished with kitchenettes, TVs and private terraces, and the family team will bring you pizzas and breakfast to your cabin on request. Be warned: they book up months in advance. €€

**A Casa Niulinca** Av de la scala; https://facebook.com/acasaniulinca. Calacuccia's best restaurant has a huge, shaded terrace off the main road above the lake. Salads,

omelettes and burgers make up the bulk of the menu and the slick service and liberal portions can't be faulted. The prices are reasonable, too. €

**Grand Hotel de la Scala** 39 avenue de Valdoniello; http://grandhoteldelascala.com. The imposing terracotta edifice of this eco-labelled hotel, built in the 1930s, is a mere hint of the Art Deco splendour that awaits inside. Each one of the 30 rooms is a miniature masterpiece, with carefully chosen contemporary furnishings, elaborate headboards and gleaming bathrooms with traditional brass faucets. The mountain-view pool is the icing on the cake. €€€€

## Lac de Nino

Few sights are as enchanting as the **Lac de Nino**, a glimmering expanse of sky-blue set amid a lush grassy plateau speckled with *pozzines* (small natural pools) with the chiselled silhouette of the Rotondo massif rising up in the background. Scrambling down into the high alpine valley at 1,743m is one of the highlights of the GR20, and you'll often spot wild horses and pigs grazing by the waterholes or along the Tavignano River, which flows out from the lake. If you're not hiking the GR20, the most popular trail to the lake sets out from the **Maison Forestière de Poppaghia** (12km southwest of Calacuccia along the D84) and takes up to five hours to hike a total of 10km there and back. It's a moderately difficult route, and you'll need proper hiking shoes and plenty of water.

# Corte and around

Stacked up the side of a wedge-shaped crag against a spectacular backdrop of granite mountains, **CORTE** epitomizes *l'âme corse*, or "Corsican soul" – a small town marooned amid a grandiose landscape, where a spirit of dogged patriotism is never far from the surface. Corte has been the home of Corsican nationalism since the first National

Constitution was drawn up here in 1731, and was also where **Pascal Paoli**, "U Babbu di u Patria" ("Father of the Nation"), formed the island's first democratic government later in the eighteenth century. Self-consciously insular and grimly proud, it feels distinctly untainted by the motley crew of hikers, day-trippers and backpackers that descend en masse come summer. The presence of the island's only university lightens the atmosphere noticeably during term-time, when the bars and cafés lining its long main street fill with students. For the outsider, Corte's charm is concentrated in the tranquil *haute ville*, where the forbidding **citadelle** presides over a warren of narrow, cobbled streets.

## Haute Ville

The old **haute ville**, immediately above Corte's main street, cours Paoli, centres on **place Gaffory**, which is dominated by a statue of General Gian-Pietru Gaffori pointing vigorously towards the church. On its base, a bas-relief depicts the siege of the Gaffori house by the Genoese, who attacked in 1750 when the general was out of town, and his wife Faustina was left holding the fort. Their residence still stands, right behind, and you can clearly make out the bullet marks made by the besiegers.

For the best view of the citadelle, follow the signs uphill to the viewing platform, the **Belvédère**, which faces the medieval tower, suspended high above the town on its

**CORTE**

HAUTE VILLE

Museu di
a Corsica

CITADELLE

Petit Train

Palais
National

Belvédère

Oratoire St-
Théophile

Pont Vieux

PLACE DUC-
DE-PADOUE

Bank

Bank

Église de
l'Annonciation

PL DES
ARMES
PLACE
GAFFORY

PLACE
PAOLI

University

AVENUE JEAN-NICOLI

AVENUE XAVIER LUCIANI

AVENUE PRES PIERUCCI

Tavignano

Restonica

AVENUE DU 9 SEPTEMBRE

Gare
Corte

Buses to
Aleria

Casino
Hypermarket

Vallée du Tavignano

Vallée de la Restonica

Vizzavona & Ajaccio

& Bastia

Bastia

Aleria

| ● EATING | |
|---|---|
| Le 24 | 1 |
| A Bocca | 4 |
| A Casa di l'Orsu | 6 |
| Le Bips | 3 |
| Grimaldi | 2 |
| Terra Corsa | 7 |
| U Museu | 5 |

| ■ ACCOMMODATION | |
|---|---|
| HR | 4 |
| Du Nord | 3 |
| La Paix | 2 |
| Si Mea | 1 |
| U Sognu | 5 |

| ● SHOPPING | |
|---|---|
| A Casa Curtinese | 3 |
| Casa di u Legnu | 1 |
| Couteaux Corses | 2 |

N

0        100
metres

pinnacle of rock and dwarfed by the immense crags behind. The platform also gives a wonderful view of the converging rivers and encircling forest – a summer bar adds to the attraction.

Just above place Gaffori, left of the gateway to the citadelle, stands the **Palais National**, a great, solid block of a mansion that's the sole example of Genoese civic architecture in Corte. Having served as the seat of Paoli's government for a while, it became the Università di Corsica in 1765, offering free education to all (Napoleon's father studied here). The university closed in 1769 when the French took over the island after the Treaty of Versailles, not to be resurrected until 1981. Today, several modern buildings have been added, among them the Paoli Tech Engineering School, which has a focus on sustainable construction and renewable energy, among other things.

## The Citadelle and Musée de la Corse

Charge; includes English-language audio guide • http://museudiacorsica.corsica

7

The monumental gateway just behind the Palais National leads from place Poilu into the Genoese **citadelle**, Corte's principal landmark, whose lower courtyard is dominated by the modern buildings of the **Musée de la Corse**. The state-of-the-art museum houses the collection of ethnographer Révérend Père Louis Doazan, a Catholic priest who spent 27 years amassing a vast array of objects relating to the island's traditional transhumant and peasant past. The collection is principally made up of old farm implements, craft tools, and peasant clothing, but there are also some intriguing old maps, a giant Moor head sculpture, and plenty of interesting commentary on Corsica's history.

The museum's entrance ticket also admits you to the citadelle. The only such fortress in the interior of the island, the Genoese structure served as a base for the Foreign Legion from 1962 until 1984, but now houses a pretty feeble exhibition of nineteenth-century photographs. It's reached by a huge staircase of Restonica marble, which leads to the medieval tower known as the **Nid d'Aigle** (Eagle's Nest). The fortress, of which the tower is the only original part, was built in 1420, and the barracks were added during the mid-nineteenth century. These were later converted into a prison, in use as recently as World War II, when the Italian occupiers incarcerated Corsican Resistance fighters in tiny cells. Adjacent to the cells is a former **watchtower** which, at the time of Paoli's government, was inhabited by the hangman.

### ARRIVAL AND DEPARTURE

### CORTE AND AROUND

**By bus** Bus services to Corte have almost completely disappeared over recent years, but there's still an infrequent service to Aléria (https://corsicabus.org).

**By train** The *gare CFC* (04 95 46 00 97) is at the foot of the hill near the university. If you don't want to walk, the Petit Train (https://petit-train-corte.com) leaves from the roundabout one block south and heads up to the citadelle.

**Destinations** Ajaccio (3–5 daily; 2hr); Bastia (3–5 daily; 1hr 45min); Calvi (2 daily; 2hr 30min); L'Île Rousse (2 daily; 2hr).
**By car** There's free parking at the train station, from where you can walk (about 15 mins uphill) or take the Petit Train (see above). Alternatively, there's plenty of space at the underground Parking Tuffelli (charge) in town.

### INFORMATION AND GETTING AROUND

**Shuttle buses** Summer *navettes* (shuttle buses) connect to hiking trailheads at Restonica and col de Verghio; reservations are essential (http://autocars-cortenais.fr).

**Tourist office** Just inside the main gates of the citadelle, near the museum (http://corte-tourisme.com). In the same

building is the information office of the Régional de Corse (https://pnr.corsica).
**Taxis** Taxi Etienne (06 09 40 61 09) and Taxi Luciani (06 09 40 61 09) both operate 24/7 by reservation.

### ACCOMMODATION

### SEE MAP PAGE 150

**HR** 12 av du 9-septembre; http://hotel-hr.com. This converted concrete-block gendarmerie, within a short walk

**7**

## HIKING THE VALLÉE DE LA RESTONICA

Renowned for its glacier-moulded rocks and deep alpine lakes, the **Gorges de la Restonica** was, until recently, one of the island's pre-eminent day hikes, drawing tens of thousands of walkers each season. Sadly, when storms Ciarán and Domingos swept through the valley at the end of 2023, they caused severe damage to the access roads, effectively cutting off all vehicle access to the upper part of the valley. From 2024, a shuttle service has been set up to maintain access to the lower valley and the trails themselves remain accessible, but what was once a half-day family-friendly hike to and from the lakes is now a challenging full-day trek.

### ACCESS TO THE VALLEY

Access to the **Gorges de la Restonica** is via the D623, but the gorges begin about 6km along at **Tuani**, just beyond where the route penetrates the **Forêt de la Restonica**, a glorious forest of chestnut, Laricio pine and the tough maritime pine endemic to Corte. This part of the valley is still open to cars and it's possible to park at Tuani; from that point on, access is by shuttle or bike only.

From Tuani, it used to be possible to drive all the way to the **Bergeries de Grotelle**, a further 10km down the road, from where the final leg to reach the lakes was a manageable 3km on foot. Now, shuttles can only reach as far as Frassetta, about 4km south of Tuani. This means that if you want to hike all the way to the lakes, it's 18.2km there-and-back, taking an average of 8hr 30. Shuttles run from 6am to 8pm, so it's doable in a day, but it's a much greater undertaking.

### THE HIKES

Although the classic day trek is less accessible, there are still plenty of ways to walk the valley; the tourist office has put together a handy booklet detailing all of them. The easiest cover the lower valley, setting out from Corte, perhaps stopping to picnic and bathe in the many pools fed by the cascading torrent of the River Restonica, easily reached by scrambling down the rocky banks. You can also hike along alternative footpaths to reach Tuani, follow the southern slopes of Restonica, or climb up to the Plateau d'Alzu. From

of the train station, looks grim from the outside, but its 125 rooms are comfortable enough and its rates rock bottom; bathroom-less options are the best deal. €
**Du Nord** 22 cours Paoli; https://hoteldunord.corsica. Pleasant, clean place right in the centre, with plenty of Second Empire charm. Its variously priced rooms are large for the tariffs and there are also several recently renovated studio apartments. €€
**La Paix** 15 Av. de Gaulle; https://hoteldelapaix-corte.fr. There's no hiding the fact that this place could do with some modernization, but as 2-star hotels go, it's got a lot going for it. It's clean, comfortable enough, well-located, and compared to the competition, rooms are dirt cheap, even in summer. €̄

★ **Si Mea** 3 av du Pont de l'Orta; http://hotelsimea-corte. fr. In a quiet, off-track, elevated location on the eastern fringe of Corte, this small hotel occupies a renovated 1930s building set in its own grounds. The boutique-style rooms have been artfully decorated and have large beds with quality linen, plus balconies boasting panoramic views of the town and mountains. Excellent value for the price. 10–15 mins' walk from the centre. €€
**U Sognu** –Rte de la Restonica. At the foot of the valley, this campsite is a 15-minute walk from the centre. It has a good view of the citadelle, plenty of poplar trees for shade, and toilets in a converted barn. There's also a small bar and restaurant (in summer). €̄

### EATING
SEE MAP PAGE 150

**Le 24** 24 cour Paoli; https://le-24-restaurant-corte.fr. Served by an enthusiastic young crew against a backdrop of vaulted stone walls and stylish designer furniture, the food in this hip Corsican speciality place is innovative yet full of traditional flavours. Try the *brioche perdu* soaked in *Nutella* if it's on the menu. €€

**A Bocca** 5 cour Paoli; https://abocca-corte.fr. Small but stylish sushi house that offers a range of sushi, poke bowls, wraps and gyoza to eat in or takeaway. Frequented by students who appreciate its low price point, it's exceedingly fresh and makes a welcome change if you've been gorging on stews and charcuterie platters all week. €̄

Frassetta, you can also enjoy an about 5-hour there-and-back hike to the *bergeries*, which still afford spectacular views of the gorges.

Finally, if you want to reach the most famous portion of the hike, *a* well-worn path winds along the valley floor from the *bergeries* to a pair of beautiful glacial lakes. The first and larger, **Lac de Melo**, is reached after an easy one-and-a-half-hour hike through the rocks. One particularly steep part of the path has been fitted with security chains, but the scramble around the side of the passage is perfectly straightforward and much quicker. Once past Lac de Melo, press on for another forty minutes along the steeper marked trail over a moraine to the second lake, **Lac de Capitello**, the more spectacular of the pair. Hemmed in by vertical cliffs, the deep turquoise-blue pool affords fine views of the Rotondo massif on the far side of the valley.

### SHUTTLE BUSES

Daily shuttle buses organized by the Territorial Collectivity of Corsica (charge; https://www. isula.corsica/Navetta-Restonica-C13_a4624.html) leave from outside the train station in Corte between May and September with departures every half-hour or every 20 minutes in July-August. Tickets must be booked in advance using the smartphone app.

### ACCOMMODATION AND EATING

**Auberge de la Restonica** Lieu-dit Restonica, 2km southwest of Corte; http://www.aubergerestonica.com. Open May to October, this family-run restaurant serves up hearty slabs of *sanglier* and *magret de canard* seared to perfection, along with plenty of regional specialities. During the day, you can order cocktails and hang out by the pool. €€

**Camping Tuani** Tuani, 6km southwest of Corte; http:// camping-corte.com. Seasonal mid-sized campsite with shady plots for tents or caravans. There's a wood-fired pizzeria and river access, so you can cool off with a swim

– what more could you need after a day's hiking? €
★**Dominique Colonna** Lieu-dit Restonica, 2km southwest of Corte; http://dominique-colonna.com/. Snuggled in a leafy enclave at the mouth of the gorge, this 4-star is a masterpiece of contemporary woodland chic, blending exquisite design with its stunning natural backdrop. The forest-enveloped swimming pool and riverside massage house are ripe for post-hike pampering, while the beautifully furnished rooms exude tranquillity. €€€€

**A Casa di l'Orsu** 4 Rue Mgr Sauveur Casanova. Meat lovers will be in heaven at this restaurant, which serves a mean *tagliatelle au sanglier* and a rich *lentilles au figatellu* that will fill you up until the next day. There are also several vegetarian dishes. Cash only. €€

**Le Bips** 14 cours Paoli. Popular budget restaurant on the main drag, serving copious pasta dishes, salads, steaks and some local specialities at down-to-earth rates. Later on in the evening, its focus is very much on drinking and there's always a live crowd there until late. €

**Grimaldi** 15 cours Paoli https://www.grimaldi-corse.com. A local institution since the turn of the twentieth century, this master chocolatier and patisserie sells a gourmet selection of handmade chocolates, cakes, and pastries infused with the flavours of Corsica – think myrtle, clementines, citron

and wild thyme. It's also a *salon de thé* where the breakfast formule comes with arguably the best croissant in town. €

**Terra Corsa** 3 Rue Mgr Sauveur Casanova. This is about as local as it gets, with ingredients sourced directly from local family farms and charcuterie boards served with generous slabs of *terrine de figatelli* and fig jam. The lunchtime menus are great value, offering dishes like *cannelloni au brocciu* and *fiadone*. €

**U Museu** Rampe Ribanelle in the haute ville at the foot of the citadelle, 30m down rue Colonel-Feracci; http://restaurant-umuseu.com. One of the best-looking restaurants in town, perched on a terrace at the foot of the citadelle walls. Try the *menu corse*, featuring lasagne in wild boar sauce, trout and *tripettes*. Great value for money, and the house wines are local AOC. €€

### SHOPPING
SEE MAP PAGE 150

**A Casa Curtinese** 9 Rue du Vieux Marché. Said to be Corsica's oldest epicerie, this tangerine-coloured shop is bursting at the seams with local products. Rummage through the charmingly cluttered shelves and you'll find

delicious chestnut creams, immortelle balm, and *canistrelli* in a dozen flavours. Most unique are the sachets of fresh maquis herbs, of which there are at least two dozen types.

**Casa di u Legnu** 2 Rue du Vieux Marché. Behind the paint-

peeling door, this little shop specializes in hand-crafted wooden items made from authentic Corsican olive wood. The shaped chopping boards make a popular souvenir.
**Couteaux Corses** 3 Rue de l'Ancien Collège; https://

couteaux-corses.fr. Another time-honored Corsican craft is on display at this artisan knife-maker. The traditional shepherd's knives are crafted from delicately embossed Damascus steel with oak or ram's horn handles.

## Gorges du Tavignano

A deep cleft of ruddy granite beginning 5km to the west of Corte, the **Gorges du Tavignano** offers one of central Corsica's great walks, marked in orange paint flashes alongside the broad cascading River Tavignano. You can pick up the trail from opposite the Chapelle Sainte-Croix in Corte's *haute ville* and follow it as far as the Lac de Nino (see page 149), 30km west of the town, where it joins the GR20. To reach the *Refuge de la Sega* (see below), it's about a 5-hour walk, at which point you're about halfway to the lake. Most people, though, just follow the trail until the *Passerelle du Rossulinu*, a landmark footbridge that crosses the river, before retracing their steps back to town (about 4hr 30min there and back).

### ACCOMMODATION AND EATING — GORGES DU TAVIGNANO

**Refuge de la Sega** http://pnr-resa.corsica. Situated at 1192m amid glorious pine forest, this ranks among Corsica's best-run *refuges* and serves as a welcome stop off on the long trek up the valley to Lac de Nino. Choose between dorm beds or a bivouac with half or full-board board that includes a filling breakfast, evening meal and a packed lunch for the next day. Dorm beds have to be booked through the PNRC website and meals in advance by phone. €

# Venachese

South of Corte, the rolling agricultural lands and dense forests of the Venachese region are ringed by the craggy ridges of the Monte d'Oru and Monte Cardu massifs. Dotted with small villages and remote shepherd's huts, where old transhumance traditions are still kept alive today, it's little surprise that this region is famous for its cheese.

The principal villages of **Venaco**, **Vivario** and **Vizzavona** all lie along the smooth-driving T20, which follows the line of the scenic yet slow-moving railway, gliding over the Vecchio River and plunging through the pine-clad slopes of the **Forêt de Vizzavona**. Most visitors to this region fall into two camps: those hiking and canyoning through the wild gorges and those pottering around the rural villages and attending traditional village fêtes.

### GETTING AROUND — VENACHESE

While driving is by far the most convenient way to explore, Venaco, Vivario, Vizzavona and Bocognano can all be reached by train along the Corte – Ajaccio route.

## Venaco

South of Corte, one of the first villages you'll come to is **Venaco**, home of the celebrated "U Venachese", a soft cheese made with a mix of raw sheep and goat's milk. Cheese fans won't want to miss the annual cheese fair, *A fiera di u Casgiu* (May; https://fromages-corse.org), which has been held in Venaco since 1996 and features the island's most revered cheesemakers.

### ACCOMMODATION — VENACO

**Peridundellu** http://campingvenaco.e-monsite.com/. Quiet rural campsite by a local farmhouse with spotless facilities and access to laundry, fridges and a dump point. The friendly hosts will prepare dinner on request and deliver fresh baguettes and croissants to your campsite in the morning. €

# Vivario

The Vecchio River flows south from Venaco where the looming grey boulders of the **vallée du Verghellu** provide gentle terrain for rock climbers and canyoners to cut their teeth. Just north of Vivario, where the railway soars over the river, you'll find the so-called **Pont Eiffel**, a hulking viaduct that rises dramatically over the gorge – the work of none other than Gustave Eiffel himself.

Just outside of town, you can scale the small hill to see the ruins of the Pasciola fort, one of just two towers (the other is in neighbouring Vizzavona) built by the French in 1771 after their victory over the Paolists saw the end of the Corsican

## CANYONING TOURS

Wherever you go in Corsica, you'll see advertisements for the island's most popular outdoor craze, canyoning, a high-octane mix of hiking, scrambling, swimming and abseiling that promises to get your adrenaline pumping. Taking place around the natural river canyons and waterfalls of central and south Corsica, most tours include cliff jumps and slides; some also involve ziplines or additional obstacles. Canyoning tours are typically available from May to September or early October, and they can book up quickly in July and August, so plan ahead.

### CHOOSING A CANYONING TOUR

Canyoning excursions can vary hugely in technical difficulty, activity level and height, so it's important to be honest with yourself about both your fitness level and your fear level. Most canyoning operators provide clear details about what is involved – for example, more "adventurous" tours may include high jumps and abseils, while more "sporty" or "experienced" tours may involve up to six hours of quite intense activity. There are also beginner or "discovery" tours that are better suited to first-timers, children (some routes are suitable for kids from 5-6 years, depending on their size) and more nervous adventurers. It's also worth noting the length and pace of the tour and which parts are optional – jumps and slides should never be compulsory. Don't be afraid to ask questions and follow the advice of the instructors who have likely dealt with hundreds if not thousands of first-time canyoners. Although only a few tour companies advertise having English-speaking guides, many do, but it's best to double-check before booking.

### WHERE TO GO

There are several different canyoning destinations throughout central and south Corsica, but unless you're really into the sport, it's better to pick the closest and most suitable for your level rather than setting your heart on a specific location. The views and thrills are going to be unforgettable wherever you go and your canyoning guide is best placed to choose the most suitable destination based on current conditions.

**Altipiani** (Corte; https://canyon-corte.com/en) run canyoning tours for all levels in Verghellu canyon, south of Corte, as well as more challenging tours in Corsica, Petra-Leccia and Vecchio canyons.

**Corsica Natura** (Bocagnano; https://corsicanatura-activites.fr) offer canyoning in Richiusa canyon, south of the Vizzavona forest, and some gentler options along the Vecchio River. They also have caving tours and a treetop adventure park.

**Canyon Corse** (Ajaccio; https://canyon-corse.com) have English-speaking guides and operate tours in the Verghellu and Richiusa canyons, as well as more advanced routes in Zoicu canyon.

**In Terra Corsa** (Ponte Leccia; https://interracorsa.com) operate in the less-frequented canyons around Monte-Cinto and the Asco and Golo valleys (see page 147).

**Corsica Forest** (https://corsica-forest.com) run tours at Purcaraccia, Pulischellu and Vacca canyons within the famous Aiguilles de Bavella (see page 125) in South Corsica.

7

Republic. Intended to be one of a string of defensive towers to help the French military gain control over the nationalist mountain territories, the project was soon abandoned once they realized the engineering feat required to build in such an unforgiving landscape.

## ACCOMMODATION VIVARIO

**U Campanile** Place de l'Eglise, 20219 Vivario; http://hotel-restaurant-ucampanile.com. Housed in an old stone family home, this 2-star hotel is remarkably good value. The five rooms are heated and air-conditioned, and while the decor won't win any awards, there's everything you need for a good night's sleep, plus a decent restaurant serving local dishes. €

**Chez Jean-Pierre** Rue Principale, 20219 Vivario; https://www.facebook.com/barchezjeanpierre.vivario. If you want to experience true Corsican hospitality, this is the place. They serve a range of grills, cooked up on the terrace barbecue in front of you, and are always happy to accommodate the needs of hungry hikers. €€

## Vizzavona

Tall Lariccio pine and beech trees tower up over the roadside as you reach **Vizzavona** and the sweeping **Forêt de Vizzavona** that unfurls across the mountainsides. The GR20 can be joined from the roadside, where an about 2-hour there-and-back section weaves through the wooded ravine and culminates in a rocky scramble down to the **Cascade des Anglais** waterfalls. Swimming beneath the falls became a popular pastime for the British aristocrats who frequented the village at the turn of the twentieth century, hence the name. By the train station in Vizzavona, you can see the sombre, long-abandoned ruins of the grand Hôtel de la Forêt where they once stayed.

## ACCOMMODATION VIZZAVONA

**Casa Alta** Just off the T20, north of the village; https://www.casa-alta.fr/. Charming traditional stone manor in a tranquil forest setting. This *chambres d'hôtes* has five rooms, each individually styled and breakfast is included. €€€
**Le Vizzavona** Hameau de Vizzavona Gare; http://www.

hotel-vizzavona.com/. This grand old *maison de maître* dates back to 1901 and has been beautifully renovated. Behind the burgundy shutters are huge wood-floored rooms with elegant furnishings and tasteful artworks. The choice to not fit TVs is fitting with the peaceful surroundings. €€

## Bocognano

The forest views are most dazzling as you glide over the **Col de Vizzavona** mountain pass, after which the thickset pines give way to leafy chestnut trees as you arrive in the village of **Bocognano**. On the crest of the Gravona Valley, the small village has its moment in the limelight each December when it hosts the island's biggest chestnut festival, **Fiera di a Castagna** (https://fieradiacastagna.com), three days of food-centred celebrations that bring together farmers, artisans and musicians from all around Corsica.

While you're there, the **Ecomuseum U Palazzu** (charge) is also worth a peek, a small ethnology museum housed in Napoleon Bonaparte's summer house.

## INFORMATION, ACCOMMODATION AND EATING BOCOGNANO

**Tourist Office** U Palazzu Quartier (https://celavuprunelli.corsica/en/).
**Casa Santa Lucia** Mingardo; http://casasantalucia.fr. Traditional stone house with a stunning terrace and swimming pool that looks out over an expanse of forested hills. There are three rooms with luxurious stone bathrooms and bathtubs, plus you'll have access to the kitchen and lounge. €€

**A Tanedda (l'Auberge)** Route du busso; +33495274244. The atmospheric terrace with twinkling lights and a view out over the beautiful mountains makes this a romantic spot for evening dining. Everything on the menu is homemade (and delicious), but the *tiramisu a la châtaigne* is the star of the show – you absolutely must leave space for it. The lightning-fast service is either a pro or con, depending on your preference. €€

# Bozio

Sandwiched between the chestnut-fringed farmlands of Castagniccia and the forested green belt of the Venachese, **Bozio** gets little love from tourists passing through. In fact, unless you're hiking the Mare à Mare Nord trail, which slinks through on its way to Corte, you're unlikely to step foot in this leafy enclave of central Corsica. A deeply religious and historically nationalist region – the village of Bustanicu was responsible for the start of the Corsican revolt of 1729, when the people protested against a new tax imposed by the Genoese – it's equally known for its *paghjelle,* a form of polyphonic chanting that you'll hear echoing through the region's churches. Said churches are also a trove of architectural rarities, and a little-known footpath, the Chapel Trail, takes in the highlights. In the **Santa Maria Assunta** chapel in Favalello hides a seventh-century lintel and some remarkable fifteenth-century frescoes; in neighbouring Sermano, the Romanesque **chapel of San Nicolao** is adorned with elaborate fifteenth-century frescos. Over in the next town, Alando, the **Saint-François-de-Bozio Convent** was the site where the decisive 1757 battle between Emmanuel Matra and General Pascal Paoli's army took place.

7

## ACCOMMODATION AND EATING                                    BOZIO

**Auberge U Fragnu** Convento, Alando. Secreted away in an old stone mill, this restaurant serves farm-to-table dishes and the region's finest cheeses and charcuterie. There are just two *menus* on offer, but you can't go wrong by trusting the chefs – they are also happy to offer vegetarian or other alternatives if you ask. €̄

★ **Couvent d'Alando** Facing the convent, Alando; http:// chambresdhotes-corte.fr/. In a prime location by the old convent, this *chambres d'hôtes* has five delightful rooms that are light, spacious and luxurious, all with unique touches. In one, painted driftwood and buffed stones create a stunning mosaic in the bathroom; in another, there's an intricately carved wooden headboard. It's worth taking advantage of the *table d'hôtes* option – host Marie-Laure is a talented chef, and the ingredients are all local and bio. €̄

**Table du village U fragnu** Santa Lucia Di Mercurio. This village restaurant's mountain view terrace is always brimming with locals. All the meat is locally sourced, as is the charcuterie, which is served with sweet fig jam and sweet *mytre* liquor. Save room for the homemade desserts. €̄

TRADITIONAL RESTAURANT IN CALVI PORT

# Contexts

# History

"Corsica is France, but it is not French," Paul Theroux wrote about Corsica back in the 1970s. It's a paradox that has been echoed by Corsicans since it was incorporated into France two centuries prior, and it's central to understanding the island today. Set on the western Mediterranean trade routes, Corsica has always been of strategic and commercial appeal. Greeks, Carthaginians and Romans all left their mark, while five centuries under the Republic of Genoa resulted in a revolt, the establishment of the short-lived Corsican Republic in 1755 and the eventual ceding of the island to the French in 1768.

Corsica's troubles, however, were far from over and the islanders' ambitions for independence were far from quashed. As Theroux rightly observed and travellers will quickly discover, the island remains distinctly "not French". Nearly two and half centuries of French rule have had a limited influence, and many Corsicans remain committed to their indigenous heritage, Catholic traditions and native language, along with – to the chagrin of many French presidents –their enduring fight for autonomy. It's a theme that's dominated Corsican politics over the past decades, leading to violent protests, bombings and uprisings that settled down thanks to a permanent ceasefire in 2014 but flared up again in 2022.

## Early civilisations

While archaeologists still maintain theories of palaeolithic settlement in Corsica, concurrent with that of neighbouring Sardinia, for the moment, the earliest traces of occupation date back to the Mesolithic era. Traces of stone industries and excavated burial sites point to human occupation in Corsica as early as 9,000 BC, while the oldest human skeleton found on the island is the "Lady of Bonifacio" c.6570 BC, discovered by François de Lanfranchi in 1972 in Araguina-Sennola cave near Bonifacio.

Widespread inhabitation of the island is known throughout the Neolithic Era, with the founding of villages, agricultural practices and animal husbandry. Corsica's most significant prehistoric sites include Filitosa, inhabited since c 6,000 BC and best known for its 2-3-metre-tall menhirs (c 1500 BC), which feature human faces. Other megalithic monuments can be seen at Cauria near Sartène and the Bronze Age village of Castello di Cucuruzzu in the southern Alta Rocca mountains.

## Greeks, Carthaginians and Romans

The Greeks arrived in Corsica from Phocaea in 565 BC, founding the city of Alalia (now Aléria) along the east coast. They were soon followed by the Etruscans and Carthaginians, who, in a rare alliance, managed to reclaim Corsican territory from the Greeks during the Battle of Alalia in 540-535 BC. While the Etruscans took control of

| 6,500 BC | 4,000 BC | 565 BC | 540-535 BC |
|---|---|---|---|
| Corsica's oldest skeleton,"The Lady of Bonifacio". | Erection of megalithic structures at Filitosa. | Greeks from Phocaea found the city of Alalia (now Aléria). | Battle of Alalia sees Allied Etruscans and Carthaginians reclaim territory from the Greeks. |

Alalia, the Greeks maintained a presence on the island until the arrival of the Romans. Interestingly, the native Corsicans, pushed back into the mountainous interiors, remained largely independent through this period.

Corsica's strategic location made it a key focus of the Punic Wars between the Roman Republic and Ancient Carthage, and the Romans invaded the island in 259 BC. The Roman city of Aléria was soon established, replacing Alalia, along with the Roman province of Sardinia and Corsica. By 115BC, the entire island was under Roman rule, and its economy was flourishing as it became a key exporter of iron, wood, honey, and wine.

The Romans stayed in Corsica for more than 500 years, through the rules of Julius Caesar, Hadrian, Caracalla and Diocletian. By 200 AD, Christianity had been introduced to the island, and the Roman cities of Mantinum (Bastia), Urcinium (Cargèse), Aiacium (Ajaccio), and Marianum (Bonifacio) had been established along the coast.

## The Middle Ages

The decline and imminent fall of the Roman Empire left Corsica once again vulnerable to invasion, and by 455AD, the Vandals had ousted the Romans. The following centuries saw the island attacked, invaded, settled, abandoned, and fought over, leaving generations of islanders fighting against foreign government.

After the Vandals came the Byzantines, who maintained rule between 534AD and 725AD during one of the island's most chaotic periods. Repeated attacks by the Vandals, the Ostrogoths, and the Lombards weakened Byzantine resolve until the island was finally annexed, albeit briefly, by the Lombards. In 774AD, Charlemagne, then King of the Franks, conquered the island and handed it over to the Pope, but again this was short lived. By the 9th century, frequent raids by the Moors from Spain and North Africa resulted in them taking control of large parts of the island while native Corsicans retreated further into the mountains.

Finally, the Papacy decided to re-stake its claim to Corsica and liberating the island from the Moors, granted it to the Republic of Pisa.

## The Italian era

From 1077 to 1284, under the Pisans, a feudal system was established in Corsica with Sinucello della Rocca appointed Count of Corsica. This is largely regarded as one of the island's most prosperous periods, both economically and culturally, although much of this progress was confined to the east – the Tuscany-facing side of the island.

Pisan Romanesque art and architecture spread through the island, and there was widespread immigration from neighbouring Tuscany. It's worth mentioning that many of Corsica's most notable churches and chapels date back to this era, and traces of Tuscan influence can be observed in regional dialects and local cuisine, especially in the north.

Despite the comparatively peaceful appearances, the Pisans still found their hold on Corsica challenged regularly by the Genoese, who took control of Bonifacio in 1195. The attacks culminated in the 1284 Battle of Meloria, in which the Genoese, now allied with the Byzantine Empire, were victorious and thus staked their claim to Corsica.

| 259 BC | 80 BC | 774 AD | 1077-1090 |
|---|---|---|---|
| Romans begin their conquest of Corsica. | The Roman City of Aléria is built. | Charlemagne conquers Corsica, bringing it under Frankish control. | Control of Corsica is given to the Papacy; it's then yielded to the Republic of Pisa. |

By now, the Corsicans were no strangers to conflict, and Genoese rule brought with it plenty more. Genoa's ownership of the island was contested by the Kingdom of Aragan and the Pope, and in 1453, struggling under the weight of its own debt, Genoa even temporarily handed over control of Corsica to its own Bank of St. George.

By the 16th century, the Republic of Genoa was back in the driving seat, but the island had become a point of contest in the struggle for supremacy between Spain and France. In 1553, Corsica had its first taste of French rule as a combined attack by French and Ottoman forces, aided by Corsican mercenary Samperu Corsu de Bastelica, succeeded in inciting a revolt of Corsicans against the Geonese and capturing the island. The French protectorate held Corsica until 1559 when it was restored to the Geonese through the treaty of Cateau-Cambrésis. Genoa reestablished control, but their increasingly oppressive rule and high taxes brought growing resentment among the islanders. The repeated attacks of coastal villages by barbary pirates added to the strain and despite building some 85 defence towers along the coast, the Genoese were largely ineffective in protecting the island.

## The fight for Corsican independence

In the end, it was the Corsicans themselves that attempted to liberate the island from the Geonese. After almost five centuries under the Republic, tensions bubbled up into a nationalist movement, initially flared by the introduction of a new tax in 1729. These early rebellions, led by Giacinto Paoli, were easily thwarted by the Geonese, but it was the start of a long and increasingly futile struggle to maintain control.

It was Pascal Paoli, son of Giacinto Paoli, who wound up leading a successful resistance movement against the Geonese and in 1755, he established the Corsican Republic. During the island's 14-year independence, Pascale Paoli was appointed General of Corsica, a Corsican Constitution was ratified, the "A Bandera Corsa" flag became the flag of Corsica, and the University of Corsica was founded in Corte. Paoli was hailed a national hero, and he remains a revered figure for Corsican nationalists to this day.

While the uprising achieved its goal of breaking the Geonese hold on the island, the future of the Corsican Republic was soon put in peril. The Republic of Genoa, struggling to maintain its last pockets of control (the cities of Calvi and Bonifacio at this point were still held by the Geonese) and exhausted by decades of fighting, made a move that few saw coming. In the 1768 Treaty of Versailles, Genoa sold Corsica to France to pay off its debts (and possibly to rid itself of the burden).

According to the Corsican Republic, France's claim to Corsica was illegitimate and one that Paoli vowed to fight. But the Corsican armies were no match for the French, and by 1769 Corsica was conquered. Paoli sought refuge in Britain, where he stayed in exile for more than 20 years, forming a long-standing alliance with British King George III.

Paoli wasn't quite done with Corsica yet. In 1789, Parisians revolted against King Louis XVI during the Storming of the Bastille, which brought about the start of the French Revolution. That year also brought two pivotal changes for Corsica. Firstly, an official decree stating that Corsica was part of France, and secondly, as a result of the decree, Paoli was officially pardoned and allowed to return to his homeland.

| 1284 | 1729-1755 | 1768 | 1769 |
| --- | --- | --- | --- |
| The Battle of Meloria leads to Genoese rule over Corsica. | Corsicans revolt; General Pasquale Paoli declares the Corsican Republic. | The Treaty of Versailles sees Genoa cede Corsica to France. | French regain control over Corsican forces; Napoleon Bonaparte is born in Ajaccio. |

## NAPOLEON BONAPARTE

On 15 August 1769, the same year that France defeated Paoli and assumed control of Corsica, **Napoleon Bonaparte** was born in Ajaccio, forever tying their fates. Napoleon's father, Carlo Buonaparte, had been part of the Corsican Republic and fought alongside Pasquale Paoli against the French. However, unlike Paoli, when the French took over, Buonaparte instead pledged allegiance to King Louis XV, embracing the new government and accepting a position as Assessor of the Royal Jurisdiction of Ajaccio. The decision proved a good one for the young Napoleon, whose noble status allowed him to leave Corsica at the age of nine, receiving a scholarship at the prestigious **Brienne military academy**.

The young Napoleon excelled at military school, earning himself entry to the **École Militaire** in Paris and graduating early. At the age of 16, he was commissioned into the artillery; when he was 20, the Revolution broke out in Paris, and the scene was set for a remarkable career.

Always an ambitious opportunist, Napoleon returned to Ajaccio in 1791, aged 22. There, he joined the local Jacobin club and – with his eye on a colonelship in the Corsican militia – enthusiastically promoted the interests of the Revolution. Despite spending his formative years in mainland France, the young Napoleon still held dear the Corsican Nationalist ideals of his parents and their hero, Pascale Paoli. An early extract from his diaries read:

*"On Corsica, I was given life, and with that life, I was also given a fierce love for this my ill-starred homeland and fierce desire for her independence. I, too, shall one day be a 'Paoli.'"*

However, things did not quite work out as hoped and, when **Pascal Paoli** returned to Corsica, the two would soon find themselves at loggerheads.

Having spent the last twenty years in London, Paoli was pro-English and had developed a profound distaste for revolutionary excesses. Napoleon's French allegiance and his Jacobin views antagonised the older man, and his military conduct didn't enhance his standing at all. Elected second-in-command of the volunteer militia, Napoleon was involved in an unsuccessful attempt to wrest control of the Citadelle from royalist sympathisers. He thus took much of the blame when, in reprisal for the killing of one of the militiamen, several people were gunned down in Ajaccio, an incident which engendered eight days of civil war. In June 1793, Napoleon and his family were chased back to the mainland by the Paolists.

Napoleon promptly renounced any special allegiance he had ever felt for Corsica. He Gallicised the spelling of his name, preferring the French "Napoléon" to his baptismal Napoleone. And, although he was later to speak with nostalgia about the scents of the Corsican countryside, he put the city of his birth fourth on the list of places he would like to be buried.

Paoli seized his opportunity, returning to Corsica, where he promptly stood for election and was elected president of the department. It was a move that France would come to regret, as Paoli soon distanced himself from the French Revolutionaries and, seeing an opportunity to free Corsica from the French, sought help from the British Kings. It was a mutually beneficial proposition, with Corsica providing King George III with a much sought-after Mediterranean base and, for a brief period, the Anglo-Corsican Kingdom was established. The takeover was far from smooth, and by 1796,

| 1797 | 1811 | 1914-1918 | 1942-1943 |
| --- | --- | --- | --- |
| Napoleon Bonaparte becomes First Consul, leader of the French Republic. | Corsica officially becomes a department of the French Republic. | More than 12,000 Corsican soldiers die on the French battlefields in WWI. | Corsica is occupied by Italian and German forces during WWII; in 1943 it becomes the first part of France to be liberated. |

British troops had pulled out, returning the island to the French. Paoli, once again, found himself in exile in Britain, this time for good.

## The French island

By 1799, following Napoleon's coup d'état, France's Napoleonic era began, and by 1804, Napoleon was crowned Emperor of the French. During this time, Corsica was largely neglected by the French mainland and even briefly fell into British hands again in 1814 towards the end of the Napoleonic Wars. Throughout the 19th century, the island remained one of France's poorest departments, and violent rivalry between native Corsican clans grew.

Support of the French, however, seemed to grow. Mandatory primary school education was introduced, meaning that children learnt French from a young age; civil servant positions were among the best-paid on the island; and the introduction of steamboats facilitated easier travel to the mainland. Many Corsicans chose to emigrate to France or other countries within the French Empire or to serve in the French army, further enabling the permeation of French culture.

## World War I and II

World War I hit Corsica hard. Corsicans were resoundingly pro-Allied and responded in droves to the call to arms, while the island itself was used as a prisoner-of-war camp and war hospital. Post-WWI, having lost a large proportion of its men (an estimated 12,000 soldiers), Corsica was plunged into recession. Many Corsicans left for the mainland and agricultural industries, suffering worker shortages, never fully recovered.

During World War II, Corsica fell into the Vichy-controlled French Zone Libre and was occupied by large numbers of Germans and Italians. Starting in November 1942, the occupation was short-lived but brutal, with the Corsican Maquis (the resistance) fighting a strong battle. By October 1943, in the wake of the Italian armistice, the island became the first part of France to be liberated. For the rest of the war, it served as an important military hub, home to several US Air Force bases and a strategic player in the liberation of France.

Once again robbed of its men and receiving little aid to rebuild its industry and infrastructure after the war, Corsica's economic challenges worsened, and emigration soared. The problems were further exacerbated in the 1960s when, after Algeria won independence from France, an exodus of tens of thousands of *"pied-noirs"* (French and European settlers who had been living in Algeria for generations) returned to France, large numbers of whom settled in Corsica. The redistribution of land and subsidies to these new settlers incensed the local population, who felt they had long been neglected by the French government, and there was a growing demand for political reform. The unextinguished flames of Corsican Nationalism had been fanned.

## The resurgence of nationalism

Corsica's uneasy relationship with the mainland has worsened in recent decades. Economic neglect and the French government's reluctance to encourage Corsican

| 1976 | 1982 | 1998 | 2014 |
|---|---|---|---|
| Militant group FLNC is formed; multiple bomb attacks target the French government in Corsica. | Corsica is granted special administrative status, gaining greater autonomy within France. | FLNC continue bomb attacks and protests; French official Claude Érignac is assassinated. | FLNC declares a permanent ceasefire between Corsican Nationalists and the French government. |

language and culture spawned a nationalist movement in the early 1970s, whose clandestine armed wing, the FLNC (Fronte di Liberazione Nazionale di a Corsica), and its various offshoots were until recently engaged in a bloody conflict with the state.

Relations between the island's hardline nationalists and Paris may be perennially fraught, but there's little support among ordinary islanders for total independence. Bankrolled by Paris and Brussels, Corsica is the most heavily subsidised region of France. Moreover, Corsicans are exempt from social security contributions and the island as a whole enjoys preferential tax status.

Opinion, however, remains divided on the best way forward for the island. While centre-right parties push for an all-out promotion of tourism as a socio-economic cure-all, local nationalist groups resist large-scale development, claiming it will irrevocably damage the pristine environment visitors come to enjoy. Meanwhile, bombings of second homes – a feature of island life since the 1980s – gave way to a marked increase in assassinations and counter-killings, most of them linked to organised crime and corruption rather than feuds between nationalist factions, as in the past. By the early 2010s, Corsica had the highest per capita murder rate of any European region – a statistic attributed by locals to the failure of the French government to address ingrained social and economic problems, but which has roots deep in the island's cultural DNA. Tensions reached a head in 1998 with the assassination of French prefect Claude Érignac, which shocked the entire nation. Five years later, Corsican nationalist militant Yvan Colonna was arrested for his murder and sentenced to life imprisonment.

The extent to which violence had become a symptom of mob influence rather than part of the liberation struggle was dramatically underlined in June 2014 when the FLNC announced a definitive end to its armed conflict with the French state. The announcement came in the wake of a particularly bloody period for the island, during which several prominent figures, including politicians, lawyers and civil servants, were gunned down.

## An autonomous future

Mainland politics often seems to bear little reflection of those in Corsica; this was particularly illustrated in the 2017 elections when Macron's landslide victory didn't involve his party gaining a single seat on the island. Prior to the 2022 elections, violent protests kicked off following the news that Colonna had been killed in prison; in their wake, Le Pen's right-wing nationalist party received almost a third more votes than Macron's party.

However, despite his lack of support, in late 2023, Macron became the first French President to openly endorse Corsican autonomy within the French Republic, and by March 2024, a deal for the recognition of an autonomous status had been proposed.

Corsica's troubled underbelly, thankfully, is largely invisible to visitors. The once ubiquitous political graffiti and bullet-scarred signposts are fast becoming a thing of the past, while the drive-by shootings and mafia activity that still arise tend to occur well away from the resorts.

| 2018 | 2020-21 | 2022 | 2024 |
|---|---|---|---|
| Corsica's two departments become a territorial collectivity with incresed legislative powers for the Corsican Assembly. | The Covid-19 pandemic hits Corsica hard, especially its tourism industry. | Riots sweep Corsica after Nationalist Yvan Colonna, convicted for Claude Érignac's assassination, is murdered. | The French government reaches an agreement for Corsican autonomy. |

# Wildlife

Cloaked in thick forests and harsh maquis, the impenetrable mountains that once sheltered fleeing bandits and guerrilla troops have also allowed biodiversity to flourish. Even today, only a small fraction of the island has been urbanised, and settlements are concentrated along the coast, leaving vast swaths of the mountainous interior wild and untamed.

## Scents of the maquis

Corsica's high alpine peaks and sandy Mediterranean shores are sewn together by dense maquis, dry scrubland that covers some 40% of the island and nurtures a huge variety of plants and aromatic herbs. Corsica's second nickname, the "Fragrant Isle" comes from the heady aromas that diffuse through the mountains during the spring and summer, when the hillsides erupt with colour and the scent of the maquis carries down to the coast. Napoleon Bonaparte is famously quoted as saying, "*From the scent of its shrubland, from afar, with my eyes closed, I would recognise Corsica*". The French Emperor had a well-documented love of cologne, and many historians have pondered the link between his strong sense of smell and the nostalgic aromas of his homeland.

The island's unique ecosystem provides the perfect terrain for the maquis to thrive. Old and abandoned soils, pristine mountain air and water, the ever-changing altitude, and the warm Mediterranean climate combine to grow a thick, evergreen undergrowth that dominates the island. This bushy, thorny scrubland blankets the hills and valleys up to about 1,000 metres, studded with olive groves, orange trees, and sweet chestnut trees.

Some 2,000 plant species have been documented in the Corsican maquis, including common species like eucalyptus, juniper, rosemary, heather, sage, mint, thyme and lavender. There are also seventy-eight species endemic to the island, including the purple-flowering *crocus corsicus*, the strong-flavoured Corsican mint (*Mentha requienii*), the winter-blooming Corsican hellebore *(Helleborus argutifolius) and* St. John's Wart, often used as a natural anti-depressant. Among the 40 species of orchid found on Corsica, two species – conrad's ophrys and nurra's orchid – are unique to the island, as is Corsican butterwort (*pinguicula corsica*), a small carnivorous plant that blooms around the high-altitude pozzine meadows.

Many of the plants and flowers are harvested for their aromatic oils, distinct flavours, or medicinal properties, and used in local foods or beauty products. Myrtle or *myrte*, which produces small berries resembling blueberries (not to be confused with *myrtille,* which is French for blueberry), is often used in Corsican cuisine, made into sauces or liqueurs that pair well with meat dishes. *Arbutus*, sometimes known as strawberry tree for its red-orange fruits, is often made into jams and sauces. Olive trees (*oliviers*) are bountiful, some up to 2,000 years old, and olive oil cultivation dates back to ancient times. In local legend, this olive oil is also used to protect against "*l'occhiu*", the Evil Eye. The yellow-flowering *immortelle* (*Helichrysum italicum*), known for its curry-like fragrance as well as its healing and anti-ageing properties, is often used in aromatherapy and cosmetic products.

The evergreen maquis is a continuously changing palette of colours, with each season bringing different blooms. White heather is the first of the spring blooms, typically starting in February, and by mid-April, the maquis is a riot of colour, lasting until mid-June. In summer, yellow-flowering agave speckles the maquis, and the diminutive Corsican bees (*Apis mellifera mellifera corsica*) are hard at work. The endemic bees have been a protected species since 1982, preventing the introduction of other species into the territory and thus preserving the purity of the much-celebrated AOP Corsican honey.

In autumn, more than 500 species of wild mushrooms grow in the damp shade of the undergrowth, from winter chanterelles, oyster mushrooms, and morels to the rare bronze bolete (dark cap). As winter sets in, the strong scent of the maquis is but a faint memory, but the late-blooming aloe still adds some pops of red.

## Mountain fauna

Much of Corsica's mountain landscapes and its wildlife are under the management of the Parc Naturel Régional de Corse, and conservation efforts are in place to protect many of its native animals. The small but mighty Corsican mouflon (big-horned sheep) have inhabited the island since ancient times and are now a protected species, but they tend to stick to the high mountain plateaus or forests. Corsican red deer were reintroduced to the island in the 1990s after being extirpated in the 1970s. Much easier to spot are the ubiquitous wild boar (*sanglier*) and Corsican black pigs (*porcu nustrale*), which often wander onto the mountain roads in their hunt for fallen chestnuts, acorns, and other succulents.

## Birds of Corsica

Corsica's coastal cliffs and lagoons provide habitats for many migratory birds as well as several endemic species. Sadly, the past decades have witnessed many species fall into decline and conservation programmes, run by the Parc Naturel Régional de Corse (PNRC) with financial support from the European Commission, have become essential to their survival.

The high cliffs of the *réserve naturelle de Scandola* on Corsica's northwest coast, along with the *calanques de Piana* to the south, are one of the primary habitats for seabirds and raptors, which can often be spotted swooping over the cliffs. Osprey and peregrine falcon make their nests on the high cliffs, and you might spot great cormorant, alpine swift, Audouin's gull, yelkouan shearwater, Mediterranean shag, rock dove, common sandpiper, and cory's shearwater, among others. To the north, red kites are most commonly spotted along the shores of the Balagne, as well as along the east coast.

Inland, the main targets for birdwatchers are the Corsican nuthatch, only found on Corsica, typically in the high-altitude pine forests and the Corsican finch, found on Corsica and neighbouring Sardinia, as are Marmora's Warbler. Golden eagles and bearded vultures (Lammergeier) once reigned over Corsica's skies, especially in the Asco Valley, Restonica Valley, and the gorges of Scala di Santa Regina. However, populations have been in decline over the past decades. Bearded vultures reached dangerously low levels in 2020, but ongoing efforts by the PNRC under the EU's LIFE programme (https://www.gypaetecorse.com/en/) have seen numbers slowly creeping up. They remain a critically endangered species, and sightings are far less common than they once were.

More common bird species in Corsica include the blue rock thrush, passerine, sylvia warblers, blackbird, and bluebird. Flamingoes can also be spotted around the Étang de Biguglia, south of Bastia, in the summer months.

## Marine life

Corsica is renowned for its red coral colonies, some of the last remaining in the Mediterranean, but the prized corals are just the tip of the island's fascinating marine ecosystems. Fish are abundant in the plankton-rich waters all around the island, including Mediterranean tuna, swordfish, monkfish, catfish, and leerfish, as well as bass, grouper, whiting, mullet, and dentex.

Two marine reserves – the **Parc naturel marin du Cap Corse et de l'Agriate** (https://parc-marin-cap-corse-agriate.fr/) and the **Réserve naturelle des Bouches de Bonifacio** (https://rnbb.fr) – also protect a wide variety of marine life, and are the best sites to spot dolphins and whales around the island. Groupers, moray and conger eels, scorpion fish, and colourful wrasses are the most sought-after sightings for snorkelers and scuba divers, along with sea urchins, octopus, cuttlefish, and large schools of barracuda.

# Music

Corsica has a long tradition of polyphonic music that was first documented around medieval times but likely dates back to the early Christian era. Influenced by hymns and Gregorian chants, Corsican polyphonic music soon developed its own unique identity, blending the traditional harmonies of sacred music with the rich storytelling of folk music.

## Polyphonic music

Traditional polyphonic music is *a capella*, featuring multiple voices singing in harmony together without instrumental accompaniment. Typically performed by male singers, the music is structured around three distinct vocal parts: *a terza* (the third), *a bassu* (the bass), and *a seconda* (the second or leading voice). Groups, known as *cunfraternita* or brotherhoods, generally have between three and eight voices, with the *seconda* considered the most important as it leads the melody, and the *bassu* and the *terza* enriching the harmonies.

Different types of polyphonic songs include *lamentu* (funeral songs), *paghjella* (hymns or chants), *sirinati* (love songs), *tribbieri* (harvest songs) and *nanna* (lullabies). Uniquely, the *voceru* is sung only by women, while the *cuntrastu* is traditionally a two-part melody performed by a male and female pair. Polyphonic performances are often an integral part of religious festivals, feasts, and funerals, as well as secular occasions such as community gatherings and family celebrations.

## The voice of the resistance

The most famous of all polyphonic songs is Corsica's self-proclaimed national anthem, Dio vi salvi Regina ("God save you Queen" in Italian), which was adopted by islanders during the declaration of independence from the Republic of Genoa in 1755. Although there is no formal recognition of the national anthem, it's known around the island and is traditionally performed at the end of music concerts.

The popularity of polyphonic music ebbed during the early years of French rule, along with the islanders waning enthusiasm for independence. However, it experienced a resurgence in the 1970s, closely linked to the rise in nationalism. New styles of polyphonic music began to branch out from the original sacred hymns, with songs reflecting the changing cultural landscape and the ongoing struggle for freedom.

Dozens of bands have sprung up on the island over the past half-century, the most popular being *A Filetta*, *I Muvrini*, and *Barbara Furtuna*, who have helped bring the tradition into the international spotlight. Many of the groups blend traditional vocal techniques with contemporary pop influences and instrumental elements, but strong storytelling remains the primary focus.

The best way to experience Corsican polyphonic music is to attend a live performance, and concerts are held at churches and music venues around the island. The village of Pigna in the Balagne has a rich music scene with regular concerts, and there's also the annual *Rencontres de Chants Polyphoniques* festival (www.rencontrespolyphoniques.com) held in Calvi each September, which brings together local acts along with other polyphonic groups from around Europe. The albums listed below provide a selection of contemporary Corsican polyphonic music.

**CORSICAN POLYPHONIC MUSIC**

**A Filetta Intantu (2002)** www.afiletta.com. This international release by the all-male a cappella group A

Filetta, named after a Corsican fern, is a masterful example of Corsican polyphony.

**I Muvrini A Strada (2000)** www.muvrini.com. Best of compilation from one of Corsica's best-known musical groups. The Bernardini brothers combine traditional polyphonic harmonies with folk music instrumentals.

**Barbara Furtuna In Santa Pace (2012)** www.barbara-furtuna.fr. Second album from this popular quartet, which puts a modern twist on Corsican polyphony and explores themes of loss, love, and spirituality.

**Jean-Paul Poletti et le Chœur de Sartène 20 Anni (2015)** http://choeurdesartene.fr. In celebration of the choral group's 20th anniversary, this record was recorded live at the Imperial Chapel of Ajaccio.

# Books

There are few books in the English language that focus solely on Corsica, and books devoted to the history of France rarely touch on Corsica. The few that do exist – and are worth reading – are detailed below, along with some history books that provide context for the Meditteranean region. The best books in this selection are marked by a ★ symbol.

## HISTORY

**Christopher Hibbert** *The French Revolution*. Well-paced and entertaining narrative treatment by a master historian.

**Colin Jones** *The Cambridge Illustrated History of France*. A political and social history of France from prehistoric times to the mid-1990s, concentrating on issues of regionalism, gender, race and class. Good illustrations and a friendly, non-academic writing style.

★ **Andrew Roberts** *Napoleon: A Life*. An enthusiastic and engagingly written biography of France's emperor that includes Napoleon's early life on the island and how his Corsican roots shaped his character and ambitions.

**Jean McIntosh Turfa** *The Etruscan World*. A deep dive into Etruscan history and anthropology that brings together the work of more than 60 scholars and researchers to shine light on the ancient civilisation. While Corsica itself is only a side note, it provides fascinating insight into the early Mediterranean cultures of Sardinia, Corsica and Sicily.

## TRAVEL & GUIDES

**Brian Bouldrey** *Honorable Bandit: A Walk Across Corsica*. This 2007 book is a first-hand account of the author's 2-week hike along the famous GR-20. Accompanied by his friend, Petra, it's a personal journey that's both inspiring and revealing.

★ **Dorothy Carrington** *Granite Island: A Portrait of Corsica*. Published in 2008, this travel memoir is born from the British author's many years in Corsica and weaves in her complex observations on Corsican history, politics and the struggle for freedom, and the individualistic island culture.

**Cicerone** *Corsica (GR20)*. This comprehensive, easy-to-follow walking guide includes detailed route descriptions for the entire GR20. Recommendations for accommodation, refreshments and facilities are included, plus IGN 1:25,000 maps of the full route.

**Dave Gosney** *Finding Birds in Corscia;* birders-store.co.uk. Written in 2022, this birdwatching bible has maps, GPS coordinates, and tips to help you spot Corsican Nuthatch, Pallid Harrier, Marmora's Warbler, and more.

**Gillian Price** *Walking in Corsica: Long-Distance and Short Walks*. This book covers 18 hikes, among them three long-distance routes - Mare e Monti, Mare-Mare Nord, and Mare-Mare Sud. Covering coast, forest, and mountain, it's an ideal introduction to hiking in Corsica and includes descriptions, maps, and practical tips.

## COMIC BOOKS

**René Goscinny and Albert Uderzo** *Asterix in Corsica*. This 1973 comic from the classic Asterix series takes Asterix and Obelix back to Corsica in 50 BC where the duo team up with a native Corsican chief to stave off Julius Caesar's army.

# French

French can be a deceptively familiar language because of the number
of words and structures it shares with English. Despite this, it's far from
easy, though the bare essentials are not difficult to master and can
make all the difference. Even just saying "Bonjour Madame/Monsieur"
and then gesticulating will often get you a smile and helpful service.
People working in tourist offices, hotels and so on almost always speak
English and tend to use it when you're struggling to speak French.

## Pronunciation

One easy rule to remember is that **consonants** at the ends of words are usually silent:
the most obvious example is Paris, pronounced "Paree", while the phrase *pas plus tard*
(not later) sounds something like "pa-plu-tarr". The exception is when the following
word begins with a vowel, in which case you generally run the two together: *pas
après* (not after) becomes "pazaprey". Otherwise, consonants are much the same as in
English, except that: *ch* is always "sh", *c* is "s", *h* is silent, *th* is the same as "t", and *r* is
growled (or rolled). And to complicate things a little, *ll* after *i* usually sounds like the
"y" in yes – though there are exceptions, including common words like *ville* (city), and
*mille* (thousand). And *w* is "v", except when it's in a borrowed English word, like *le
whisky* or *un weekend*.

Vowels are the hardest sounds to get exactly right, but they rarely differ enough from
English to make comprehension a problem. The most obvious differences are that *au*
sounds like the "o" in "over"; *aujourd'hui* (today) is thus pronounced "oh-jor-dwi".
Another one to listen out for is *oi*, which sounds like "wa"; *toi* (to you) thus sounds like
"twa". Lastly, adding "m" or "n" to a vowel, as in *en* or *un*, adds a nasal sound, as if you
said just the vowel with a cold.

## Basic words and phrases

French nouns are divided into masculine and feminine. This causes difficulties with
adjectives, whose endings have to change to suit the nouns they qualify – you can talk
about *un château blanc* (a white castle), for example, but *une tour blanche* (a white
tower). If you're not sure, stick to the simpler masculine form – as used in this glossary.

### ESSENTIALS

| | |
|---|---|
| **hello (morning or afternoon)** bonjour | **this one** ceci |
| **hello (evening)** bonsoir | **that one** celà |
| **good night** bonne nuit | **open** ouvert |
| **goodbye** au revoir | **closed** fermé |
| **thank you** merci | **big** grand |
| **please** s'il vous plaît | **small** petit |
| **sorry** pardon/Je m'excuse | **more** plus |
| **excuse me** pardon | **less** moins |
| **yes** oui | **a little** un peu |
| **no** non | **a lot** beaucoup |
| **OK/agreed** d'accord | **inexpensive** pas cher/bon marché |
| **help!** au secours! | **expensive** cher |
| **here** ici | **good** bon |
| **there** là | **bad** mauvais |

| | |
|---|---|
| **hot** chaud | **entrance** entrée |
| **cold** froid | **exit** sortie |
| **with** avec | **man** un homme |
| **without** sans | **woman** une femme (pronounced "fam") |

## NUMBERS

| | |
|---|---|
| **1** un | **21** vingt-et-un |
| **2** deux | **22** vingt-deux |
| **3** trois | **30** trente |
| **4** quatre | **40** quarante |
| **5** cinq | **50** cinquante |
| **6** six | **60** soixante |
| **7** sept | **70** soixante-dix |
| **8** huit | **75** soixante-quinze |
| **9** neuf | **80** quatre-vingts |
| **10** dix | **90** quatre-vingt-dix |
| **11** onze | **95** quatre-vingt-quinze |
| **12** douze | **100** cent |
| **13** treize | **101** cent-et-un |
| **14** quatorze | **200** deux cents |
| **15** quinze | **300** trois cents |
| **16** seize | **500** cinq cents |
| **17** dix-sept | **1000** mille |
| **18** dix-huit | **2000** deux mille |
| **19** dix-neuf | **5000** cinq mille |
| **20** vingt | **1,000,000** un million |

## TIME

| | |
|---|---|
| **today** aujourd'hui | **now** maintenant |
| **yesterday** hier | **later** plus tard |
| **tomorrow** demain | **at one o'clock** à une heure |
| **in the morning** le matin | **at three o'clock** à trois heures |
| **in the afternoon** l'après-midi | **at ten thirty** à dix heures et demie |
| **in the evening** le soir | **at midday** à midi |

## DAYS AND DATES

| | |
|---|---|
| **January** janvier | **Sunday** dimanche |
| **February** février | **Monday** lundi |
| **March** mars | **Tuesday** mardi |
| **April** avril | **Wednesday** mercredi |
| **May** mai | **Thursday** jeudi |
| **June** juin | **Friday** vendredi |
| **July** juillet | **Saturday** samedi |
| **August** août | **August 1** le premier août |
| **September** septembre | **March 2** le deux mars |
| **October** octobre | **July 14** le quatorze juillet |
| **November** novembre | **November 23** le vingt-trois novembre |
| **December** décembre | **2019** deux mille dix-neuf |

## TALKING TO PEOPLE

When addressing people, a simple *bonjour* is not enough; you should always use *Monsieur* for a man, *Madame* for a woman, *Mademoiselle* for a young woman or girl. This has its uses when you've forgotten someone's name or want to attract someone's attention. "Bonjour" can be used well into the afternoon, and people may start saying "bonsoir" surprisingly early in the evening, or as a way of saying goodbye.

## PHRASEBOOKS AND COURSES

**Rough Guide French Phrasebook** Mini dictionary-style phrasebook with both English–French and French–English sections, along with cultural tips, a menu reader and downloadable scenarios read by native speakers.

**Breakthrough French** One of the best teach-yourself courses, with three levels to choose from. Each comes with a book and CD-ROM.

**The Complete Merde! The Real French You Were Never Taught at School** More than just a collection of swearwords, this book is a passkey into everyday French

and a window into French culture.

**Oxford Essential French Dictionary** Very up-to-date French–English and English–French dictionary, with help on pronunciation and verbs, and links to free online products.

**Michel Thomas** A fast-paced and effective audio course that promises "No books. No writing. No memorising", with an emphasis on spoken French, rather than conjugating verbs and sentence construction http://michelthomas.com.

**Do you speak English?** Parlez-vous anglais?
**How do you say it in French?** Comment ça se dit en français?
**What's your name?** Comment vous appelez-vous?
**My name is …** Je m'appelle …
**I'm …** Je suis …
**… English** … anglais[e]
**… Irish** … irlandais[e]
**… Scottish** … écossais[e]
**… Welsh** … gallois[e]
**… American** … américain[e]
**… Australian** …australien[ne]
**… Canadian** … canadien[ne]
**… a New Zealander** … néo-zélandais[e]

**… South African** … sud-africain[e]
**I understand** Je comprends
**I don't understand** Je ne comprends pas
**Could you speak more slowly?** S'il vous plaît, parlez moins vite
**How are you?** Comment allez-vous?/ Ça va?
**Fine, thanks** Très bien, merci
**I don't know** Je ne sais pas
**Let's go** Allons-y
**See you tomorrow** À demain
**See you soon** À bientôt
**Leave me alone (aggressive)** Laissez-moi tranquille
**Please help me** Aidez-moi, s'il vous plaît

## FINDING THE WAY

**bus** autobus/bus/car
**bus station** gare routière
**bus stop** arrêt
**car** voiture
**train/taxi/ferry** train/taxi/bac or ferry
**boat** bâteau
**plane** avion
**shuttle** navette
**train station** gare (SNCF)
**platform** quai
**What time does it leave?** Il part à quelle heure?
**What time does it arrive?** Il arrive à quelle heure?
**a ticket to …** un billet pour …
**single ticket** aller simple
**return ticket** aller retour
**validate/stamp your ticket** compostez votre billet
**valid for** valable pour
**ticket office** vente de billets
**how many kilometres?** combien de kilomètres?
**how many hours?** combien d'heures?
**hitchhiking** autostop
**on foot** à pied
**Where are you going?** Vous allez où?
**I'm going to …** Je vais à …

**I want to get off at …** Je voudrais descendre à …
**the road to …** la route pour …
**near** près/pas loin
**far** loin
**left** à gauche
**right** à droite
**straight on** tout droit
**on the other side of** à l'autre côté de
**on the corner of** à l'angle de
**next to** à côté de
**behind** derrière
**in front of** devant
**before** avant
**after** après
**under** sous
**to cross** traverser
**bridge** pont
**town centre** centre ville
**all through roads (road sign)** toutes directions
**other destinations (road sign)** autres directions
**upper town** ville haute/haute ville
**lower town** ville basse/basse ville
**old town** vieille ville

## QUESTIONS AND REQUESTS

The simplest way of asking a question is to start with *s'il vous plaît* (please), then name the thing you want in an interrogative tone of voice. For example:

**Where is there a bakery?** S'il vous plaît, où est la boulangerie?

**Which way is it to the Eiffel Tower?** S'il vous plaît, la route pour la Tour Eiffel?

**Can we have a room for two?** S'il vous plaît, une chambre pour deux?

**Can I have a kilo of oranges?** S'il vous plaît, un kilo d'oranges?

## QUESTION WORDS

**where?** où?

---

**SIGN LANGUAGE**

**Défense de ...** It is forbidden to ...
**Fermé** closed
**Ouvert** open
**Rez-de-chaussée (RC)** ground floor
**Sortie** exit

---

**how?** comment?
**how many/how much?** combien?
**when?** quand?
**why?** pourquoi?
**at what time?** à quelle heure?
**what is/which is?** quel est?

## ACCOMMODATION

**a room for one/two persons** une chambre pour une/deux personne(s)
**a double bed** un grand lit/ un lit matrimonial
**a room with two single beds/twin** une chambre à deux lits
**a room with a shower** une chambre avec douche
**a room with a bath** une chambre avec salle de bain
**for one/two/three nights** pour une/deux/trois nuits
**Can I see it?** Je peux la voir?
**a room on the courtyard** une chambre sur la cour
**a room over the street** une chambre sur la rue
**first floor** premier étage
**second floor** deuxième étage
**with a view** avec vue
**key** clé
**to iron** repasser
**do laundry** faire la lessive
**sheets** draps

**blankets** couvertures
**quiet** calme
**noisy** bruyant
**hot water** eau chaude
**cold water** eau froide
**Is breakfast included?** Est-ce que le petit-déjeuner est compris?
**I would like breakfast** Je voudrais prendre le petit-déjeuner
**I don't want breakfast** Je ne veux pas le petit-déjeuner
**bed and breakfast** chambres d'hôtes
**Can we camp here?** On peut camper ici?
**campsite** camping/terrain de camping
**tent** tente
**tent space** emplacement
**hostel** foyer
**youth hostel** auberge de jeunesse

## DRIVING

**service station** garage
**service** service
**to park the car** garer la voiture
**car park** un parking
**no parking** défense de stationner/ stationnement interdit
**petrol/gas station** station d'essence
**fuel** essence
**unleaded** sans plomb
**leaded** super
**diesel** gazole

**oil** huile
**air line** ligne à air
**put air in the tyres** gonfler les pneus
**battery** batterie
**the battery is dead** la batterie est morte
**plug (for appliance)** prise
**to break down** tomber en panne
**petrol can** bidon
**insurance** assurance
**green card** carte verte
**traffic lights** feux rouges

## HEALTH MATTERS

**doctor** médecin
**I don't feel well** Je ne me sens pas bien
**medicines** médicaments
**prescription** ordonnance

**I feel sick** Je suis malade
**I have a headache** J'ai mal à la tête
**stomach ache** mal à l'estomac
**period** règles

**pain** douleur
**it hurts** ça fait mal
**chemist/pharmacist** pharmacie
**hospital** hôpital

**condom** préservatif
**morning-after pill/emergency contraceptive** pilule du lendemain
**I'm allergic to …** Je suis allergique à …

## OTHER NEEDS

**bakery** boulangerie
**food shop** alimentation
**delicatessen** charcuterie, traiteur
**cake shop** pâtisserie
**cheese shop** fromagerie
**supermarket** supermarché
**to eat** manger
**to drink** boire
**tasting, eg wine** dégustation, tasting
**camping gas** camping gaz

**tobacconist** tabac
**stamps** timbres
**bank** banque
**money** argent
**toilets** toilettes
**police** police
**telephone** téléphone
**cinema** cinéma
**theatre** théâtre
**to reserve/book** réserver

## RESTAURANT PHRASES

**I'd like to reserve a table for two people, at eight thirty** Je voudrais réserver une table pour deux personnes à vingt heures trente
**I'm having the €30 set menu** Je prendrai le menu à trente euros

**Waiter! (never "garçon")** Monsieur/Madame!/ s'il vous plaît!
**the bill/check please** l'addition, s'il vous plaît

# Glossary of Corsican terms

The Corsican language is more influenced by Italian than French, but it is a language in its own right – it is not, as is often misunderstood – simply a local dialect. While French is the official language used on Corsica, you will often see Corsican terms popping up in place names and on local maps, so it's worth understanding a few key words. In addition, you may hear locals interspersing their French with Corsican words, especially greetings and common expressions. Here are some of the common terms you might come across throughout this book or while travelling around with their translations in both French and English.

## BASIC PHRASES

### CORSICAN/FRENCH/ENGLISH

**bonghjornu** *bonjour* hello (morning or afternoon)
**bona sera** *bonsoir* good evening
**avvèdeci** *au revoir* goodbye
**grazie** *merci* thank you
**scusatemi** *excusez-moi* excuse me
**fate u piacè/pè piacè** *s'il vous plaît* thank you

**benvenuti** *bienvenue* welcome
**a salute** *santé* cheers
**iè, innò** *oui/non* yes/no
**cumu state?** *comment allez-vous?* how are you?
**và bè** *ça va* I'm fine
**à dopu** *à bientôt* see you soon
**macu** *c'est bien* it's ok

## COMMON TERMS

**Arinella** A beach with fine sand.

**Bocca** A mountain pass or *col* in French.

**Capu** A mountain peak or summit.

**Cignale** The wild boar (*sanglier*) that is native to the island.

**Compru in Corsu** An item that is made in Corsica or a food/ingredient that is sourced from the island.

**Fiume** A river or *fleuve* in French.

**Fragnu** An old mill, typically used for producing olive oil.

**Machja** The maquis or interior shrubland that covers much of Corsica; also used to denote the guerrilla forces that hid in the underbrush during the French Resistance of WWII.

**Osteria** A traditional inn that typically offers Corsican cuisine and wine but sometimes offers accommodation.

**Pinzutu** Corsican's nickname for French tourists, sometimes shortened to *pins*. Translates to "point" or "pointed" and is said to be derived from the pointed hats worn by the French soldiers of Louis XV.

**Pulifunia** Corsica's traditional polyphonic music, which features multiple singers performing a cappella.

**Punta** Another word for mountain peak or summit.

**Scoglii** Rocks or used to describe a rocky path or beach.

**Stantara** Prehistoric standing stones or menhirs that date from the Bronze Age.

# Small print and index

## A ROUGH GUIDE TO ROUGH GUIDES

Published in 1982, the first Rough Guide – to Greece – was a student scheme that became a publishing phenomenon. Mark Ellingham, a recent graduate in English from Bristol University, had been travelling in Greece the previous summer and couldn't find the right guidebook. With a small group of friends he wrote his own guide, combining a contemporary, journalistic style with a thoroughly practical approach to travellers' needs.

The immediate success of the book spawned a series that rapidly covered dozens of destinations. And, in addition to impecunious backpackers, Rough Guides soon acquired a much broader readership that relished the guides' wit and inquisitiveness as much as their enthusiastic, critical approach and value-for-money ethos. These days, Rough Guides include recommendations from budget to luxury and cover more than 120 destinations around the globe, from Amsterdam to Zanzibar, all regularly updated by our team of roaming writers.

Browse all our latest guides, read inspirational features and book your trip at **roughguides.com**.

## Rough Guide credits

**Editor:** Beth Williams
**Proofreader:** Norm Longley
**Cartography:** Katie Bennett
**Picture Editor:** Piotr Kala
**Picture Manager:** Tom Smyth
**Layout:** Pradeep Thapliyal
**Publishing Technology Manager:** Rebeka Davies
**Production Operations Manager:** Katie Bennett
**Head of Publishing:** Sarah Clark

## Publishing information

First edition 2025

ISBN: 9781835292716

### Distribution

*UK, Ireland and Europe*
Apa Publications (UK) Ltd; mail@roughguides.com
*United States and Canada*
Two Rivers; ips@ingramcontent.com
*Australia and New Zealand*
Woodslane; info@woodslane.com.au
*Worldwide*
Apa Publications (UK) Ltd; mail@roughguides.com

### Special Sales, Content Licensing and CoPublishing

Rough Guides can be purchased in bulk quantities at discounted prices. We can create special editions, personalized jackets and corporate imprints tailored to your needs. mail@roughguides.com.

roughguides.com

### EU Representative

LOGOS EUROPE, 9 rue Nicolas Poussin, 17000, LA ROCHELLE, France; Contact@logoseurope.eu; +33 (0) 667937378

Printed by Finidr in Czech Republic

This book was produced using **Typefi** automated publishing software.

A catalogue record for this book is available from the British Library.

All rights reserved
© 2025 Apa Digital AG
License edition © Apa Publications Ltd UK

No part of this book may be reproduced, stored in a retrieval system, or transmitted in any form or by any means – electronic, mechanical, photocopying, recording, or otherwise – without prior written permission from Apa Publications.

Every effort has been made to ensure that this publication is accurate, free from safety risks, and provides accurate information. However, changes and errors are inevitable. The publisher is not responsible for any resulting loss, inconvenience, injury or safety concerns arising from the use of this book.

## Help us update

We've gone to a lot of effort to ensure that this edition of **The Rough Guide to Corsica** is accurate and up-to-date. However, things change – places get "discovered", transport routes are altered, restaurants and hotels raise prices or lower standards, and businesses cease trading. If you feel we've got it wrong or left something out, we'd like to know, and if you can direct us to the web address, so much the better.

Please send your comments with the subject line **"Rough Guide Corsica Update"** to mail@roughguides.com. We'll send a copy of the next edition (or any other Rough Guide if you prefer) for the very best emails.

## Acknowledgements

Thanks to everyone who helped with researching this book, especially Francoise Melard and Marie Louise Nicoli at ATC Corsica, Jeanine Pieraggi at Ouest Corsica, Hélène Battaglini at Bonifacio Tourist Office, Marine Teste at Atout France, Franck Rollin and the whole team at Hippocampe Plongee, Laura Maldonado, and our Airbnb hosts Patrice and Mathee for sharing their love of Corsica with us. A special thank you to René and Ziggy for making these island adventures even more memorable.

## ABOUT THE AUTHOR

**Zoë Smith** is a travel writer and digital editor who has written for Rough Guides titles including France, Dordogne & the Lot, Turkey, and Istanbul. She backpacked solo around South America and Southeast Asia and travelled to 50+ countries before settling in her childhood second home of France. She enjoys seeking out local cultural experiences as well as outdoor adventures like hiking, scuba diving and horse riding, and can't resist an unusual place to stay.

## Photo credits
(Key: T-top; C-centre; B-bottom; L-left; R-right)

All images **Shutterstock**

**Cover:** Evisa **iStock**

# Index

# Map symbols

The symbols below are used on maps throughout the book

| | | | | | | | |
|---|---|---|---|---|---|---|---|
| – – – | Chapter boundary | ✈ | Airport | ✚ | Hospital | ◆ | Forest |
| | Road | ★ | Transport stop | ◠ | Cave | ▲ | Peak |
| | Pedestrian road | P | Parking | ⁙ | Ruins | ⊠ | Gate |
| | Steps | ▼ | Place of interest | ⚲ | Church/chapel | ⇥ | Church |
| | Railway | ✉ | Post office | ⛪ | Monastery | | Building |
| – – – | Footpath | ⓘ | Tourist office | ☩ | Windmill | | Park |
| | Ferry | ⚱ | Museum | ⛷ | Ski resort | ⊞ | Cemetery |
| | Wall | ✺ | Viewpoint | ♜ | Tower | | |

## Listings key

| | |
|---|---|
| ■ | Accommodation |
| ● | Eating |
| ■ | Drinking/nightlife |
| ● | Shopping |

# YOUR TAILOR-MADE TRIP
## STARTS HERE

**Tailor-made trips and unique adventures crafted by local experts**

Rough Guides has been inspiring travellers with lively and thought-provoking guidebooks for more than 35 years. Now we're linking you up with selected local experts to craft your dream trip. They will put together your perfect itinerary and book it at local rates.

Don't follow the crowd – find your own path.

# HOW ROUGHGUIDES.COM/TRIPS WORKS

### STEP 1
Pick your dream destination, tell us what you want and submit an enquiry.

### STEP 2
Fill in a short form to tell your local expert about your dream trip and preferences.

### STEP 3
Our local expert will craft your tailor-made itinerary. You'll be able to tweak and refine it until you're completely satisfied.

### STEP 4
Book online with ease, pack your bags and enjoy the trip! Our local expert will be on hand 24/7 while you're on the road.

# BENEFITS OF PLANNING AND BOOKING AT ROUGHGUIDES.COM/TRIPS

### PLAN YOUR ADVENTURE WITH LOCAL EXPERTS

Rough Guides' English-speaking local experts are hand-picked, based on their experience in the travel industry and their impeccable standards of customer service.

### SAVE TIME AND GET ACCESS TO LOCAL KNOWLEDGE

When a local expert plans your trip, you save time and money when you book, even during high season. You won't be charged for using a credit card either.

### MAKE TRAVEL A BREEZE: BOOK WITH PEACE OF MIND

Enjoy stress-free travel when you use Rough Guides' secure online booking platform. All bookings come with a money-back guarantee.

# WHAT DO OTHER TRAVELLERS THINK ABOUT ROUGH GUIDES TRIPS?

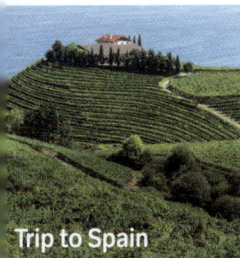

**Trip to Spain**

This Spain tour company did a fantastic job to make our dream trip perfect. We gave them our travel budget, told them where we would like to go, and they did all of the planning. Our drivers and tour guides were always on time and very knowledgable. The hotel accommodations were better than we would have found on our own. Only one time did we end up in a location that we had not intended to be in. We called the 24 hour phone number, and they immediately fixed the situation.

**Don A, USA** ★★★★★

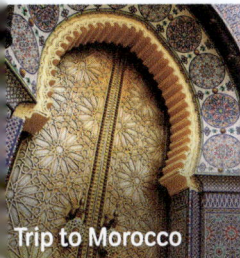

**Trip to Morocco**

Our trip was fantastic! Transportation, accommodations, guides – all were well chosen! The hotels were well situated, well appointed and had helpful, friendly staff. All of the guides we had were very knowledgeable, patient, and flexible with our varied interests in the different sites. We particularly enjoyed the side trip to Tangier! Well done! The itinerary you arranged for us allowed maximum coverage of the country with time in each city for seeing the important places.

**Sharon, USA** ★★★★★

# PLAN AND BOOK YOUR TRIP AT
## ROUGHGUIDES.COM/TRIPS